Words, Words, Words!

Ready-to-Use Games and Activities for Vocabulary Building, Grades 7–12

Jack Umstatter

JOSSEY-BASS
A Wiley Imprint
www.josseybass.com

To my wife, Chris, and daughters, Kate and Maureen,
for their love and care.

To my former colleague Denis Thompson, whose teaching skills
and knowledge touched thousands of students and inspired
hundreds of teachers to love learning.

Published by Jossey-Bass
A Wiley Imprint
989 Market Street, San Francisco, CA 94103-1741   www.josseybass.com

Jossey-Bass books and products are available through most bookstores. To contact Jossey-Bass directly call our Customer Care Department within the U.S. at 800-956-7739, outside the U.S. at 317-572-3986 or fax 317-572-4002.

Jossey-Bass also publishes its books in a variety of electronic formats. Some content that appears in print may not be available in electronic books.

ISBN: 0-7879-7116-2

Printed in the United States of America
FIRST EDITION
PB Printing   10 9 8 7 6 5 4 3 2 1

CONTENTS

Unit 5   How We Act

Unit 6   Words from Mythology

Unit 7   The Big and Small of It All

Unit 8   Tell It Like It Is

Unit 9   The Sciences (Naturally!)

Unit 10   Mathematically Inclined

Unit 11   How We Move

Unit 12   Write On!

Unit 13   Popular SAT Words

Unit 14   What We'd Like Said About Us

Unit 15   To a Degree

Unit 16   All Types of People

Unit 17   An Interesting Combination of Words

Unit 18   All in the Family

Unit 19   Skilled—Or Not So Skilled

Unit 20 Here, There, and Everywhere

Unit 21 Smart—Or Not So Smart

Unit 22 A Bit Different

Unit 23 How (or Not How) to Say It

Unit 24 Gone!

Unit 25   Age

Unit 26   Who Wants to Be Called That?

Unit 27   How Much—Or How Little

Unit 28   Social Studies Class

Unit 29   Science Class

Unit 30   All About the Senses

Review Test   Units 28–30   **259**

ABOUT THE AUTHOR

Jack Umstatter has taught English on both the junior high school and senior high school levels since 1972. He has also taught education at Dowling College in Oakdale, New York, for the past thirteen years and English at Suffolk County Community College for the past two years. Mr. Umstatter currently teaches English and co-chairs the English department in the Cold Spring Harbor School District on Long Island.

The author of thirteen publications, including *Hooked on Literature!* (1994), *201 Ready-to-Use Word Games for the English Classroom* (1994), *Brain Games!* (1996), *Hooked on English!* (1997), the six-volume *Writing Skills Curriculum Library* (1999), *Grammar Grabbers!* (2000), *Where Words Come From* (2002), and *English Brainstormers!* (2002), Mr. Umstatter has been selected Teacher of the Year several times, was elected to *Who's Who Among America's Teachers*, and has appeared in *Contemporary Authors*.

ACKNOWLEDGMENTS

Thanks to my editor, Dr. Steve Thompson, whose skillful guidance and constant encouragement made this writing experience very enjoyable.

Thanks to my publisher, Paul Foster, for his strong support and confidence.

Thanks to my wife, Chris, for her loving inspiration and valued assistance in completing this resource.

Thanks also to Diane Turso, my proofreader, who has been a terrific help in many of my writings.

Many definitions were taken from *Webster's New World Dictionary*, Third College Edition, published by Prentice Hall.

Some definitions, synonyms, and antonyms were taken from *Roget's Thesaurus*, published by Bantam Books.

ABOUT THIS RESOURCE

The English language contains nearly 600,000 common words—far more than are contained in any other of the world's major languages. With so many words to learn, students can easily become overwhelmed by the enormity of the task. As we already know, reading is one very effective way to increase vocabulary. Yet, if students do not engage in reading as much as they should (a common accusation), there need to be other avenues to expand a student's vocabulary. The "drill and kill" method of studying vocabulary does not readily engage students. Neither do the large, alphabetized lists of the "most commonly used words" or "most commonly found words on this or that state exam." What students need (think of the typical adolescent) is, as singer Rod Stewart says, "a reason to believe," a convincing motivation and method to learn new words. Telling them that a stronger vocabulary often increases one's chances for success in life, or that knowing more words can contribute to a higher score of important standardized exams, especially the college admissions examinations, will not necessarily convince students.

Words, Words, Words! Ready-to-Use Games and Activities for Vocabulary Building, Grades 7–12, features proven, practical, and fun-filled methods to help your students increase their vocabulary—and enjoy doing so! The resource is divided into thirty thematic units, each containing fifteen interrelated words. Each word's pronunciation, part(s) of speech, and use in illustrative sentences allow the students a greater awareness and appreciation of that word. Plus, students will benefit from the "Helpful Hints" that accompany some of these words. Since the words in each unit are thematically related, the students will readily see each word's associations, similarities, and differences. Additionally, each unit features four different ready-to-use activities to reinforce the unit's words. These classroom-tested activities include crossword puzzles, matching columns, magic squares, jumbles, word finds, cloze and close readings, multiple choice, concealed quotations, riddles, and more. They can be used as quick time fillers, competitions, tests, quizzes, make-up quizzes, or extra credit assignments. You choose if you would like to utilize them for individual, group, or entire class formats. A twenty-five-question test is found after each three units. Thus, your students will become more motivated and excited about studying vocabulary. In turn, you will save yourself much-needed time, since every one of the resource's activities is ready-to-use and has an easy-to-use answer key.

In 1961, the American poet Robert Frost said, "Life is tons of discipline. Your first discipline is your vocabulary." A year later, British novelist Evelyn Waugh wrote, "One forgets words as one forgets names. One's vocabulary needs constant fertilizing or it will die." With *Words, Words, Words! Ready-to-Use Games and Activities for Vocabulary Building, Grades 7–12*, you can help your students improve and continually fertilize their first discipline. Plus, as my students and I have done, both you and your students will enjoy the experience!

Jack Umstatter

Unit 1
PLACES

PLACES

1. **asylum:** (n) sanctuary, refuge, institution for the mentally ill

    Since the mentally ill man had trouble living alone, he was placed in an *asylum* last week.

    syn: haven, retreat, hideaway, shelter

2. **bungalow:** (n) one-story cottage

    Our family enjoys renting the *bungalow* on Brooks Lake each summer.

    syn: cabin, summerhouse

    Helpful Hint: A bungaLOW is a building that is usually LOW to the ground.

3. **cavern:** (n) a large cave

    The scientists want to revisit this *cavern* to check for possible changes in the rock formations.

    Family words: cavernous (adj)

    Helpful Hint: A CAVErn is a large CAVE.

4. **depot:** (n) storehouse; warehouse; railroad or bus station

    The truck driver dropped the sixteen large boxes at the grain *depot*.

    My mother will pick up my sister at the train *depot* at six o'clock tonight.

    syn: terminal, terminus

5. **galley:** (n) a long, low ancient ship propelled by oars; the kitchen of a ship or airplane

    We drew pictures of an immense *galley* that included the slaves and convicts who were on board.

    The documentary revealed that many slaves were harshly treated as they rowed in the *galley* of this antique ship.

6. **hearth:** (n) stone floor of a fireplace

    Please do not leave the newspapers on the *hearth*, as they could easily ignite from the sparks.

7. **labyrinth:** (n) structure containing an intricate network of winding passages that are hard to follow without losing one's way; a maze

    Daedulus, the father of Icarus, constructed mythology's most famous *labyrinth* at the request of Crete's King Minos.

    syn: intricacy, confusion, tangle

8. **lagoon:** (n) an area of shallow salt water

    We wandered near this peaceful *lagoon* while we were vacationing here last summer.

9. **landmark:** (n) a prominent feature of a landscape

    The Golden Gate Bridge is a California *landmark*.

    syn: milestone, watershed, highlight, feature

PLACES (continued)

10. **metropolis:** (n) a large city or center

    Which is your favorite North American *metropolis*—New York, Los Angeles, Atlanta, or Boston?

    syn: hub, seat

11. **monastery:** (n) residence for monks

    The monks living in that *monastery* have taken certain vows including poverty, obedience, and silence.

    Helpful Hint: MONks live in a MONastery.

12. **peninsula:** (n) land with water on three sides

    Bordered by the Atlantic Ocean and the Gulf of Mexico, Florida is a world-famous *peninsula*.

    Helpful Hint: A PENinsula is often shaped like a PEN.

13. **plateau:** (n) an elevated tract of flat land

    The view from this large *plateau* is both magnificent and breathtaking.

    syn: tableland, plain, highland, mesa

    Helpful Hint: A PLATEAU and a PLATE are both flat!

14. **quay:** (n) wharf; dock

    Workers called stevedores load and unload the ships that dock at this *quay*.

    syn: pier, landing

15. **vestibule:** (n) a small entrance hall or room, either to a building or to a larger room

    My father greeted our New Year's Eve guests in the *vestibule* before escorting them into the living room.

    syn: foyer, antechamber, hallway, entry

    Helpful Hint: Leave your VEST in the VESTibule before you walk into the living room.

1-1   A LARGE CITY, A DOCK, AND MORE

One of the answers in this crossword puzzle has to do with a large city. Another has to do with a dock. So there's a start. Fill in the answers to the fifteen clues below.

Across

1. prominent feature of a landscape
6. land with water on three sides
8. small entrance hall either to a building or to a larger room
10. storehouse; warehouse; railroad or bus station
12. structure containing an intricate network of winding passages
14. institution for the mentally ill; refuge; place of protection

Down

1. an area of shallow water
2. residence for monks
3. dock; wharf; pier
4. large cave
5. large city or center
7. elevated tract of flat land
9. long, low usually single-decked ship propelled by oars and sails used in ancient and medieval times; kitchen of a ship
11. one-story cottage
13. stone floor of a fireplace

1-2   THE LETTERS C AND R STAND FOR THEMSELVES

Today is your day to play detective. The fifteen words from Unit 1 have been disguised in this activity. Code letters have been substituted for the letters of the words, except that the real letter C is still the letter C in the substitute code, and the letter R is still the letter R in the substitute code. The other letters found in the Code Letters column have been given substitutes. Use the Letter Substitution Code to track your letters. Write the correct letters in the appropriate spaces. If you have done all of this correctly, you have decoded the fifteen words and are a good detective!

Code Letters	**Real Letters**
1. CUWDRT	CAV __ R __
2. NQUBDUH	__ __ A __ __ A __
3. NDTLTOHQU	__ __ __ __ __ __ __ __ A
4. QUKVRLTBA	__ A __ __ R __ __ __ __
5. SYTUOBDRV	__ __ __ A __ __ __ R __
6. ADURBA	__ __ A R __ __
7. PDNYB	__ __ __ __ __
8. SDBRYNYQLO	__ __ __ __ __ __ __ __ __ __
9. MUQQDV	__ A __ __ __ __
10. UOVQHS	A __ __ __ __ __
11. QUTPSURG	__ A __ __ __ A R __
12. WDOBLKHQD	V __ __ __ __ __ __ __ __
13. QUMYYT	__ A __ __ __ __
14. KHTMUQYE	__ __ __ __ A __ __ __
15. IHUV	__ __ A __

Letter Substitution Code Used:

Code Letters: A B C D E G H I K L M N O P Q R S T U V W Y

Real Letters: __ __ C __ __ __ __ __ __ __ __ __ __ __ __ R __ __ A __ V __

1-3   FIND THE THREE WORDS

Choose the correct word and then write it in the appropriate blank. After each sentence, a number is written within parentheses. That number signifies the letter that should be written at the bottom of this page. If you have correctly written the fifteen letters in order, you have spelled out three five-letter words. The first word means to soothe; the second is something you need for a printer; the third is where many actors earn their living.

asylum	depot	labyrinth	metropolis	plateau
bungalow	galley	lagoon	monastery	quay
cavern	hearth	landmark	peninsula	vestibule

1. While exploring a(n) _____ in England in the 1900s, scientist Arthur Ogilvy found the jawbone of a man, now dated at 31,000 years old. **(2)**

2. My father catches many fish in the _____ that eventually empties into the Caribbean Sea. **(1)**

3. Our science teacher told us about a unique type of bird _____ found in the woods near our school. **(4)**

4. We spotted several horses on the distant plains as we stood atop the _____. **(6)**

5. Our hotel is just down the block from the _____, where many ships pull into port each day. **(4)**

6. Since this old palace has so many confusing long and narrow hallways, we thought that we were in a(n) _____. **(8)**

7. Grandfather enjoyed moving to the peaceful countryside after living and working for so many years in the noisy and crowded _____. **(5)**

8. Only the northern portion of this _____ does not have a coastline. **(5)**

9. Please explain what types of activity took place down in the ship's _____. **(5)**

10. The Eiffel Tower in Paris is a world-famous _____. **(7)**

11. Our small group waited for ten minutes in the building's _____ before we were escorted into the large conference room to meet our state representative. **(3)**

12. Hundreds of monks have lived in this magnificent _____ during the past two hundred years. **(6)**

13. Our family cat lies near the _____ to keep warm during those cold winter nights. **(3)**

14. Each summer, my friend's family lives in a lakeside _____ that was built nearly fifty years ago. **(4)**

15. How many bus and train riders use this _____ each week? **(2)**

_____

1-4   A COLORFUL MATCHING COLUMN

Match the word in Column A with its definition in Column B. Then write the two-letter answer on the line after the number in Column A. Last, write the two-letter answers (in order) at the bottom of the page. If your answers are correct, you will understand the title of this activity.

Column A

1. _____ asylum

2. _____ bungalow

3. _____ cavern

4. _____ depot

5. _____ galley

6. _____ hearth

7. _____ labyrinth

8. _____ lagoon

9. _____ landmark

10. _____ metropolis

11. _____ monastery

12. _____ peninsula

13. _____ plateau

14. _____ quay

15. _____ vestibule

Column B

bl. residence for monks

br. sanctuary, refuge; institution for the mentally ill

di. wharf; dock

ed. large city or center

eo. stone floor of a fireplace

er. prominent feature of a landscape

go. small entrance hall or room

in. elevated tract of flat land

ng. area of shallow saltwater

np. large cave

ow. one-story cottage

pl. log, low ancient ship propelled by oars

ra. structure containing an intricate network of winding passages

ue. land with water on three sides

ur. storehouse; warehouse; railroad or bus station

_____

_____

_____

Unit 2

BEG, BORROW, AND STEAL

BEG, BORROW, AND STEAL

1. **accumulate:** (v) to collect over a period of time

   Since my grandfather and my father have given me their comic book collections, I have been able to *accumulate* many comic books these past few years.

   syn: gather, amass, heap, pile; **ant:** get rid of, spend, throw out, give away

   family words: accumulation (n)

   Helpful Hint: If you start too LATE, you cannot accumuLATE too much!

2. **bankrupt:** (adj) legally unable to pay debts; (v) to cause to become bankrupt

   Unfortunately, many of these companies are *bankrupt* due to poor management and inferior service.

   A bad economy will *bankrupt* companies very easily.

   syn: insolvent, destitute, broke, in the red (adj); **ant:** solvent, flourishing, in the black (adj)

   family words: bankruptcy (n)

3. **cache:** (n) safe place to hide things; (v) to hide or store

   The explorers hid their food supplies in the *cache* deep within the forest.

   These criminals *cached* their loot in the basement closet.

   syn: storehouse, hideout, hideaway, repository, stockpile, reserve (n)

   Helpful Hint: People often hide CASH in the CACHE.

4. **counterfeit:** (n) an imitation made to deceive; forgery; (adj) made in imitation so as to deceive; pretended or forged; (v) to make an imitation or fraud; to pretend; to feign

   Experts quickly informed us that this painting was nothing more than a *counterfeit*.

   After the criminal was caught passing *counterfeit* $100 bills in this county, he was arrested.

   The convict had *counterfeited* these $100 bills.

   syn: copy, fake, reproduction (n); false, spurious, fake, bogus (adj); **ant:** genuine, authentic, real (adj)

   family words: counterfeiter (n)

   Helpful Hint: The criminal placed the COUNTERfeit bills on the COUNTER.

5. **embezzle:** (v) to steal (money, etc., entrusted to one's care); to take by fraud for one's own use

   O. Henry, the author of the short story "The Gift of the Magi," was charged with trying to *embezzle* money when he worked as a bank teller in an Austin, Texas, bank.

   syn: pilfer, peculate

   family words: embezzlement, embezzler (n)

6. **entreat:** (v) to ask earnestly; to appeal; to plead

   The four prisoners *entreated* their captors to treat them mercifully.

   syn: beg, implore, beseech, petition

   family words: entreatingly (adv); entreaty, entreatment (n)

   Helpful Hint: The children would enTREAT Mom for an after-dinner TREAT.

7. **hoard:** (v) to accumulate and hide or to keep in reserve; (n) a supply stored up or hidden

   Before he changed his selfish ways, Ebenezer Scrooge, a character in Charles Dickens's "A Christmas Carol," loved to *hoard* money.

   All of us were surprised when he showed us his *hoard* of cash.

   syn: collect, amass, save, store; **ant:** disperse, squander, spend, scatter, use up

   family words: hoarder (n)

BEG, BORROW, AND STEAL (continued)

8. **implore:** (v) to ask or beg earnestly for

   Seeing the helpless dog near the curb, the young girl *implored* nearby adults to assist her in getting the animal to the vet.

   syn: entreat, beseech, plead, importune

   family words: imploringly (adv)

9. **larceny:** (n) theft of property

   Many notorious bank robbers, such as Butch Cassidy and the Sundance Kid, were later charged with *larceny*.

   syn: stealing, embezzlement, swindling, burglary, robbery

   family words: larcenist, larcener (n); larcenous (adj); larcenously (adv)

10. **mendicant:** (n) one who begs

    Since he rarely has money to buy himself a cup of coffee, a *mendicant* will often ask passers-by for some change.

    syn: beggar, panhandler

    family words: mendicancy, mendacity (n)

    Helpful Hint: When asked, "Why don't you patch up your clothes?" the beggar replied, "MEND I CAN'T!"

11. **mortgage:** (n) pledge to pay back debt; (v) to put an advance claim or liability on

    My parents had taken out a twenty-five-year *mortgage* when they purchased their new home.

    Ricardo's parents *mortgaged* their home and now owe the bank quite a bit of money.

    syn: promise, pawn, encumber

    family words: mortgaged (adj); mortgager (n)

    Helpful Hint: MORT GAGE always paid his MORTGAGE on time.

12. **pilfer:** (v) to steal (especially small sums or petty objects); filch

    I hope you never *pilfer* money from the poor box at church.

    syn: purloin, snatch, rifle

    family words: pilferer (n)

13. **plagiarize:** (v) to take ideas or writings from another person or source and pass them off as your own

    The teacher found that several students had *plagiarized* their essays from the Internet.

    syn: pirate, copy, steal, borrow, infringe

    family words: plagiarizer (n)

    Helpful Hint: The PLAY GUYS tried to PLAGIARIZE the play.

14. **thief:** (n) one who steals; one guilty of theft or larceny

    Caught by the police, the *thief* handed over the stolen money.

    syn: filcher, robber, burglar, pilferer, swindler

15. **usurp:** (v) to take or assume power, or a position, or the rights to something and hold in possession by force or without right

    The violent protestors tried to *usurp* the throne from the reigning king.

    syn: take over, seize, commandeer, wrest, exact

    family words: usurper (n)

2-1   START WITH A CAPITAL

Here are fifteen words from Unit 2 and one other word—a country's capital. Match each word with its definition by writing the correct number in the appropriate box. Let's start with Washington, DC, a capital. You'll see that the number 10 has been placed in the box with the letter P. Do the same for the other fifteen words and their definitions. If your answers are correct, all rows, columns, and the two diagonals will add up to the same number.

A. haggle   **E.** habitat   **I.** accumulate   **M.** miser
B. implore   **F.** mortgage   **J.** dwindle   **N.** pilfer
C. counterfeit   **G.** cache   **K.** entreat   **O.** larceny
D. mendicant   **H.** bankrupt   **L.** hoard   **P.** Washington, DC

1. pledge to pay back debt, especially on a house or piece of property
2. collect over a period of time
3. theft of property
4. beggar
5. a greedy, stingy person
6. to beg
7. legally unable to pay one's debts
8. to ask earnestly
9. forged imitation
10. capital of the United States
11. to decrease in size or amount
12. natural home
13. to get and store away money or goods; to accumulate and hide or keep in reserve
14. safe place to hide things
15. argue about the terms of something
16. to steal

A=	B=	C=	D=
E=	F=	G=	H=
I=	J=	K=	L=
M=	N=	O=	P=10

Magic Number:

_____

2-2   PATRIOTISM IS IN!

Match each word in Column A with its opposite from Column B. Write the two-letter answers from Column B on the line next to the proper answer in Column A. When your answers are correct, you will spell out the last names of three famous American patriots. Write the two-letter answers (in order) at the bottom of this page.

Column A

1. _____ accumulate

2. _____ bankrupt

3. _____ counterfeit

4. _____ embezzle

5. _____ hoard

6. _____ larceny

7. _____ mendicant

8. _____ mortgage

9. _____ plagiarize

10. _____ thief

11. _____ usurp

Column B

an. to write one's own ideas in an honest way

da. donation

er. genuine

ff. solvent; able to pay one's debts

fr. the act of lending money to another

in. to legally give power to another

je. to spend freely

kl. one who donates

ms. one who gives money to beggars

na. small amount

so. to give money to another

_____

_____

_____

2-3 SLIDING ALONG

Circle the synonym for each of the twelve words. Then write the letter on the line next to the number. If your answers are correct, not only will you spell out a popular wintertime activity, but you will also see how this activity's title makes sense.

1. _____ **accumulate**   (r) to deceive   (s) to collect over a period of time   (t) to forget

2. _____ **cache**   (n) safe place to hide things   (o) dock   (p) forged items

3. _____ **counterfeit**   (m) blessing   (n) opportunity   (o) an imitation made to deceive

4. _____ **embezzle**   (u) to spend freely   (v) to memorize   (w) to steal

5. _____ **hoard**   (a) school of fish   (b) a supply stored up or hidden   (c) a weather vane

6. _____ **implore**   (o) to beg   (p) to remind   (q) to remember

7. _____ **larceny**   (a) theft of propert   (b) donations   (c) starting fires

8. _____ **mendicant**   (q) one who repairs automobiles   (r) beggar   (s) loser

9. _____ **mortgage**   (c) tuition payment   (d) pledge to pay back debt   (e) insurance for the homeowner

10. _____ **plagiarize**   (h) to take a course in college   (i) to take ideas or writings from another person   (j) to have fun

11. _____ **thief**   (n) one who steals   (o) chef   (p) coach

12. _____ **usurp**   (f) to make a funny sound while drinking a cold drink   (g) to take or assume power, or a position, or the rights to something by force   (h) to bring happiness to another person

What is the popular winter time activity? _____

2-4   NO NEED TO BEG, BORROW, OR STEAL

If you know your words from Unit 2, there is no need to beg, borrow, or steal any answers in this word-find puzzle. Simply circle the fifteen words from Unit 2 in this puzzle. (The words are found horizontally, vertically, and diagonally.) The number of letters found in each word is listed next to the word's definition.

```
h o a r d k a c c u m u l a t e m m y m
n x v p e h w t k h k x z b t b o e p p
h k r j m p g j p m n n k j y t r n j g
p w y z b v f z i q p m b q k f t d n p
m i b l e a h s l y d b i h p y g i r z
b n m b z p n x f w d h x s f z a c z k
c p k p z d s k e j w s r t e y g a d w
h a g g l e l a r c e n y h z r e n l w
d k c p e o n c c u k d w k f x t t x h
w g x h l c r v h b p t f w q p q g j g
i y c z e l k e h c s t w m t j p z z s
n c o u n t e r f e i t e n t r e a t y
d d t h h p b c d t v h f x h y n y k k
l l d d t t k y c b j m b p w w d c s p
e b d t w l v z p b s v b h f x s t h k
```

a greedy, stingy person (5)

argue about the terms of something (6)

beggar (9)

to steal (8)

collect over a period of time (10)

forged imitation (11)

legally unable to pay one's debts (8)

pledge to pay back debt, especially on a house or piece of property (8)

safe place to hide things (5)

theft of property (7)

to ask earnestly (7)

to beg (7)

to decrease in size or amount (7)

to get and store away money or goods (5)

to steal (6)

Unit 3

WHAT'S THAT YOU SAY?

WHAT'S THAT YOU SAY?

1. **anecdote:** (n) a short account of an incident in someone's life

    My uncle loves to entertain us with his *anecdotes* about his life as a sailor.

    syn: tale, story, narrative

    Helpful Hint: ANN ECDOTE loved to relate her favorite ANECDOTE.

2. **aver:** (v) to declare to be true; to state positively; to affirm

    I firmly *aver* that I was not there when the robbery occurred.

    syn: attest, swear; **ant:** deny, refute, dispute

3. **braggart:** (n) one who boasts or brags

    It is usually boring and never easy to listen to a *braggart* relate tales of his deeds.

    syn: swaggerer, showoff

    family words: bragging (adj)

4. **concur:** (v) to agree

    Most of the classmates *concur* with Robert's suggestion on how to solve the Thanksgiving dance problem.

    syn: accede, approve, assent, consent; **ant:** disagree, object, dissent

    Helpful Hint: The prefix "con-" means *with* and the root word "cur" means *to run*. Thus, concur means to "run with" or "to agree."

5. **counsel:** (v) to advise; to give advice; (n) discussion and deliberation; advice; lawyer

    Mrs. O'Neill will often *counsel* her young children about home safety.

    Whenever Manuel encounters a major problem, he will often seek his father's *counsel*.

    She hired an experienced *counsel* to help him with his legal case.

    syn: urge, favor, instruct, advocate (v); consultation, deliberation, advisement (n)

6. **fabricate:** (v) to make, build, construct, especially by assembling parts already manufactured; to make up a story or lie; invent

    Since I have always found Teresa to be truthful, I cannot believe that she would ever *fabricate* such a farfetched story.

    syn: (for "to make") assemble, manufacture, create; (for "to invent") concoct, feign, contrive, make up

    family words: fabricator, fabrication (n)

7. **frank:** (adj) candid; honest

    Because she wanted me to be *frank* with her, I had to tell her the painful truth as to why she had not been selected for the team.

    syn: open, straightforward, unconcealed, undisguised, direct; **ant:** guarded, ambiguous, constrained, veiled

    family words: frankness (n)

    Helpful Hint: My friend FRANK is always very honest. He's FRANK in more ways than one!

8. **gist:** (n) the basic idea of

    Not having the time to tell her friends the entire incident, Juanita gave them only the *gist* of the event.

    syn: substance, point, core, essence, sense, crux

    Helpful Hint: Please do not tell the entire story. JUST the GIST is fine with me!

WHAT'S THAT YOU SAY? (continued)

9. **interrogate:** (v) to ask questions formally in examining

   Our lawyer, Ms. Louden, began to *interrogate* the witness to see what he remembered about the accident.

   syn: question, inquire, query; **ant:** answer, reply, respond

   family words: interrogator, interrogation (n); interrogative (adj)

10. **murmur:** (v) to make a low, indistinct, continuous sound; (n) a low, indistinct, continuous sound, as of a stream or far-off voices; a mumbled or muttered complaint

    Please speak clearly. Do not *murmur* your response.

    Ursula found the stream's *murmur* to be quite relaxing.

    syn: hum, drone, buzz (v); buzz, rustle, purr (n)

    family words: murmurer, murmuration (n); murmuring (adj)

11. **mute:** (adj) not speaking; voluntarily silent; unable to speak; not spoken; (n) a person who does not speak

    Rather than telling what he knew of the accident, the eyewitness remained *mute*.

    The narrator of Kesey's novel, *One Flew over the Cuckoo's Nest*, poses as a *mute*.

    syn: dumb, wordless, soundless, mum (adj); **ant:** voiced, sounded, spoken, talkative, audible (adj)

    family words: mutely (adv); muteness (n)

    Helpful Hint: The young, silent boy thought that it was cute to be MUTE.

12. **narrate:** (v) to tell a story

    My teacher can *narrate* a story as well as anyone I know.

    syn: describe, relate, recount, detail

    family words: narrator, narration (n); narrative (adj)

13. **negotiate:** (v) to make arrangements with a view to reaching an agreement; to try to settle; (v) to surmount; to cross

    Our mayor tried to *negotiate* a deal between the town's workers and the city council.

    The champion cyclist had little trouble *negotiating* the mountain's curves.

    syn: bargain, arrange, mediate, intercede

    family words: negotiator, negotiation (n)

14. **pun:** (n) play on words; (v) to make a pun or puns

    "Most of the houses in France are made of plaster of Paris" is an example of a *pun*.

    Henrietta loves to *pun*, especially since her friends enjoy hearing her clever word play.

    family words: punster (n)

    Helpful Hint: It is fun to hear a good PUN. Play on, words!

15. **reassure:** (v) to give confidence to

    Let me *reassure* you that you have a really good chance of making the cheerleading team.

    syn: convince, persuade, ensure; **ant:** question

    family words: reassurance (n); reassuringly (adv)

    Helpful Hint: Need confidence? Not only will I ASSURE you, but I will also REASSURE you!

3-1   RELATING THEM

On the lines provided, express the relationship between each pair of words or phrases.

1. braggart : humble _____

2. counsel : advise _____

3. reassure : lack of confidence _____

4. anecdote : lengthy _____

5. mute : able to be heard _____

6. fabricate : invent _____

7. narrate : anecdote _____

8. concur : disagree _____

9. aver : to deny _____

10. murmur : roar _____

11. pun : clever _____

12. frank : dishonest _____

13. gist : main point _____

14. interrogate : answer _____

15. negotiate : stir up trouble _____

3-2   EGO MAN

Fill in each blank with one of the following words. Each word is used only once.

anecdote	concur	frank	murmur	negotiate
avers	counsel	gist	mute	pun
braggart	fabricate	interrogated	narrate	reassure

First, let me _____(1) you that I am telling you the truth. I did not
_____(2) this story. Please understand that I do not intend to tell you the
entire story. Instead, I will tell you the _____(3) of what happened that day
to a guy named Ego Man.

My older brother, Sam, the one who loves to tell an interesting _____(4)
now and then, has always been very _____(5) with me. Since he tells it
like it is, he _____(6) that this really happened. Last week, he started to
_____(7) a story about Ego Man, this not-too-smart _____(8)
who loves to talk about himself and how terrific he is.

Sam related the story of how Ego Man had attempted to _____(9) a dis-
pute between two of his soccer teammates. These other two players had been arguing with each
other throughout the practice. Thinking he possessed the wisdom of Solomon, not to mention
superb conflict-resolution skills, Ego Man tried to _____(10) his teammates.
Neither would _____(11) with his suggestions on how to stop arguing with each
other. Both players felt that Ego Man made them appear foolish as he _____(12)
them with all sorts of foolish questions in front of the other players. Feeling uneasy and
not wanting to give a clear response, each guy answered Ego Man's questions with a
_____(13) that could hardly be heard. It was almost as though the players
wished they could suddenly become _____(14), unable to respond to Ego
Man's silly questions. Finally, after several insulting responses by these two players, including
a clever _____(15) on the word *gymnasium*, Ego Man became so frustrated
that he walked away in disgust (and confusion).

3-3 WHO IS THEODORE GEISEL?

Somewhere in this puzzle you will find out (if you do not already know) why Theodore Geisel is famous. You will also fill in the words from Unit 3 (and other words) along the way. Have fun!

Across

  5. to invent; to make up
  9. Italy's monetary unit
 10. the skin on your head
 14. to agree
 16. short, amusing story
 20. to tell a story
 21. silent
 22. to give confidence

Down

  1. main idea of a story
  2. the famous children's author, Theodore Geisel, used Dr. _____ as his pen name
  3. nursery rhyme Jack's companion
  4. to ask questions
  5. candid; honest
  6. one who boasts or brags
  7. to state
  8. New York's capital city
 11. play on words
 12. to try to bring two sides together
 13. game played mostly with the feet
 15. to advise
 17. exit's opposite
 18. Paris is its capital
 19. low, indistinct sound

3-4   THREE-LETTER ADJECTIVES

Ten of the words from Unit 3 have been broken up into two parts. The first part of the word is in Column A, and the second part is in Column B. The definitions of these ten words are found in Column C. Each of the groups of letters in these three columns has a letter next to it. Match the three correct parts and then, at the bottom of this page, write the three-letter adjective that you have spelled out.

Column A	Column B	Column C
1. a **(t)**	assure **(o)**	low, indistinct sound **(t)**
2. anec **(o)**	ate **(r)**	one who boasts **(d)**
3. brag **(o)**	cur **(o)**	short, amusing story **(d)**
4. con **(p)**	dote **(d)**	to advise **(y)**
5. coun **(s)**	gart **(l)**	to agree **(t)**
6. inter **(b)**	iate **(c)**	to ask questions **(g)**
7. mur **(w)**	mur **(e)**	to give confidence **(w)**
8. narr **(d)**	rogate **(i)**	to state **(n)**
9. negot **(i)**	scl **(h)**	to tell a story **(y)**
10. re **(l)**	ver **(a)**	to try to settle **(e)**

1. _____   6. _____

2. _____   7. _____

3. _____   8. _____

4. _____   9. _____

5. _____   10. _____

3-5   UNITS 1–3 CROSSWORD PUZZLE REVIEW

Fill in the blanks with words from Units 1 to 3. Good luck!

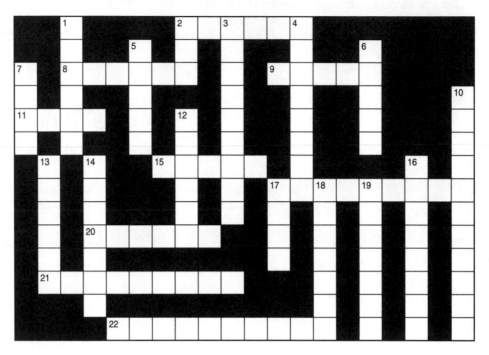

Across

2. to steal in small quantities
8. an area of shallow salt water
9. safe place to hide things
11. to declare to be true
15. candid; honest
17. beggar
20. a large cave
21. residence for monks
22. collect over a period of time

Down

1. a long, low ancient ship propelled by oars; kitchen area
2. play on words
3. structure containing an intricate network of winding passages that are hard to follow without losing one's way; a maze
4. to give confidence
5. a supply stored up or hidden; accumulate and hide or keep in reserve
6. storehouse; warehouse
7. dock; pier
10. an imitation made to deceive; forgery
12. to make a low, indistinct continuous sound
13. place of protection
14. theft of property
16. legally unable to pay debts
17. silent
18. to tell a story
19. to beg

Words, Words, Words!

Units 1–3   REVIEW TEST

Directions: Please circle the correct **synonym.** Then write the answer's corresponding letter on the line next to the question's number. Each question is worth four points.

1. ____ **cavern**   (a) small house   (b) large cave   (c) mountain resort

2. ____ **peninsula**   (a) land with water on three sides   (b) ocean's bottom   (c) island

3. ____ **quay**   (a) door opener   (b) ship   (c) wharf or dock

4. ____ **accumulate**   (a) collect over a period of time   (b) to steal   (c) send to another country

5. ____ **embezzle**   (a) to work in a bank   (b) to steal   (c) to give to the poor

6. ____ **pilfer**   (a) to steal in small quantities   (b) to take or assume power   (c) to beg

7. ____ **mortgage**   (a) owning of two or more homes   (b) beggar   (c) pledge to pay back debt

8. ____ **concur**   (a) safe place to hide things   (b) to agree   (c) place inside an airport

9. ____ **mute**   (a) arguing   (b) noisy   (c) silent

10. ____ **metropolis**   (a) large city or center   (b) prominent feature of a landscape
(c) area of shallow saltwater

Directions: Please circle the correct **antonym.** Then write the answer's corresponding letter on the line next to the question's number. Each question is worth four points.

11. ____ **bungalow**   (a) mansion   (b) small city   (c) ferocious reptile

12. ____ **plagiarize**   (a) to help another do a job   (b) to do one's own work
(c) to give secret information to another

13. ____ **reassure**   (a) to lend money to another person   (b) to inspire fear in another or oneself
(c) to give confidence to another or oneself

14. ____ **interrogate**   (a) to answer   (b) to be mute   (c) to aid another

15. ____ **usurp**   (a) one who gives money to another   (b) to give over willingly
(c) to take by force

16. ____ **counterfeit**   (a) genuine   (b) forgotten   (c) lazy

17. ____ **braggart**   (a) humble person   (b) boastful person   (c) one who is absent from school

18. ____ **bankrupt**   (a) able to pay one's bills   (b) not guilty   (c) taking out mortgages

19. ____ **frank**   (a) play on words   (b) insincere   (c) mute

20. ____ **despair**   (a) tragedy   (b) two of the same thing   (c) hope

Units 1–3   REVIEW TEST (continued)

Directions: Please circle the word that correctly **completes** the sentence. Then write the answer's corresponding letter on the line next to the question's number. Each question is worth four points.

21. ____ Rather than relating the lengthy story, he just gave us the   **(a) cache**   **(b) gist**   **(c) pun**   of the incident.

22. ____ The peacemaker tried to   **(a) negotiate**   **(b) interrogate**   **(c) hoard**   a deal that would bring the two warring parties together.

23. ____ The Seattle Space Needle is the city's most famous   **(a) labyrinth**   **(b) plateau**   **(c) landmark**.

24. ____ We studied all about the monks who had lived in this   **(a) lagoon**   **(b) monastery**   **(c) depot**   where they prayed, worked, and studied in silence.

25. ____ With thousands of dollars that they could not account for stored in their car's trunk, the two men were accused of   **(a) larceny**   **(b) asylum**   **(c) labyrinth.**

Unit 4

CLEAN YOUR ROOM!

CLEAN YOUR ROOM!

1. **amend:** (v) to make better; to improve; to correct; to change or revise (a law or legislative bill)

   I have to *amend* my poor eating habits and start to eat healthy foods.

   How do you plan to *amend* the current law so that more people are happy with it?

   syn: ameliorate, strengthen; **ant:** worsen, weaken, pollute

   family words: amendable (adj); amender (n)

   Helpful Hint: The Bill of Rights, the U.S. Constitution's first ten AMENDments, changed and improved the Constitution.

2. **cram:** (v) to fill (a space) beyond normal capacity by pressing or squeezing; to stuff into; to pack full or too full; to stuff

   How many more toys can we *cram* into that toy chest?

   syn: squeeze, compress, saturate, glut

   family words: crammer (n)

3. **despair:** (v) to give up hope; (n) loss of hope

   As long as you have the slightest bit of hope, you should not *despair*.

   None of the people here think that *despair* is the way to go in difficult times.

   syn: lose heart, despond (v); hopelessness, discouragement, depression (n)

   family words: despairing (adj); despairingly (adv)

4. **eave:** (n) roof overhang

   The *eave* of the house next to ours almost touches our roof's eave.

   Helpful Hint: EVE stood beneath her roof's EAVE to shelter herself from the rain.

5. **eccentric:** (adj) odd; unusual; (n) one who is odd or unusual

   The *eccentric* man uses a knife and fork when he eats his candy bar.

   There was the *eccentric*, doing odd things at every turn.

   syn: unconventional, strange, bizarre, weird; **ant:** conventional, ordinary, regular, normal

   family words: eccentricity (n); eccentrically (adv)

   Helpful Hint: The prefix "ec-" means *away from*, and the root "centr" means *in the center*. Thus, ECCENTRIC means "away from the center" (or what is normal or typical).

6. **forbidding:** (adj) looking dangerous or threatening; (v) not allowing

   The storm clouds in the distance looked quite *forbidding*.

   His aunt was *forbidding* him from going to the concert that night.

   syn: frightening, scary, horrifying (adj); prohibiting, banning, excluding (v); **ant:** pleasant, agreeable, friendly, encouraging (adj); allow, permit, sanction, let (v)

   family words: forbiddingly (adv); forbidden (adj)

7. **germinate:** (v) to begin to grow, as from a spore, seed or bud; to start developing or growing

   How long will it take for these seeds to *germinate*?

   syn: sprout, push up

   family words: germination (n); germinative (adj)

CLEAN YOUR ROOM! (continued)

8. **habitat:** (n) natural home

   The jungle is the lion's *habitat*.

   Helpful Hint: It became a HABIT for the bird to go to its HABITAT.

9. **imply:** (v) to suggest; to hint; to intimate

   I did not mean to *imply* that you are not that talented.

   syn: insinuate, connote, allude, signify

   family words: implication (n); implicated (adj)

10. **maze:** (n) confusing pathway

    My mother often feels as though she is in a *maze* in that large supermarket.

    syn: meander, tangle, snarl, complex

    Helpful Hint: I was AMAZED that I made it through the confusing MAZE.

11. **ordeal:** (n) difficult or painful experience

    Running the 26.2 marathon was an *ordeal* for the relatively new distance runner.

    syn: trial, tribulation, torment; **ant:** joy, delight, pleasure

12. **prohibit:** (v) to forbid; to outlaw

    If this law *prohibits* my walking the dog in the park, I guess that I will have to take him home.

    syn: ban, prevent, deny; **ant:** allow, permit, legalize, encourage

    family words: prohibiter, prohibitor, prohibition (n); prohibitive (adj); prohibitively (adv)

    Helpful Hint: A PRO is PROhibited from smoking on the baseball field.

13. **scour:** (v) to clean by vigorous scrubbing

    Steve had to *scour* that pot in order to remove the stubborn stains.

    syn: wash, brush

    family words: scourer (n)

14. **spacious:** (adj) large; having more than enough room or space

    No one felt crowded in the *spacious* reception hall that we had rented for my sister's wedding.

    syn: roomy, commodious, sizable; **ant:** cramped, crowded, small

    family words: spaciousness (n); spaciously (adv)

    Helpful Hint: A SPACIOUS room has much SPACE.

15. **utterly:** (adv) completely; totally

    Never have I felt so *utterly* helpless as when I tried to catch that greased pig.

    syn: extremely, thoroughly

4-1   FIND THE PROVERB

A proverb is a wise saying. "An apple a day keeps the doctor away" and "He who hesitates is lost" are two familiar proverbs. Match each word in Column A with its OPPOSITE in Column B by writing the two-letter answer on the appropriate line. Then write each two-letter answer (in order) at the bottom of this page. If your answers are correct, you will spell out a familiar proverb. We have helped you by giving one of the answers.

Column A	**Column B**
1. _____ amend	**ar.** have confidence
2. _____ cram	**bi.** causing pleasure
3. _____ despair	**ca.** state directly
4. _____ eccentric	**ee.** to place or insert comfortably, leaving sufficient room
5. _____ forbidding	**ne.** pleasant experience
6. _____ germinate	**he.** to leave dirty
7. _____ imply	**ly.** normal
8. _____ maze	**rd.** to wither
9. _he_ ordeal	**rm.** incomplete; partial
10. _____ prohibit	**st.** to allow
11. _____ scour	**tc.** clear path
12. _____ spacious	**th.** to leave as is
13. _____ utterly	**wo.** small and cramped

The proverb is _____

_____

_____

4-2   THERE ONCE WAS A MAN . . .

A limerick is a five-line poem that often starts with the words "There once was a man . . . " A limerick follows a specific rhyming pattern. Lines 1, 2, and 5 rhyme with each other. Lines 3 and 4 rhyme with each other. Use each of the following fifteen words only once in the six limericks below. Have fun!

amend	eave	germinate	maze	scour
cram	eccentric	habitat	ordeal	spacious
despair	forbidding	imply	prohibit	utterly

There once was a(n) _____ (1) named Steve
Whom we saw hanging from the roof's _____ (2).
We thought he was kidding
With act so _____ (3).
Yet we knew we should help and not leave.

There once was a wise woman named Clair
Who told us, "Be brave; don't _____."(4)
On her we could _____ (5) depend.
There was nothing in her to _____ (6).
She was a lady so smart and so fair!

There once was a guy named Gus
Who lived in a house quite _____ (7).
No bad news would he ever _____ (8)
When he had some for Chris or for Guy.
And that was the same for the rest of us!

Mom hoped that her seeds would _____ (9).
Each spring she planted on the same date.
But birds picked at this and that.
For this was their spring _____ (10),
And Mom could only try to tolerate!

We never looked forward to the hour
When Dad would point to the sink and say, "_____" (11).
We thought it an _____ (12),
So we'd often yell and squeal
Til' Dad would then point to the shower.

There once was a dangerous teen craze
To run through this darkened old _____ (13).
So we'd spread out or _____ (14)
Run with Bob, Ken, or Pam
Til' the cops did _____ (15) that phase.

4-3   LOOK FOR THOSE SECOND LETTERS

Write the correct word from Unit 4 in the appropriate space. Each word is used once. Then write the second letter of each answer (in order) on the line at the bottom of this page. If your answers are correct, you will spell out three words.

amend	eave	germinate	maze	scour
cram	eccentric	habitat	ordeal	spacious
despair	forbidding	imply	prohibit	utterly

1. _____ to clean by vigorous scrubbing

2. _____ difficult or painful experience

3. _____ to give up hope

4. _____ confusing pathway

5. _____ to suggest; not to state directly

6. _____ to stuff into

7. _____ causing fear

8. _____ roof overhang

9. _____ to change

10. _____ odd; unusual

11. _____ natural home

12. _____ to forbid

13. _____ large; having more than enough room or space

14. _____ to begin to grow

15. _____ completely

_____

_____

4-4   TWO WORDS AND TWO GIRLS

Write the correct word in each blank. Each word is used once. Then circle the next-to-last letter of each answer. Write those letters (in order) at the bottom of this page. If your answers are correct, you will spell out two words and two girls' names. Good luck!

amend	eave	germinate	maze	scour
cram	eccentric	habitat	ordeal	spacious
despair	forbidding	imply	prohibit	utterly

1. Due to car problems and numerous traffic jams, what we thought would be a great weekend vacation turned into nothing less than a(n) _____.

2. My father had to get a ladder to repair the rain-damaged _____.

3. My brother and I tried to _____ our sports equipment into the car's small trunk.

4. State laws _____ motorists from using cell phones while the car is moving.

5. The politician's proposal that taxes should be double next year is _____ ridiculous to some taxpayers.

6. Since the bathroom had not been cleaned in a while, we wanted to _____ every part of it.

7. Now that I have witnessed that horrible automobile accident, I will admit that I have never seen such a _____ event.

8. People who have confidence in themselves and their abilities tend not to _____ when difficulties arise.

9. These seeds tend to _____ several weeks after they have been planted.

10. Rather than directly state what I felt, I had to _____ to her what I thought she had done wrong.

11. The _____ older man used a knife and fork to eat his candy bar.

12. That neighborhood's roads are so complicated and confusing that it reminds me of a _____.

13. None of us realized how _____ our school's cafeteria is until we visited another school's tiny eating area.

14. The Bill of Rights proves that the Founding Fathers felt it was necessary to _____ the Constitution.

15. Does it seem that this animal caged in this zoo misses its former _____?

_____

Unit 5

HOW WE ACT

HOW WE ACT

1. **abnormal:** (adj) not typical

    After hearing the decision that they did not like, the group members began to act in an *abnormal* way.

    syn: unusual, irregular, odd; **ant:** normal, usual, standard, ordinary

    family words: abnormality (n); abnormally (adv)

    Helpful Hint: The prefix "ab-" means *away from*. Thus, *abnormal* behavior is *away from* the regular behavior.

2. **brood:** (v) to worry about; to think about something in a distressed or troubled way; (n) the offspring of animals; all the children in a family; a group of a particular breed or kind

    Try not to *brood* over the fact that you did not make the team.

    We met the *brood* as they were walking toward the park that night.

    syn: fret, pine, mope, ponder (v)

3. **casual:** (adj) not formal

    Since you do not have to dress formally, select some *casual* outfit to wear.

    syn: nonchalant, unconcerned, cool, calm; **ant:** planned, formal

    family words: casualness (n); casually (adv)

4. **caustic:** (adj) harsh; severe; biting

    The gas station attendant had a *caustic* tone that irritated my brother, who was trying to be genial.

    syn: corrosive, gnawing, destructive; **ant:** neutral, gentle, soothing

    family words: causticity (n); caustically (adv)

    Helpful Hint: For what CAUSE was he so CAUSTIC and spiteful to his friend?

5. **crude:** (adj) lacking taste and tact

    Behave properly; do not act in a *crude* fashion.

    syn: unrefined, ill-mannered, churlish; **ant:** refined, polished, well-mannered

    family words: crudeness (n); crudely (adv)

    Helpful Hint: It is RUDE to be CRUDE. So be tasteful and tactful!

6. **enchant:** (v) to charm greatly

    The young girl was *enchanted* by the stories she read before bedtime.

    syn: bewitch, hypnotize, mesmerize

    family words: enchanter, enchantress (n)

    Helpful Hint: Her AUNT wanted to ENCHANT the crowd at the musical concert.

7. **hospitable:** (adj) friendly

    It was nice to see someone treat us in a *hospitable* manner after the crude treatment we had received earlier.

    syn: neighborly, welcoming, convivial; **ant:** antisocial, aloof, unsociable

    family words: hospitably (adv)

    Helpful Hint: The HOSPITABLE HOSPITAL workers helped the patients.

HOW WE ACT (continued)

8. **insinuate:** (v) to introduce or work into gradually, indirectly, and artfully; to hint

    Are you trying to *insinuate* that I should carry all the groceries into the house?

    syn: suggest, imply, intimate

    family words: insinuator, insinuation (n); insinuatingly (adv); insinuative (adj)

9. **meddle:** (v) to interfere; to intrude

    My grandmother minds her own business and never *meddles* in the affairs of other people.

    syn: intrude, tamper; **ant:** hold aloof, refrain, avoid

    family words: meddler (n)

    Helpful Hint: You will not deserve a MEDAL when you MEDDLE in other people's business! Stay away!

10. **nurture:** (v) to promote the development of

    Her teacher *nurtured* Tamika's dancing skills.

    syn: feed, nourish, sustain, cultivate

    family words: nurturant, nurtural (adj); nurturer (n)

11. **oppress:** (v) to overpower; to keep down by the cruel use of authority

    Our government believes in freedom and will not *oppress* any of its citizens.

    syn: subjugate, abuse, tyrannize, persecute; **ant:** liberate, emancipate, free

    family words: oppressor (n); oppressive (adj); oppressively (adv)

    Helpful Hint: When you PRESS down on others, you are cruel to them. When you OPPRESS others, you are cruel to them.

12. **pamper:** (v) to gratify to excess

    The family members loved to *pamper* themselves with manicures, pedicures, and other luxuries.

    syn: coddle, spoil, indulge

    family words: pamperer (n)

13. **procure:** (v) to obtain; to acquire

    How can I *procure* a pass to get into the museum?

    syn: acquire, get, secure; **ant:** lose

    family words: procurement, procurer (n); procurable (adj)

    Helpful Hint: The PRO baseball player wanted to PROcure another great contract.

14. **snare:** (v) to catch by trapping; (n) a device used to capture someone or something

    The hunters attempted to *snare* the wild animal for several hours.

    Unfortunately, the *snare* did not attract the prey, and we could not capture the animal.

    syn: noose, trap (n)

    family words: snarer (n)

    Helpful Hint: Do you DARE to SNARE a wolf out of its lair?

15. **tamper:** (v) to meddle with

    It is not smart to *tamper* with that rough group of students.

    syn: interfere, fiddle

    family words: tamperer (n)

    Helpful Hint: Do not TAMPER with a tough guy from TAMPA!

5-1 CLUMPS OF LETTERS

Fill in the blanks with the words from the Unit 5 group below. The numbers after the definition indicate the letters that you should write (in order) at the bottom of this page. If your letters are correct, you will spell out seven different words.

abnormal	caustic	hospitable	nurture	procure
brood	crude	insinuate	oppress	snare
casual	enchant	meddle	pamper	tamper

1. __ __ __ __ __: to think about something in a distressed or troubled way **(2,3)**

2. __ __ __ __ __ __: gratify to excess **(3,4)**

3. __ __ __ __ __ __ __: to charm greatly **(3,4)**

4. _____: to overpower; to keep down by the cruel use of authority **(5,6,7)**

5. __ __ __ __ __ __: to meddle with **(4,5)**

6. __ __ __ __ __ __ __: to promote the development of **(3,4)**

7. __ __ __ __ __ __ __ __: not typical **(6,7)**

8. __ __ __ __ __ __ __ __ __: hint **(8,9)**

9. __ __ __ __ __: to catch by trapping **(2,3)**

10. __ __ __ __ __ __: to interfere **(1,2)**

11. __ __ __ __ __ __: not formal **(3,4)**

12. __ __ __ __ __ __ __ __ __: friendly **(5,6)**

13. __ __ __ __ __ __: to obtain **(2,5)**

14. __ __ __ __ __: lacking taste and tact; unrefined **(4,5)**

15. __ __ __ __ __ __: biting, harsh, severe **(4,5)**

Word #1: _____ (definitions 1 and 2)

Word #2: _____ (definitions 3 and 4)

Word #3: _____ (definitions 5 and 6)

Word #4: _____ (definitions 7 and 8)

Word #5: _____ (definitions 9 and 10)

Word #6: _____ (definitions 11 and 12)

Word #7: _____ (definitions 13, 14, and 15)

5-2   WHY START WITH SOMETHING CRUDE?

It is okay to start with something crude here since *crude* is the first answer! Each of the words below is used only once. Fill in your answers to complete each sentence.

abnormal	caustic	hospitable	nurture	procure
brood	crude	insinuate	oppress	snare
casual	enchant	meddle	pamper	tamper

1. Rather than behaving in the accepted calm and refined way, Ralph acted in a(n) _____ manner.

2. The group strongly believed in the freedom of speech and refused to _____ its members from expressing their true feelings.

3. Nobody should be so forward as to _____ in another's person's business.

4. Even though we lost the heated soccer match, our coach advised us to move on and not to _____ over the loss.

5. There is little sense in your trying to _____ with the evidence in this controversial trial.

6. The owners of the resort that we stay in each summer believe that all of their workers should act in a(n) _____ fashion toward the resort's guests.

7. Are you trying to _____ that we have not told you the truth?

8. Julie finished her report on the animals' _____ behaviors.

9. Because his parents wanted to _____ a love for the arts in Josh, they often took him to Broadway plays and musicals.

10. Please tell me how I may _____ a tape of last night's humorous TV show.

11. The doctor's _____ response to my concerns lessened my fears about the problem.

12. These angry, biting remarks had been delivered in a very _____ way.

13. Wanting me to become a strong and independent young man, my older brother refused to _____ me when I played sports with him.

14. What is the best method to _____ this wild animal without doing it any harm?

15. My grandfather would _____ us with his stories of the "good old days."

5-3   WHAT IS AN AMAZON?

Match the fifteen words below with their definitions. Write the correct number in the appropriate box. If your answers are correct, the columns, rows, and the two diagonals will add up to the same number. Plus, you will have figured out what an Amazon is!

A. hospitable　　**E.** Amazon　　**I.** oppress　　**M.** abnormal
B. brood　　　　**F.** crude　　　**J.** enchant　　**N.** snare
C. tamper　　　 **G.** procure　　**K.** casual　　 **O.** insinuate
D. caustic　　　 **H.** meddle　　**L.** pamper　　**P.** nurture

1. to interfere

2. not typical

3. to worry about

4. not formal

5. to charm greatly

6. to meddle with

7. to promote the development of

8. South American river; large female warrior

9. hint

10. lacking taste and tact

11. to overpower

12. harsh; biting; severe

13. friendly

14. to gratify to excess

15. to obtain

16. to catch by trapping

A=	B=	C=	D=
E=	F=	G=	H=
I=	J=	K=	L=
M=	N=	O=	P=

Magic Number:

_____

5-4 MUSIC TO YOUR EARS

Match the words in Column A with their definitions in Column B. Write the two-letter answers in the spaces next to the appropriate number in Column A. Then write the fifteen two-letter answers (in order) at the bottom of this page. If your answers are correct, you will spell out six different types of music.

Column A	Column B
1. _____ abnormal	**ae.** to meddle with
2. _____ brood	**bl.** not formal; in a relaxed manner
3. _____ casual	**ck.** to worry about
4. _____ caustic	**co.** to promote the development of
5. _____ crude	**gg.** to catch by trapping
6. _____ enchant	**ho.** friendly
7. _____ hospitable	**ip.** to charm greatly
8. _____ insinuate	**is.** to interfere
9. _____ meddle	**ja.** to overpower
10. _____ nurture	**pd.** hint
11. _____ oppress	**re.** to obtain
12. _____ pamper	**ro.** not typical
13. _____ procure	**sh.** lacking taste and tact
14. _____ snare	**ue.** harsh; biting; sarcastic
15. _____ tamper	**zz.** to gratify to excess

Six types of music: _____

_____

Unit 6

WORDS FROM MYTHOLOGY

WORDS FROM MYTHOLOGY

1. **ambrosia:** (n) the food of the gods

   Nectar was the favorite drink of the gods on Mount Olympus, and *ambrosia* was their favorite food.

   family words: ambrosial (adj)

   Helpful Hint: The modern-day goddess AMBER loved to eat AMBROSIA.

2. **atlas:** (n) a book of maps

   Our social studies teacher taught us how to use an *atlas* when trying to locate a country.

   Helpful Hint: AT LAST, I found my ATLAS. Now I know how to get there!

3. **centaur:** (n) monster with the head and arms of a man and the body and legs of a horse

   Last night I had a nightmare in which I was chased by the mythological *centaur*.

4. **echo:** (n) the repetition of sound; (v) to repeat another's words or ideas; to repeat or reflect sound from a surface

   The tour guide's *echo* could be heard from a distance in the cavern.

   We heard our voices *echo* as we shouted while walking through the tunnel leading to the beach.

   syn: reverberation (n); copy (v)

   family words: echoey (adj)

5. **Herculean:** (adj) very powerful or courageous

   All of the athletes featured in the World's Strongest Man competition had *Herculean* strength.

   syn: heroic, prodigious, titanic, mighty; **ant:** weak

6. **hygiene:** (n) sanitary practice

   Health teachers emphasize the importance of good *hygiene* to prevent sickness.

   syn: sanitation, cleanliness

   family words: hygienic (adj); hygienically (adv)

   Helpful Hint: White-tooted and germ-free GENE had great HYGIENE.

7. **iridescent:** (adj) showing shifting changes in color from different angles

   The entertainer's *iridescent* outfit was not a distraction to the audience members.

   family words: iridescence (n); iridescently (adv)

8. **jovial:** (adj) full of hearty, playful good humor; genial

   Friendly Uncle Hermie is one of the most *jovial* people I have ever met.

   syn: merry, mirthful, cheerful; **ant:** cheerless, somber

   family words: joviality (n); jovially (adj)

   Helpful Hint: JOVIAL JOVE was playful and had good humor. By JOVE!

9. **mentor:** (n) a wise, loyal advisor

   The patient guidance of my *mentor*, Mrs. Persol, helped me immensely in this year's science competition.

   syn: guide, master, guru

   family words: mentorship (n)

10. **mercurial:** (adj) having the qualities of the god Mercury, such as eloquence, cleverness, shrewdness, and thievishness; having qualities suggestive of mercury; quick, quick-witted, changeable

    Kenny's *mercurial* qualities included his keen sense of humor and his clever comments on many topics.

    syn: lively, ingenious

    family words: mercurialness (n); mercurially (adv)

11. **nemesis:** (n) just punishment; anyone or anything by which, it seems, one must inevitably be defeated or frustrated

    When it came to academic classes, biology was my friend's *nemesis*, for he seldom scored above 70 percent on any quiz or test.

    syn: retribution, retaliation

    Helpful Hint: MY SIS always bettered her NEMESIS.

12. **odyssey:** (n) any extended wandering or journey

    My grandparents began their three-month *odyssey* to distant countries, including China and Japan.

    syn: pilgrimage, expedition, voyage

    Helpful Hint: Her two-month ODYSSEY took her across MANY A SEA!

13. **panic:** (n) sudden fear; (v) to react to a crisis with great fear

    Unfortunately *panic* set in when the dance club began to go up in flames.

    Several police officers told the crowd to stay cool and not to *panic*.

    syn: terror, dread, alarm (n); terrify, frighten, unnerve (v)

    family words: panicky (adj)

14. **tantalize:** (v) to tease or disappoint by promising or showing something desirable and then withholding it

    It is not wise to *tantalize* a dog with a juicy bone that you do not plan on giving to him.

    family words: tantalization, tantalizer (n)

    Helpful Hint: It can be harmful to TANTALIZE these hungry GUYS with French FRIES.

15. **zephyr:** (n) a soft, gentle breeze

    The *zephyr* on that lazy spring afternoon made all of us very drowsy.

6-1   A MONSTROUS AFFAIR TO SAY THE LEAST

Using the words from the list below, select and then write the most appropriate word in each blank. Each word is used only once.

ambrosia	echo	iridescent	mercurial	panic
atlas	Herculean	jovial	nemesis	tantalize
centaur	hygiene	mentor	odyssey	zephyr

Have you ever had a nightmare in which you go on a(n) _____(1) and meet up with a cruel man of _____(2) strength accompanied by a monster known as the _____(3)? In this nightmare both of these monsters appear to be quite dirty. Both apparently lack proper _____(4). Now perhaps if you possessed the _____(5) qualities to outwit them or were quite _____(6) and outgoing, you might not be able to challenge these foes. Even if you had a trusty _____(7) to discuss your plan of escape, or a(n) _____(8) to help you find your route away to a safe destination, you could still be in a very tough predicament. Did you think you could _____(9) the villains by appealing to their taste buds with delicious _____(10) that had been enjoyed by the gods of mythology? That probably would not work. Your yelling so loudly hoping that your possible rescuers would hear your _____(11) would probably also be ineffective! Trying to blind them with your _____(12) clothing would not work either. Ugh! What are you to do?

Just as _____(13) is about to set in, you wake up and feel the relaxing _____(14) coming off the lake outside your window. You suddenly realize that neither of these monsters is your real-life _____(15). Then your alarm clock rings, and you know that you must get ready for another day of school. Such is life!

6-2 HEADLINES!

Match the underlined portion of each headline with a word from the group below. Each word is used only once.

Ambrosia	Echo	Iridescent	Mercurial	Panic
Atlas	Herculean	Jovial	Nemesis	Tantalize
Centaur	Hygiene	Mentor	Odyssey	Zephyr

1. _____ Gods Pig Out on <u>Their Own Food</u>!

2. _____ <u>Coach</u> Motivates Gymnast to Olympic Gold!

3. _____ <u>Great Fear</u> Forces Sports Fans to Exit Arena!

4. _____ <u>Friendly and Outgoing Woman</u> Wins Hospitality Award!

5. _____ <u>Gentle Breeze</u> Comforts Island Vacationers!

6. _____ West Virginia Family Starts <u>Cross-Country Trip</u>!

7. _____ Doctors Say, "Don't Let Supersize Portions <u>Tempt</u> You!"

8. _____ Kid Finds Rare <u>Book of Maps</u> in Abandoned House!

9. _____ Man with <u>Great</u> Strength Lifts Triple His Weight!

10. _____ Hunter Hears His Voice <u>Repeat Itself</u> in Canyon!

11. _____ Nurse Lectures on <u>Good Sanitary Practices</u>!

12. _____ Student Claims to See <u>Monster with the Head and Arms of a Man and the Body and Legs of a Horse</u>!

13. _____ Football Team Loses to Its <u>Rival Opponent</u>!

14. _____ <u>Shifting Changes in Color</u> of Sky Amazes Scientists!

15. _____ The <u>Quick-Witted, Shrewd</u> Student Outwits the Others!

6-3   FIVE WILL GET YOU FORTY

First, match these fifteen words with their definitions by writing the number from Column B next to the correct word in Column A. Then write the number next to the word under the correct group, A, B, or C below. If your numbers are correct, each group should add up to 40. Thus, five (words) will get you forty (points). Good luck!

Column A	Column B
___ ambrosia	1. showing shifting changes in color
___ atlas	2. book of maps
___ centaur	3. having the qualities of a god
___ echo	4. gentle breeze
___ Herculean	5. genial; happy
___ hygiene	6. to entice; to tempt
___ iridescent	7. very powerful or courageous
___ jovial	8. sanitary practice
___ mentor	9. food of the gods
___ mercurial	10. journey
___ nemesis	11. monster with the head and arms of a man and the body and legs of a horse
___ odyssey	12. a wise, loyal advisor
___ panic	13. opponent
___ tantalize	14. the repetition of a sound
___ zephyr	15. sudden fear; to react to a crisis with great fear

Group A	Group B	Group C
___ centaur	___ ambrosia	___ echo
___ hygiene	___ atlas	___ mercurial
___ iridescent	___ Herculean	___ nemesis
___ jovial	___ mentor	___ tantalize
___ panic	___ odyssey	___ zephyr

6-4   START WITH ZEUS

Zeus was the chief Greek god. So let us start with him. The number 12 has been placed in the box with the L in it. Then match the other words from mythology with their correct definitions. Write the correct number in each appropriate box. Each is used only once. If your answers are correct, all the rows, columns, and the two diagonals will add up to the same number.

A. tantalize	**E.** iridescent	**I.** nemesis	**M.** echo
B. Herculean	**F.** centaur	**J.** odyssey	**N.** mentor
C. panic	**G.** atlas	**K.** hygiene	**O.** ambrosia
D. zephyr	**H.** jovial	**L.** Zeus	**P.** mercurial

1. full of hearty, playful good humor
2. to tease or disappoint by promising or showing something desirable and then withholding it
3. very powerful or courageous
4. book of maps
5. any extended wandering or journey
6. the food of the gods
7. shrewd, clever, quick-witted
8. just punishment; anyone or anything by which, it seems, one must inevitably be defeated or frustrated
9. sanitary practice
10. wise, loyal advisor
11. the repetition of sound
12. chief of the Greek gods
13. showing shifting changes in color from different angles
14. soft, gentle breeze
15. sudden fear
16. monster with the head and arms of a man and the body and legs of a horse

A=	B=	C=	D=
E=	F=	G=	H=
I=	J=	K=	L=12
M=	N=	O=	P=

Magic Number:

_____

Units 4–6   REVIEW TEST

Directions: Please circle the correct **synonym.** Then write the answer's corresponding letter on the line next to the question's number. Each question is worth four points.

1. ____ **amend**   (a) to improve   (b) to worsen   (c) to connect

2. ____ **eave**   (a) relaxation   (b) roof overhanging   (c) building post

3. ____ **forbidding**   (a) looking dangerous or threatening   (b) allowing   (c) poor

4. ____ **imply**   (a) to state directly   (b) to bring together   (c) to suggest

5. ____ **scour**   (a) to handle   (b) to clean by vigorous scrubbing   (c) to recycle

6. ____ **utterly**   (a) kindly   (b) respectfully   (c) completely

7. ____ **brood**   (a) highway   (b) offspring of animals   (c) corner

8. ____ **insinuate**   (a) to give up   (b) to do something wrong   (c) to hint

9. ____ **nurture**   (a) to promote the development of   (b) to keep down   (c) to baffle

10. ____ **snare**   (a) device used to capture someone or something   (b) picture   (c) lake

Directions: Please circle the correct **antonym.** Then write the answer's corresponding letter on the line next to the question's number. Each question is worth four points.

11. ____ **eccentric**   (a) forgetful   (b) loud   (c) conventional

12. ____ **ordeal**   (a) destruction   (b) determination   (c) delight

13. ____ **prohibit**   (a) to listen to   (b) to legalize   (c) to joke with

14. ____ **spacious**   (a) crowded   (b) memorable   (c) laughing

15. ____ **abnormal**   (a) frightful   (b) rigid   (c) standard

16. ____ **casual**   (a) planned   (b) serialized   (c) long

17. ____ **hospitable**   (a) antisocial   (b) darkened   (c) shivering

18. ____ **meddle**   (a) to interfere   (b) to avoid   (c) to ease

19. ____ **oppress**   (a) to hinder   (b) to emancipate   (c) to keep down

20. ____ **Herculean**   (a) original   (b) epic   (c) weak

Units 4–6   REVIEW TEST (continued)

Directions: Please circle the word that correctly **completes** the sentence. Then write the answer's corresponding letter on the line next to the question's number. Each question is worth four points.

21. ____ Jason used the help of his _____ to do so well on these exams.
    (a) odyssey   (b) mentor   (c) nemesis

22. ____ Because he was laughing so heartily, you could see that Raina was in a(n)
    _____ mood.   **(a) jovial   (b) iridescent   (c) mercurial**

23. ____ Once the fire began to spread, the boys were filled with _____.
    (a) zephyr   (b) nemesis   (c) panic

24. ____ With all this available space, is it smart to _____ your belongings into
    one small corner?   **(a) germinate   (b) cram   (c) imply**

25. ____ The coach's _____ remarks hurt these two players.
    (a) caustic   (b) iridescent   (c) mercurial

Unit 7

THE BIG AND SMALL OF IT ALL

THE BIG AND SMALL OF IT ALL

1. budget: (n) a plan for one's expenditures; (v) to plan expenses according to a budget

We made sure that we stayed within our *budget*.

Since you will be busy, make sure you *budget* your time well.

syn: funds, resources (n); to make financial arrangements (v)

family words: budgeter (n); budgetary (adj)

2. bulky: (adj) large; having great bulk; massive; awkwardly large; big and clumsy

Carrying the *bulky* rug up the apartment building's five flights was not easy.

syn: sizable, huge, considerable, unwieldy; **ant:** small, little, miniature

family words: bulkiness (n); bulkily (adv)

Helpful Hint: Would you call the massive Hulk "BULKY HULKY" to his face?

3. capacity: (n) the amount of space that can be filled; room for holding; content or volume; mental ability

This stadium is perfect for a large concert since it has a seating *capacity* of 75,000.

Her memory *capacity* showed when she recited all the U.S. presidents' names.

syn: size, expanse, magnitude

family words: capacious (adj)

4. curtail: (v) to cut short; reduce; abridge

We will have to *curtail* the meeting due to the snowstorm.

syn: abbreviate, lessen, diminish; **ant:** expand, extend, lengthen

family words: curtailment (n)

Helpful Hint: *Curt* means short, in a sort of verbally, rude way. *Curtail* means "to cut short (in size)," much like the way one who is curt does (emotionally) to others.

5. deprive: (v) to take something away from forcibly; dispossess; to keep from having, using, or enjoying

His doctor warned him that on this diet he should not *deprive* himself of nutritious foods.

syn: strip, rob, divest, hinder; **ant:** give, add, assist

family words: deprivation (n); deprived (adj)

6. duplicate: (n) an exact copy or reproduction; replica; facsimile; (adj) double; having two similar parts; (v) to make double or twofold; to make an exact copy

The artist was asked to make a *duplicate* of her original plan for the mural.

These *duplicate* parts should really be labeled to avoid confusion.

Though many people felt that nobody could *duplicate* the feat, the record has been broken twice already!

syn: likeness, imitation (n); to reproduce, to replicate (v); **ant:** original, pattern, model, archetype (n)

family words: duplication (n); duplicable (adj)

Helpful Hint: DUPLICATE and REPLICATE both mean to make copies.

7. dwindle: (v) to continue to become smaller or less; diminish; shrink

Our hopes for victory began to *dwindle* when we saw the early election returns.

syn: waste, lessen; **ant:** increase, grow, multiply, add, augment

8. essential: (adj) absolutely necessary; indispensable; (n) something necessary or fundamental

Is this baseball player *essential* to the team's possible success this season?

What *essential* to the group's success are we missing?

syn: fundamental, vital; **ant:** secondary, accessory, auxiliary

family words: essentially (adv)

9. **extraneous:** (adj) coming from outside; foreign; not truly or properly belonging; not relevant; not essential; not pertinent

Several *extraneous* pictures were included in the yearbook photos that the publisher sent to our editors.

family words: extraneousness (n); extraneously (adv)

Helpful Hint: EXTRANEOUS is EXTRA, that which is not needed.

10. **humongous:** (adj) of enormous size or extent; very large or great

The *humongous* cartoon character's size scared the little child.

Helpful Hint: HUMONGOUS is a combination of HUGE and ENORMOUS.

11. **increase:** (v) to become greater in size, amount, degree; to add to; to augment; (n) an increasing or becoming increased; growth; enlargement

These weightlifters want to *increase* the number of pounds that they lift.

I plan to ask the boss for an *increase* in my salary.

syn: extend, enlarge, expand, amplify; **ant:** diminish, lessen, decrease

family words: increaser (n); increasable (adj)

12. **massive:** (adj) big and solid; bulky; ponderous; large and imposing or impressive; large-scale

Jerry, a rather small competitor, knew that he was no match for his more *massive* wrestling opponent.

syn: huge, heavy, dense; **ant:** light, airy

family words: massiveness (n); massively (adv)

Helpful Hint: If it is MASSIVE, it has great MASS, size, or bulk.

13. **morsel:** (n) a small bite or portion of food; a small piece or amount; bit; a tasty dish; (v) to divide into or distribute in small portions

Fluffy, our loyal dog, will eat every *morsel* of food left over from our breakfast, lunch, or dinner.

Do you think we should *morsel* the food so that everybody can have a taste?

syn: taste, tidbit, scrap, piece (n)

Helpful Hint: Please don't ask for MORE after you have eaten the last MORSEL.

14. **penalize:** (v) to make punishable; to set a penalty for; to impose a penalty on; to put at a disadvantage

This referee told both managers that he would *penalize* the team whose pitcher threw the ball close to the opposing batter's body.

syn: punish, fine, discipline

family words: penalization, penalty (n)

15. **surplus:** (n) a quantity or amount over and above what is needed and used; something left over; excess; (adj) forming a surplus; extra; excess

Do not count on the government to have a *surplus* of money in these tight fiscal times.

These *surplus* instruments can be used by our junior high musicians who do not own instruments.

syn: overage, remainder; **ant:** shortage, shortfall, lack

Helpful Hint: PLUS means more. So does SURPLUS!

7-1 FIFTEEN AND FIVE

Fifteen words from Unit 7 and five rivers from around the world are the answers to these twenty clues in this crossword puzzle. Fill in the correct letters and let the rivers flow!

Across

1. to keep on becoming or making smaller or less; diminish
5. to cut short; reduce; abridge
6. the amount of space that can be filled; content or volume
10. Italian river
11. South America's longest river
14. a plan for one's expenditures
16. absolutely necessary; indispensable; something necessary or fundamental
18. small bite or portion of food; a small piece or amount

Down

2. an exact copy or reproduction; replica; facsimile
3. of enormous size or extent; very large or great
4. an African river
6. another African river
7. to become greater in size, amount, or degree; add to; augment
8. famous Chinese river
9. big and solid; bulky; ponderous
12. coming from outside; foreign; not truly or properly belonging
13. to make punishable; to put at a disadvantage
14. big and clumsy; awkwardly large
15. to take something away from forcibly
17. quantity or amount over and above what is needed and used; something left over

7-2   FLOATING LIKE A BUTTERFLY

If you correctly match these fifteen words in Column A with their definitions in Column B, you will spell out a quote by a famous American, followed by his name and his occupation (when he was quoted). Write each two-letter answer on the line after the appropriate number. Then write those thirty letters (in order) at the bottom of this page. Two answers have already been done for you. Do well!

Column A	Column B
1. ____ budget	**ad.** growth; enlargement
2. ____ bulky	~~**al.**~~ big and solid
3. ____ capacity	**ea.** to keep from having
4. **GR** curtail	**er.** excess or more than is needed
5. ____ deprive	~~**gr.**~~ to cut short; reduce; abridge
6. ____ diminish	**ha.** to decrease in size or amount
7. ____ duplicate	**he.** the amount of space that can be filled
8. ____ dwarfish	**ia.** a plan for one's expenditures
9. ____ dwindle	**ib.** a small piece
10. ____ humongous	**mm.** of enormous size or extent; very large or great
11. ____ increase	**mt.** awkwardly large
12. **AL** massive	**mu.** small in size
13. ____ morsel	**ox.** to set a penalty for; to impose a penalty on
14. ____ penalize	**st.** an exact copy; to make an exact copy
15. ____ surplus	**te.** to reduce in size

Quote: _____

Name: _____

Occupation: _____

7-3 SPINNING AROUND

The activity's title might seem a bit odd, but once you have selected the fifteen correct answers, you will see that the title does make sense. Start your spinning by circling the correct answer for each analogy. Then write the fifteen letters (in order) below. The three words you spell out with these consecutive letters will prove the "spinning around" idea. Good luck!

1. budget : plan
  P. water : harbor
  Q. review : film
  R. apex : curtain
  S. golf : sport

2. increase : decrease
  A. safe : insecure
  B. tall : height
  C. silent : hushed
  D. jam : fruit

3. deprive : provide
  P. water : harbor
  R. rob : take away
  S. bird : creature
  T. hearty : feeble

4. surplus : excess
  U. depot : storehouse
  V. ballad : singer
  W. enthusiastic : deadened
  X. tripod : camera

5. capacity : space
  Q. fertilizer : texture
  R. sound : decibels
  S. clown : circus
  T. triangle : geometry

6. duplicate : exact copy
  M. tent : camping
  N. labyrinth : maze
  O. moisture : dehumidifier
  P. stem : flower

7. decrease : lessen
  L. oil : lighten
  M. weigh : think about
  N. infect : cleanse
  O. accumulate : disperse

8. massive : small and flabby
  A. eccentric : typical
  B. nurture : promote the development of
  C. hoard : supply stored or hidden
  D. scour : clean vigorously

9. bulky : awkwardly large
  R. cram : stuff into
  S. amend : remain the same
  T. narrate : listen to a story
  U. germinate : wither and die

10. dwarfish : large in size
  Q. hospitable : friendly
  R. abnormal : atypical
  S. counterfeit : genuine
  T. oppress : overpower

11. penalize : reward
  O. discount : reduce
  P. instigate : end
  Q. find : enemy
  R. flatten : crush

12. dwindle : decrease
  I. responsible : irresponsible
  J. assure : disengage
  K. immature : grown up
  L. friendly : sociable

13. morsel : large
  U. professor : unintelligent
  V. daisy : dreaded
  W. forest : burned
  X. canary : three-legged

14. humongous : enormous
  Q. joyous : unhappy
  R. bright : dull
  S. tall : short
  T. condensed : shortened

15. curtail : cut short
  L. chap : moisten
  M. vacate : fill
  N. debate : convince
  O. comprehend : understand

Name: _____ Date: _____ Period: _____

7-4   CHANGE A LETTER (OR TWO)

This activity will test your vocabulary, spelling, and word play abilities. The answers to these fifteen sentences are there, but they are a bit disguised. For numbers 1 through 10, one letter has been changed. Thus for #1, the correct answer is *(a) play* because we have changed the letter *n* in *plan* to the letter *y* to make the word *play*. For numbers 11 through 15, we have changed two consecutive letters in each of the correct answers. Now it is double the fun! Ready to get started? Go and change those letters!

Change one letter for the first ten sentences.

1. To *budget* is to (a) play (b) glow (c) sang (d) toll. plan_____

2. A package that is *bulky* is awkwardly (a) front (b) barge (c) dress (d) wrong. _____

3. *Capacity* deals with the amount of (a) grove (b) spade (c) prone (d) force. _____

4. To *curtail* is to (a) danger (b) lesson (c) police (d) growth. _____

5. To *deprive* is to keep from (a) hating (b) dating (c) raking (d) baking. _____

6. Something that is *extraneous* is not (a) tanned (b) lotion (c) weeded (d) remove. _____

7. A *duplicate* is a (a) roam (b) cozy (c) dent (d) soar. _____

8. Something that is *essential* is (a) dream (b) found (c) chant (d) seeded. _____

9. The monster that is *humongous* is (a) treat (b) beset (c) drink (d) repay. _____

10. To *penalize* is to (a) beg (b) sew (c) raw (d) wed a penalty for some wrong. _____

Change two letters for the following five sentences:

11. To *increase* is to (a) grab (b) draw (c) stay (d) dole. _____

12. To *dwindle* is to decrease in (a) crew (b) port (c) silo (d) moat or amount. _____

13. A *massive* structure is big and (a) prove (b) sound (c) gravy (d) devil. _____

14. A *morsel* is a small (a) piety (b) drape (c) cloud (d) alone. _____

15. If you have a *surplus* of helpers, you have a(n) (a) buffer (b) crumbs (c) hunger (d) except number of workers. _____

Unit 8

TELL IT LIKE IT IS

TELL IT LIKE IT IS

1. **babble:** (v) to talk foolishly; to make incoherent sounds, as a baby does; (n) prattle; blab

   We hear him *babble* too often and make sense too infrequently.

   We could not stop from laughing as we listened to the baby's constant *babble* coming from the adjoining room.

   syn: murmur, chatter, clamor

   family words: babbler (n)

2. **blurt:** (v) to say suddenly, without stopping to think; often used with "out"

   I recommend that you think before you *blurt* out something silly that makes you look foolish.

   syn: utter, exclaim, cry, sputter

   Helpful Hint: Because CURT Curt would often BLURT out, they threw him out!

3. **chatter:** (v) to make short, indistinct sounds in rapid succession, as birds, apes, and others; to talk fast, incessantly, and foolishly; (n) rapid, foolish talk

   The bingo players loved to *chatter* before the games began at the bingo hall.

   The zoo attendant told us that the *chatter* of these animals is really their way of communicating with each other.

   syn: prattle, babble, prate (v)

   family words: chatterer (n)

   Helpful Hint: What's the MATTER with their CHATTER? I'll tell you. It is too fast and foolish!

4. **consolidate:** (v) to combine into a single whole; to merge; to unite; to make or become solid

   Due to the company's financial state, the officials decided to *consolidate* the company's three factories.

   syn: combine, incorporate; **ant:** disband, diversify, separate

   family words: consolidation, consolidator (n)

   Helpful Hint: "Con" means *with*; "solid" is *solid*; therefore, if you *consolidate* something, you make it more *solid* or stronger.

5. **detest:** (v) to dislike intensely; to hate; to abhor

   People *detest* the actions of those who abuse children.

   syn: loathe, despise, abominate; **ant:** like, love, care for, admire

   family words: detester (n)

   Helpful Hint: Do you DETEST taking a TEST?

6. **expose:** (v) to lay open (to danger, attack, ridicule); to leave unprotected; to allow to be seen; to reveal, exhibit, or display

   Aware that controversy would certainly arise, the newspaper reporters still decided to *expose* the wrongdoings of the politicians.

   syn: bare, display, uncover; **ant:** conceal, hide, cover up, veil

   family words: exposer, exposition, exposure (n)

TELL IT LIKE IT IS (continued)

7. **haggle:** (v) to bargain; to argue about terms, prices; to wrangle; to chop or cut crudely; to hack; to mangle

   Many customers feel uncomfortable when they *haggle* over the item's price.

   syn: stickle, negotiate

   family words: haggler (n)

   Helpful Hint: The HAG loved to HAGGLE with the HAGGARD hardware helper.

8. **hilarious:** (adj) extremely funny; noisily merry; producing merriment

   The *hilarious* movie had all of us laughing hysterically during many of the comedic scenes.

   syn: laughable, sidesplitting, uproarious; **ant:** miserable, sad, dispirited

   family words: hilarity (n); hilariously (adv)

9. **insist:** (v) to take and maintain a stand or make a firm demand (often with "on" or "upon"); to demand strongly; to declare firmly or persistently

   We will *insist* that you remain silent throughout the examination.

   syn: urge, require, enjoin, press, persist

   family words: insister (n); insistingly (adv)

10. **mumble:** (v) to speak or say indistinctly and in a low voice, as with the mouth partly closed; mutter; murmur; (n) a mumbled sound or utterance

    When he is upset, the driver will often *mumble* to himself thinking that we cannot hear him.

    Unfortunately, those who should not have heard his *mumble* heard it.

    syn: speak unclearly, speak softly, burble (v); stammer, drone, grunt (n)

    family words: mumbler (n)

    Helpful Hint: We could not hear MR. BUMBLE'S MUMBLES.

11. **promote:** (v) to raise or advance to a higher position or rank; to further the popularity, sales, etc., of by publicizing and advertising; to move (a student) forward a grade in school; to encourage

    Last night we went to the bookstore and listened to the author *promote* her mystery novel.

    Mrs. Larsen will *promote* all of her students to the fifth grade.

    syn: (for "to raise . . .") upgrade, elevate, raise, reward (v); (for "to further the popularity . . .") sell, tout (v) **ant:** (for "to raise . . .") demote, disable, downgrade, retard (v); (for "to further . . .") discourage, condemn, denounce (v)

    family words: promoter, promotion (n); promotional (adj)

    Helpful Hint: The prefix "pro-" means *forward* or *toward*. When someone or something is *promoted*, he, she, or it is "moved forward."

12. **protest:** (v) to make objection to; to state positively; to affirm solemnly; to speak strongly against; (n) an objection; a gathering of people demonstrating their unhappiness with someone or something

    We watched the driver *protest* the fact that he was given a ticket for illegal parking.

    Those objecting to the judge's decision staged a *protest* in front of the courthouse.

    syn: demonstrate, complain, disprove, remonstrate (v); demonstration, dispute, dissent, outcry, objection (n)

    family words: protestor (n)

13. **rage:** (n) furious, uncontrolled anger; a great force, violence, or intensity; the current fashion; (v) to show violent anger in action or speech; to spread unchecked, as a disease

    The angry bicyclist tried to control her *rage* after the cabbie cut her off.

    Can you believe that this type of footwear is the *rage* of Hollywood?

    Paul felt that he had to *rage* at the new ruling concerning fishing limitations.

    syn: (for "furious, uncontrolled anger") wrath, fury (n); (for "the current fashion . . ." craze, vogue, fad, style (n); storm, seethe, bluster, rave (v); **ant:** (for "furious, uncontrolled anger" equanimity, serenity, composure (n); lull, mollify, moderate (v)

    family words: ragingly (adv)

    Helpful Hint: When the already angry animal went into a RAGE, we moved him into a CAGE.

14. **rant:** (v) to talk or say in a loud, wild way; to declaim violently; to rave; (n) a ranting speech

    My brother will *rant* against the mistreatment of animals.

    After we played a horrible first half, the coach delivered an unforgettable *rant*.

    syn: spout (v); angry outburst, tirade, rage (n); **ant:** murmur, whisper, mutter, mumble (n) (v)

    family words: rant (n)

    Helpful Hint: To cure his patient's anger problem, the therapist told the angry person to calmly say, "I CAN'T RANT. I CAN'T RANT. I CAN'T RANT."

15. **understate:** (v) to state too weakly; to make a weaker statement than is needed; to state in a restrained style

    There is no way that Jerry will *understate* the importance of getting out to vote in this very important election.

    family words: understatement (n)

    Helpful Hint: UNDERSTATE and OVERSTATE are opposites.

8-1 IT'S WHAT THEY SAID

Although we probably should not have been doing so, we have been listening in on some people's conversations and thought you could help us fill in the correct word for each blank. From the words below, select the correct word that completes each quote. Each word is used only once.

babble	expose	haggle	mumble	rage
blurt	consolidate	hilarious	promote	rant
chatter	detest	insist	protest	understate

1. "I _____ such rude and cruel behavior by those who should be protecting the less fortunate people in their charge," Molly said to her sister Marcia.

2. Julio responded, "If you want them to change their behavior, you should _____ on it immediately."

3. "Do you think I should _____ you to the next grade if you continue to earn low grades and seldom do your homework?" the teacher asked the student.

4. "Did the coach deliver his usual halftime _____ to motivate his players to do better in the second half of the game?" Steve asked Henry.

5. "Will the television stations cover the large human rights _____ at City Hall tomorrow?" Jessie asked Roberto.

6. "Why do you always seem to _____ out such silly remarks at the most serious times, Kenny?"

7. Cheryl told Pauline," My mom has heard the older man often _____ to himself when he is walking down our street."

8. "How do you expect people to listen to your _____ when everybody else is talking quite seriously?" the professor asked Frankie.

9. "Let's have some fun and go down to the street fair to _____ over the prices with the merchants," Ollie said to Rich.

10. "Instead of speaking in a civilized manner, why do you feel the need to _____ if such rude talk does not help your cause?" Marilyn asked her boyfriend.

11. "Have you recently heard the _____ of the birds in the trees outside the school?" the principal asked our class members.

12. "I do not want to _____ the importance of this year's election since it certainly will have a large influence on all of us," the mayor told the crowd.

13. "In order to save the town money, we will need to _____ several departments and work even more diligently than before," the clerk reported to the town official.

14. Mom warned Teddy, "Try not to _____ yourself to the temptations that could harm your health."

15. "That _____ comedy show had me laughing for a long time," the taxi driver told the passenger.

8-2 YOU ONLY HEAR ITS FIRST LETTER

One of the words in this Magic Square has a unique trait. You only hear its first letter—and no others! Match that word with its definition by writing the correct number in the appropriate box within the Magic Square. Do the same for the other words. If your answers are correct, the numbers in each row, column, and the two diagonals will add up to the same total. Good luck!

A=	B=	C=	D=
E=	F=	G=	H=
I=	J=	K=	L=
M=	N=	O=	P=

Magic Number:

_____

A. hilarious	**E.** mumble	**I.** haggle	**M.** queue
B. blurt	**F.** babble	**J.** chatter	**N.** expose
C. protest	**G.** consolidate	**K.** detest	**O.** promote
D. insist	**H.** rage	**L.** understate	**P.** rant

1. to say suddenly, without stopping to think
2. to combine into a single whole; merge; unite
3. to dislike intensely; hate; abhor
4. to lay open to danger; to reveal or display
5. a line or row; to get in a line
6. to state too weakly; to state in a restrained style
7. furious, uncontrolled anger; to spread unchecked, as a disease
8. extremely funny; noisily merry
9. to talk or say in a loud, wild way; rave
10. to bargain; to argue about prices
11. to speak or say indistinctly and in a low voice
12. to declare firmly
13. to make objection to; to speak strongly against
14. to talk foolishly; to make incoherent sounds, as a baby does
15. to make short, indistinct sounds in rapid succession, as birds do
16. to raise or advance to a higher position or rank; to move a student forward in school

8-3 O! THOSE PREFIXES ENDING WITH O!

Six prefixes, all ending with the letter *o*, are found in the answer key to this activity. Match the words in Column A with their definitions in Column B. Write the two-letter answers on the line after each Column A number. Distinguish between the three NO answers by writing "1st no," "2nd no," and "3rd no" on the line next to the correct Column A word. Then write the fifteen two-letter answers in order at the bottom of this page. These are the six prefixes that end with *o*. Do you know their definitions? O, how smart you are if you can do all this perfectly!

Column A

1. _____ babble
2. _____ blurt
3. _____ chatter
4. _____ consolidate
5. _____ detest
6. _____ expose
7. _____ haggle
8. _____ hilarious
9. _____ insist
10. _____ mumble
11. _____ promote
12. _____ protest
13. _____ rage
14. _____ rant
15. _____ understate

Column B

bi. to abhor; to dislike intensely

bl. to reveal, exhibit, or display; to lay open to danger or ridicule

ch. to rise to a higher position or rank; to move (a student) forward a grade in school

do. to speak or say indistinctly and in a low voice, as with mouth partly closed; mutter; murmur

eu. to strongly demand; to take and maintain a stand or make a firm demand

ge. to talk foolishly; to make incoherent sounds as a baby does; prattle; blab

ho. to make short, indistinct sounds in rapid succession, as birds and apes do; rapid, foolish talk

io. to bargain; to argue about terms and prices

mo. to talk or say in a loud, wild way; declaim violently

no. (the "1st no.") to combine into a single whole; merge; unite

no. (the "2nd no.") furious, uncontrolled anger; a great force, violence, or intensity

no. (the "3rd no.") to state too weakly; to make a statement weaker than is needed

op. to say suddenly, without stopping to think

ps. extremely funny; noisily merry

ro. to make objection to; to speak strongly against

_____

_____

8-4   UNDER THE SEA

You might think that there is something fishy going on here. Let us assure you, there is not! Yet, if you answer all these fifteen questions correctly by writing the correct two-letter combination next to the question's number, you will spell out the names of six sea creatures. Write these six sea creatures at the bottom of this page. So pick up your pen or pencil and start to find those sea creatures!

1. _____ Ernie usually downplays his accomplishments. Thus, Ernie is a guy who
(ca) understates (ll) protests (lf) mumbles.

2. _____ Ricardo often makes objections to the new school rules. Ricardo **(rp) protests
(on) promotes (et) babbles.**

3. _____ Ruth likes to argue about the cost of items with the salesperson. Ruth **(fl) haggles
(ag) detests (oo) exposes.**

4. _____ Jimmy will speak indistinctly in a low voice, often with his mouth partly closed.
Jimmy **(ol) rants (uo) blurts (ou) mumbles.**

5. _____ Karen talks foolishly and makes incoherent sounds. Karen **(nd) babbles
(rt) consolidates (re) insists.**

6. _____ Stuart raves and talks in a loud, wild manner. Stuart **(ee) promotes (er) rants
(fe) haggles.**

7. _____ Kim takes a stand and makes firm demands. Kim **(ir) detests (fl) insists
(ot) chatters.**

8. _____ Mrs. McKenna, our teacher, moved all our class members to the next grade level.
She **(ff) haggled (cc) mumbled (uk) promoted us students.**

9. _____ Sonia frequently talks out without stopping to think. She **(eb) blurts out
(st) exposes (uy) rants.**

10. _____ Juan is extremely funny and produces merriment in those around him. Juan is
(tt) consolidate (as) hilarious (we) promote.

11. _____ Reese lost control of his emotions and displayed furious, uncontrolled anger.
Reese **was in a (at) chatter (al) detest (st) rage.**

12. _____ Beth intensely dislikes the new method of selecting the All-Star team. She
(te) consolidates (un) detests (so) babbles.

13. _____ Hal was left unprotected and was allowed to be seen by others. Hal was
(aw) exposed (rr) detested (ss) hilarious.

14. _____ Several companies were merged and combined into a single whole. These companies
were **(ha) consolidated (ah) haggled (in) protested.**

15. _____ The group members were talking fast, incessantly, and foolishly. They were
(po) detesting (le) chattering (on) insisting.

_____

_____

Words, Words, Words!

Unit 9

THE SCIENCES (NATURALLY!)

THE SCIENCES (NATURALLY!)

1. chronic: (adj) lasting a long time or recurring often; having had an ailment for a long time; perpetual; constant; by habit; habitual; (n) a chronic patient

His *chronic* cough prevented his participating in strenuous athletic events.

The nurses were quite friendly with the *chronic* who were often in the hospital for one illness or another.

syn: continuing, ongoing (adj); **ant:** temporary, brief, acute, short (adj)

family words: chronicity (n); chronically (adv)

Helpful Hint: The prefix "chron-" means *time*. Associate CHRONIC and TIME—all the time!

2. dread: (v) to anticipate with anxiety, alarm, or apprehension; to fear intensely; (n) intense fear; fear mixed with awe or reverence

Since he was not skilled in math, Oscar came to *dread* taking tests in that class.

That movie filled audience members with a sense of *dread* concerning swimming and sharks.

syn: cower, worry, shudder (v); fright, terror, horror (n)

family words: dreadful (adj); dreadfully (adv)

Helpful Hint: Visit a cemetery at midnight? No way! Fred had a DREAD of the DEAD!!

3. genetics: (n): branch of biology that deals with heredity

His study of *genetics* made him skilled in predicting a person's physical characteristics.

4. heredity: (n) carrying over of characteristics from parent to offspring by means of genes in the chromosomes

If your sibling resembles your father in looks, *heredity* has probably played a big part.

5. immune: (adj) protected against something harmful

This vaccination should make you *immune* to catching the disease.

syn: exempt, invulnerable; **ant:** liable, vulnerable, exposed

family words: immunity, immunization (n)

Helpful Hint: *Immune* comes from a Latin word meaning "free from." Thus, if you are *immune*, you are "free from" a disease, something bad, or something dangerous.

6. infect: (v) to contaminate or invade with a disease-producing organism

Fearing that a germ might *infect* his open cut, Kerry immediately placed a bandage on the wound.

syn: disease, afflict, sicken

family words: infector, infection (n)

Helpful Hint: The doctor told the sick patient, "I had SUSPECTED that you had been INFECTED."

7. **microbe:** (n) a microscopic organism (any individual animal or plant having diverse organs and parts that function together as a whole to maintain life and its activities)

> Only through a powerful microscope could we see the *microbe*.

family words: microbial, microbic (adj)

Helpful Hint: *Microbe* comes from the words meaning "small life." That is exactly what a microbe is—small life!

8. **molecule:** (n) the smallest particle of an element

> When you study the element, you will probably also study the *microbe*, the element's smallest part.

family words: molecular (adj)

9. **mutation:** (n) change, as in nature, form, or qualities; variation in inheritable characteristics in a germ cell of an individual plant or animal; mutant

> The dog with that very obvious physical difference is an example of a *mutation*.

family words: mutational (adj); mutationally (adv)

Helpful Hint: Need some words that mean "a change"? MUTATION, DIVERSIFICATION, TRANSFORMATION, and ALTERATION are all in that range!

10. **nutrient:** (n) a nutritious ingredient in food; (adj) nutritional, nourishing, healthful

> If you want to be healthy, eat foods with many *nutrients*.

> The *nutrient* chart illustrated the healthy foods we can eat.

11. **offspring:** (n) progeny; descendant

> My great-grandmother's *offspring* numbered nearly one hundred people.

syn: offshoot, spawn, generation; **ant:** ancestor, forebear, forerunner

12. **prevent:** (v) to keep from happening

> Sunscreen will help *prevent* skin cancer.

syn: avert, forestall, preclude, deter; **ant:** cause, instigate, provoke, abet

family words: prevention, preventer (n); preventable (adj)

13. **species:** (n) a distinct kind; variety; class

> We researched several *species* of this creature.

syn: sort, type, category

14. **symbiosis:** (n) a relationship of mutual interdependence

> It was fascinating to learn about the *symbiosis* of these two helpful and dependent animals.

Helpful Hint: The word *symbiosis* comes from two parts—"sym-" (living together) and "bio-" (life). *Symbiosis*—living life together!

15. **trait:** (n) a distinguishing quality or characteristic, as of personality

> The family's most outstanding physical *trait* is their height.

syn: feature, attribute

Helpful Hint: Dad passed on his "handsome gene" to his son, Brian. What a GREAT TREAT to get such a GREAT TRAIT!

9-1 SEARCHING FOR THOSE SCIENCE WORDS

The fifteen science words from Unit 9 are hidden in this word-find puzzle. The words are placed horizontally, vertically, and diagonally. Circle the fifteen hidden words, and then, on a separate sheet of paper, define these fifteen words.

```
p w q t n x s o f f s p r i n g j x d v
r w t z m u j y h m g x i n n v g r j
e j y y q r t k m e u s g m h f d b e d
v c j r h z h r m b r t q y m v e s a y
e c h r o n i c i o i e a k m u n c d x
n y s f n d f c c e l o d t f j n k t g
t c h p m l k g r f n e s i i y n e x p
g m w y e s s q o k c t c i t o t l z t
n e c p q c p m b d z r t u s y n y p r
g s n s n p i k e n x a k v l x w n w h
x m h e z j j e p l b h b y e q q d h
w g w v t p r q s s j t d k h n h b j d
y m f x x i x v p d s k x h g q f y k h
v v x v n v c m w j p g y k k l g p m x
v b t y w x p s g m f b b g q h r j z w
```

Copyright © 2004 by John Wiley & Sons, Inc.

chronic	heredity	microbe	nutrient	species
dread	immune	molecule	offspring	symbiosis
genetics	infect	mutation	prevent	trait

9-2 LET'S START WITH "NO" FOR SOME OF THESE

Nine of these twenty-four clues begin with the letters *no*. So start with *no* for those nine clues, and then you are on your own (scientifically speaking) for the other fifteen clues that are all about science terms. Start with *no*, and yes, get the others done as well.

Across

2. progeny; descendant
6. lasting a long time or recurring often
10. at the present time
11. a microscopic organism
12. body part on the face
13. to eat
14. variety; class
16. characteristic
17. announcement or warning
18. zero
19. distinguished; renowned
20. change, as in nature, form, qualities
21. idea

Down

1. the smallest particle of an element
3. a relationship of mutual interdependence
4. to contaminate or invade
5. branch of biology that deals with heredity
7. carrying over of characteristics from parent to offspring by means of genes in the chromosomes
8. protected against something harmful
9. to anticipate with anxiety, alarm, or apprehension; fear intensely
12. a nutritious ingredient in food
13. opposite of south
15. keep from happening
18. one of the eight parts of speech

9-3 FINDING THE THREE-LETTER WORDS

Using the words from the list below, fill in each blank within these fifteen sentences. Each word is used only once. Then circle the number letter of the correct answer indicated after the sentence. Write that letter on the appropriate line at the bottom of this page. So if number one is correct, you have inserted the word *species* and have written the letter *p* on the line below. The definition of each three-letter word appears below the fifteen sentences.

chronic	heredity	microbes	nutrients	species
dread	immune	molecule	offspring	symbiosis
genetics	infect	mutations	prevent	traits

1. The scientist had never come across such an interesting _____ **species** _____ of bird in all her life. **(2)**

2. Since my dad and mom are each only five-feet six-inches tall, the laws of _____ were strongly against my ever becoming a National Basketball Association center of seven foot or more. **(3)**

3. In _____, or "living together," one member of the pair benefits from the relationship, and the other may benefit, be injured, or be relatively unaffected. **(2)**

4. Viruses, fungi, and bacteria are various types of _____, the tiny creatures that are unable to be seen without using a microscope. **(6)**

5. Height and hair type are inherited _____. **(3)**

6. Many people argue that we need strict laws to regulate _____, the branch of biology that deals with heredity. **(3)**

7. Because he smoked so much throughout his life, the man had unfortunately developed a _____ cough. **(6)**

8. _____ may result in changes that seriously affect the health of an individual, family, or population. **(1)**

9. You can often _____ illness by eating healthy foods and getting enough exercise. **(1)**

10. The germ began to _____ my father's finger. **(4)**

11. My mother makes sure that our lawn gets the proper _____ so it can grow to be plush and beautiful. **(4)**

12. I _____ having to go to the dentist. **(2)**

13. Hoping to make her daughter _____ to the virus, the mother had her daughter vaccinated. **(4)**

14. The _____ of the god and goddess include many other minor gods and goddesses. **(4)**

15. Our class studied the structure of the DNA _____. **(4)**

Sentences 1-3   **p**_____ : to peer or snoop; to raise, move, or force with a tool

Sentences 4-6   _____ : to prohibit

Sentences 7-9   _____ : a mischievous child

Sentences 10-12   _____ : to make a mistake

Sentences 13-15   _____ : to employ or utilize

Name: _____ Date: _____ Period: _____

9-4 FIGURING OUT THE SCIENCE WORDS

The fifteen words from Unit 9 are listed in this cryptolist. Each letter in Column A is the code letter for the real letter in Column B. Thus, "C" is the code letter for "E," "I" is the code letter for "H," and "M" is used for "R." Use your Letter Substitution Code below to help you along. Fill in the letters in Column B.

Column A (Code)	**Column B (Real)**
1. ICMCYGEL	H E R E __ __ __ __
2. VOCHGCV	__ __ E __ __ E __
3. HIMNFGH	__ H R __ __ __ __
4. PCFCEGHV	__ E __ E __ __ __ __
5. BGHMNUC	__ __ __ R __ __ E
6. GBBAFC	__ __ __ __ __ E
7. GFDCHE	__ __ __ E __ __
8. YMCRY	__ R E __ __
9. NDDVOMGFP	__ __ __ __ __ R __ __ __
10. VLBUGNVGV	__ __ __ __ __ __ __ __ __
11. BNSCHASC	__ __ __ E __ __ __ E
12. FAEMGCFE	__ __ __ R __ E __ __
13. OMCTCFE	__ R E __ E __ __
14. BAEREGNF	__ __ __ __ __ __ __ __
15. EMRGE	__ R __ __ __

Letter Substitution Code

Code: A B C D E F G H I L M N O P R S T U V Y

Letter: __ __ E __ __ __ __ H __ R __ __ __ __ __ __ __ __ __ __

Units 7–9 REVIEW TEST

Directions: Please circle the correct **synonym.** Then write the answer's corresponding letter on the line next to the question's number. Each question is worth four points.

1. ____ **curtail** (a) expand (b) cut short (c) select

2. ____ **dwindle** (a) increase (b) forecast (c) diminish

3. ____ **humongous** (a) tiny (b) very large or great (c) necessary

4. ____ **blurt** (a) to say something without stopping to think (b) to answer incorrectly
     (c) to think carefully before speaking

5. ____ **haggle** (a) to argue about terms or prices (b) to predict (c) to agree to

6. ____ **rant** (a) to state mildly (b) to question (c) to rave

7. ____ **genetics** (a) variety or class (b) branch of biology that deals with heredity
     (c) study of stars and plants

8. ____ **mutation** (a) change in form or qualities (b) exact reproduction (c) silly talk

9. ____ **offspring** (a) ancestor (b) progeny (c) cement

10. ____ **surplus** (a) lack (b) requirements (c) excess

Directions: Please circle the correct **antonym.** Then write the answer's corresponding letter on the line next to the question's number. Each question is worth four points.

11. ____ **deprive** (a) diminish (b) prevent (c) assist

12. ____ **essential** (a) accessory (b) eloquent (c) enjoined

13. ____ **increase** (a) sputter (b) lessen (c) dread

14. ____ **consolidate** (a) huge (b) disband (c) exclaim

15. ____ **mumble** (a) abbreviate (b) narrow (c) articulate

16. ____ **promote** (a) abridge (b) prattle (c) downgrade

17. ____ **prevent** (a) cause (b) remedy (c) understate

18. ____ **immune** (a) punishable (b) very funny (c) vulnerable

19. ____ **massive** (a) big and solid (b) wee (c) nourishing

20. ____ **duplicate** (a) fun (b) original (c) forest

Units 7–9 REVIEW TEST (continued)

Directions: Please circle the word that correctly **completes** the sentence. Then write the answer's corresponding letter on the line next to the question's number. Each question is worth four points.

21. ____ The financial committee needed to make changes in the planned _____.
(a) **capacity**   (b) **budget**   (c) **mutation**

22. ____ The cat chewed up the last _____ of food from her plate.
(a) **morsel**   (b) **surplus**   (c) **microbe**

23. ____ The humorous skit was very _____.
(a) **bulky**   (b) **hilarious**   (c) **essential**

24. ____ Mom selected the healthy type of cereal because it contained many
_____.   (a) **duplicates**   (b) **species**   (c) **nutrients**

25. ____ The leader stressed that she did not want to _____ the importance of
our reaching an agreement with the other party.
(a) **detest**   (b) **babble**   (c) **understate**

Unit 10

MATHEMATICALLY INCLINED

MATHEMATICALLY INCLINED

1. **bisect:** (v) to divide into two equal parts; to divide; to fork

    We were instructed to *bisect* the lines so that each new segment is two inches.

    family words: bisection, bisector (n)

    Helpful Hint: *Bisect* means "to cut" (*sect-*) into "two" (*bi-*).

2. **corresponding:** (adj) in math, a pair of nonadjacent angles, one interior and one exterior, on the same side as the transversal; these paired angles are equal if the lines cut by the transversal are parallel

    Please indicate the number of degrees in the *corresponding* angles.

3. **decimal:** (n) a fraction with an unwritten denominator of ten indicated by a point, such as ¾ = .75; (adj) of, or based, on the number 10; progressing by tens

    We transformed the fraction ¾ into the *decimal* .75.

4. **dividend:** (n) the number or quantity to be divided. In the problem "6 divided by 2 equals 3," 6 is the dividend; 2 is the divisor; and 3 is the quotient.

    When you divide the *dividend* 6 by the divisor 3 the quotient is 2.

5. **divisor:** (n) the number by which the dividend is divided to produce the quotient (see "dividend")

    Divide the dividend 12 by the *divisor* 6 and the quotient will be 2.

6. **estimate:** (n) an approximation; a general calculation; (v) to calculate approximately; to guess, to gauge, to evaluate

    Rather than count the hundreds in attendance here tonight, let us come up with an *estimate*.

    Can you *estimate* the number of cars that passed this point today?

    family words: estimation (n); estimable (adj)

7. **exponent:** (n) a small number placed to the right and above another number to show how many times that number should be multiplied by itself. If 3 has an exponent of 2, that means that 3 times 3 is 9.

    In the expression "3 to the 4th power," 4 is the *exponent*.

8. **fraction:** (n) any quantity expressed in terms of a numerator and a denominator; an indicated quotient of two whole numbers, as in ⅙ or ⅘.

    The decimal .10 is equal to the *fraction* ¹⁄₁₀.

    syn: part, portion, fragment; **ant:** whole, entirety, totality

    family words: fractional (adj)

    Helpful Hint: The prefix "fract-" means *to break* or *a part*. A *fraction* is "to break" a whole number into "parts."

9. metric: (adj) of the system of measurement based on the meter (and the gram)

The liter and the meter are terms used in the *metric* system.

family words: metrical (adj); metrication (n)

10. percent: (n) a hundredth part; percentage; (adj, adv) per hundred

Twenty is ten *percent* of 200.

family words: percentage (n)

11. perpendicular: (adj) at right angles to a given plane or line; exactly upright; straight up and down

The line that intersects this horizontal line at right angles is called the *perpendicular*.

12. property: (n) a quality common to all members of a species or class. As an example, all numbers ending with 2 are divisible by 2.

"Three times five equals five times three" is an example of the commutative *property* of mathematics.

13. proportion: (n) an equality between ratios; relationship among four quantities in which the quotient of the first divided by the second is equal to that of the third divided by the fourth

Two-thirds and four-sixths are equal *proportions*.

family words: proportional (adj)

14. quotient: (n) the result obtained when one number is divided by another (see "dividend")

In the problem "eight divided by two," the *quotient* is four.

15. symbol: (n) a written or printed mark, letter, or abbreviation standing for an object, quality, process, or quantity. The symbol for "less than" is <, and the symbol for "greater than" is >.

What is the mathematical *symbol* for "equal to"?

family words: symbolic (adj); symbolize (v)

10-1   JUST DO THE MATH

All the terms in this Magic Square deal with mathematics. In fact, one of the sixteen words is *mathematics*! Place the corresponding number in the correct box within the Magic Square, as shown by the one already done for you. If your answers are correct, all the rows, columns, and the two diagonals will add up to the same number. So now, just do the math!

A=	B=15	C=	D=
E=	F=	G=	H=
I=	J=	K=	L=
M=	N=	O=	P=

Magic Number:

_____

A. quotient   **E.** mathematics   **I.** bisect   **M.** metric
B. exponent   **F.** perpendicular   **J.** fraction   **N.** decimal
C. symbol   **G.** estimate   **K.** corresponding   **O.** property
D. proportion   **H.** divisor   **L.** dividend   **P.** percent

1. the number obtained when one number is divided by another
2. a fraction with an unwritten denominator of 10 or some power of 10, indicated by a decimal point
3. any quantity expressed in terms of a numerator and a denominator
4. sciences that include arithmetic, geometry, algebra, and calculus
5. general calculation; to calculate approximately
6. the number or quantity to be divided
7. a hundredth part; 1 is 5 _____ of 20
8. a written or printed mark, letter, or abbreviation standing for an object, quality, process, or quantity in math
9. quality common to all members of the group
10. an equality between ratios, such as 5 is to 10 and 4 is to 8
11. the number by which the dividend is divided to produce the quotient
12. pair of nonadjacent angles on the same side as the transversal
13. to divide into two equal parts
14. at right angles to a given plane
15. a small number placed to the right and above another number to show how many times that number should be multiplied by itself
16. of the system of measurement based on the meter

Words, Words, Words!

10-2   OVERHEARD IN MATH CLASS

My math teacher is a great teacher. She explains everything so well that her students usually understand the material easily. Here are fifteen sentences that I have copied from my math notebook. See if you can figure out which of the fifteen words below belongs in each blank and then write that word in the appropriate blank. Each word is used only once.

bisect	dividend	exponent	percent	proportion
corresponding	divisor	fraction	perpendicular	quotient
decimal	estimate	metric	property	symbol

1. "Place the line _____ to or at a right angle to the horizontal line."

2. "In the problem '10 divided by 2,' 10 is the dividend and 2 is the _____."

3. "Let us _____ this line, therefore dividing it into two equal parts."

4. "The following mark, >, is the _____ for 'greater than.'"

5. "Without getting perfectly exact, let us _____ how much 253 divided by 23 is."

6. "All even numbers have the following _____: They are divisible by 2."

7. "Since the transversal cuts the parallel lines, the _____ angles are equal."

8. "⅛ is an example of a _____."

9. "Grams and meters are used in the _____ system."

10. "One-fifth is the same _____ as two-tenths."

11. "In the problem '80 divided by 8,' the _____ is 80."

12. "Five is twenty _____ of 25."

13. "Six is the _____ when 60 is divided by 10."

14. "In the problem 'four cubed,' the _____ is 3."

15. "The dot in the expression .25 is called the _____ point."

10-3   WHAT IS IT CALLED?

How often have you heard someone ask, "What is it called . . . ?" Well, today is your chance to help answer this question, since all fifteen questions ask "What?" in some way. Using the words below, write the correct word in each blank.

bisect	dividend	exponent	percent	proportion
corresponding	divisor	fraction	perpendicular	quotient
decimal	estimate	metric	property	symbol

1. _____ What is the type of system based on the meter called?

2. _____ What is the approximation of a calculation called?

3. _____ What do we call the dot before the number .40, meaning 40 percent or 2 fifths?

4. _____ What is the line that is at a right angle to a horizontal line called?

5. _____ What is the number by which the dividend is divided?

6. _____ What do you call the relationship between four quantities in which the quotient of the first divided by the second is equal to that of the third divided by the fourth?

7. _____ What is the number that results when the dividend is divided by the divisor?

8. _____ What is the printed mark that stands for a mathematical process such as the sign meaning "less than"?

9. _____ What is the word that refers to the hundredth part, such as in the example "10 is what _____ of 100"?

10. _____ What do you do to a line when another divides it into two equal parts?

11. _____ What is the quality common to all members of a group, such as "all numbers greater than 0 that end with the number 0 and are divisible by 10"?

12. _____ What is the term for the number that the divisor is divided into to get the quotient?

13. _____ What is the number placed to the right and above another number to show how many times that number should be multiplied by itself?

14. _____ What is the name of the pair of nonadjacent angles, one interior and one exterior, on the same side as the transversal?

15. _____ What is the name for any quantity expressed in terms of a numerator and a denominator?

10–4 FAMOUS NAMES IN MATHEMATICS

Match these fifteen math terms in Column A with their definitions in Column B. Write the two-letter answers from Column B on the line next to the number in Column A. Then write those 30 letters in order at the bottom of this page. (One is already done for you.) If your answers are correct, you will have spelled out the names of three famous mathematicians followed by the word *math*.

Column A

1. _____ bisect

2. _____ corresponding

3. _____ decimal

4. _____ dividend

5. _____ divisor

6. _____ estimate

7. _____ exponent

8. _____ fraction

9. _____ metric

10. __th__ percent

11. _____ perpendicular

12. _____ property

13. _____ proportion

14. _____ quotient

15. _____ symbol

Column B

ag. at right angles to a given plane

ar. divide into two equal parts

as. equality between ratios

ch. a pair of nonadjacent angles, one interior and one exterior, on the same side as the transversal

cl. a small number placed to the right and above another number to show how many times that number should be multiplied by itself

ed. a number or quantity to be divided

es. the number by which the dividend is divided to produce the quotient

eu. an approximation; a general calculation

id. any quantity expressed in terms of a numerator and a denominator

im. a fraction with an unwritten denominator of 10 indicated by a point, such as .35

ma. the result obtained when one number is divided by another

or. a quality common to all members of a class, such as all odd numbers

py. of the system based on the meter

th. a written or printed mark, letter, or abbreviation standing for an object, quality, process, or quantity

ix. a hundredth part

_____

_____

_____

Unit 11
HOW WE MOVE

HOW WE MOVE

1. **ascend:** (v) to go up; to move upward; to rise; to proceed from a lower to a higher level or degree, as in rank, pitch, etc.

   It was difficult to *ascend* the twenty-seven flights of steps.

   How do you plan to *ascend* the corporate ladder of success?

   syn: arise, climb, lift off; **ant:** descend, dismount, drop

   family words: ascendible (adj); ascendancy (n)

   Helpful Hint: *Ascend* comes from the word meaning "to climb to." ASCEND and DESCEND are opposites.

2. **creep:** (v) to move along with the body close to the ground, as on hands and knees; to grow along the ground or wall, as some plants; (n) the act of creeping; (slang) a very annoying or disgusting person

   To avoid detection, the burglar had to *creep* by the sleeping guard.

   Only a *creep* would treat a dog in such a mean manner.

   syn: crawl, wriggle

   family words: creeper (n)

3. **descend:** (v) to move from a higher to a lower place; to come down or go down; to slope or extend downward

   It is usually easier to *descend* than to ascend a flight of stairs.

   syn: move down, drop, fall; **ant:** ascend, rise, soar, climb

   family words: descendible (adj)

   Helpful Hint: *Descend* comes from the word meaning "to climb down." DESCEND and ASCEND are opposites.

4. **dodge:** (v) to move or twist swiftly aside; to shift suddenly as to avoid something or someone; to evade; (n) a trick used in evading or cheating

   The runner had to *dodge* the out-of-control truck heading toward him.

   He used a *dodge* to try to dishonestly win the card game.

   syn: elude (v); twisting, turning, sidestep (n); **ant:** confront, face, meet, withstand (v)

5. **glide:** (v) to move slowly and easily, as in skating; to move by and pass gradually and almost unnoticed, as time; (n) the act of gliding; easy flow or movement

   We watched the skaters gracefully *glide* across the ice in yesterday's competition.

   Spectators were fascinated by the champion marathon runner's *glide* as she finished the grueling 26.2-mile run.

   syn: slip, slide, skate, flow (v); slide, slip (n)

   family words: glider (n)

6. hurdle: (v) to jump over (a barrier) as in a race; to overcome (an obstacle); (n) frame-like barrier over which horses or runners must leap in a special race

The firefighter had to *hurdle* the boxes in the hallway in order to reach and then rescue the crying child.

His political rival was also able to surmount each *hurdle* presented to her.

syn: vault, leap over, clear, surmount, scale (v)

family words: hurdler (n)

7. jog: (v) to move along at a slow, steady pace or trot; to engage in jogging as a form of exercise; to give a little shake, shove, or nudge; to shake up or revive (a person's memory); (n) a little shake, shove, or nudge; a slow, steady trot

Coach instructed us to *jog* around the track two times to warm up our legs for the tougher part of the workout.

To remember my classmate's name, I needed a little memory *jog* by my brother.

syn: (for "to move along") poke, plod, trudge, lumber (v); (for "to give a little shake") jostle, prod, bump (v); push, nudge (n)

family words: jogger (n)

Helpful Hint: Can you imagine a dog trying to JOG in a BOG? It's mind-boggling!

8. plod: (v) to move or walk about heavily and laboriously; to trudge; to work steadily and monotonously; to drudge; (n) the act of plodding; the sound of a heavy step

Rather than walking briskly, the worker will usually *plod* along on his way to the truck.

His distinct *plod* is memorable to anyone who has heard Timmy walk down the hall.

syn: lumber, trek, tread (v)

family words: plodder (n); ploddingly (adv)

9. ramble: (v) to walk or stroll about idly, without any special goal; to roam about; to talk or write aimlessly, without connection of ideas; (n) an aimless stroll

Carole and her boyfriend loved to *ramble* along Boston's quaint streets.

I wish that the historian would not *ramble* on about the "good old days."

After studying for three hours last night, my friends and I took a midnight *ramble* around the park's lake.

syn: (for "to walk or stroll") roam, meander, wander, rove (v); (for "to talk or write") babble, blather, digress, drivel (v); wandering, tour (n)

family words: rambler (n)

10. scamper: (v) to run or go hurriedly or quickly; (n) the act of scampering

He decided to *scamper* after he mistakenly knocked down the bully's bike.

The quarterback had a 40-yard *scamper* for the team's second touchdown.

syn: scurry, scuttle, hasten; **ant:** lag, dawdle, creep, crawl

family words: scamperer (n)

HOW WE MOVE (continued)

11. **slink:** (v) to move in a quiet or sneaking manner as from fear or guilt; to sneak

    After Kenny dropped the cola on the dining room rug, he had to *slink* away without detection.

    syn: creep, steal, skulk

    family words: slinky (adj); slinkingly (adv)

12. **sprint:** (v) to run or race at full speed, especially for a short distance; (n) a short run or race at full speed; a brief period of intense activity

    The bet was to see who could *sprint* to the streetlight the fastest.

    My uncle prefers a jog to a *sprint* any day.

    There was a *sprint* of calls between three and four o'clock today.

    family words: sprinter (n)

13. **stagger:** (v) to move unsteadily, as though about to collapse; to lose determination; to affect strongly with astonishment; (n) the act of staggering; zigzag arrangement

    All of us saw the beaten boxer *stagger* away from the match.

    We were all *staggered* by how much Laura knew about that subject.

    The patient's *stagger* was proof that she still needed to rest and recover a while longer.

    syn: (for "to move unsteadily") totter, reel, sway (v); (for "to affect strongly") stun, stupefy, astound (v)

    family words: staggerer (n)

    Helpful Hint: After the conceited guy could not lift the weights, his SWAGGER turned into a STAGGER.

14. **strut:** (v) to walk in a vain, stiff, swaggering manner; to make a display of; to show off; (n) the act of strutting; vain, swaggering gait or walk

    There was no reason for you to *strut* around after winning the musical competition.

    The proud man's *strut* displayed his superior sense of importance.

    syn: prance, parade (v); swagger, flounce (n)

    family words: strutter (n)

15. **vacate:** (v) to leave (a room, house, etc.) uninhabited; to make vacant; to make an office, position, etc., vacant

    We will *vacate* this apartment by August 31 so that the new tenants can move in the next day.

    syn: empty, make bare (v); **ant:** to fill, occupy, pack, stuff

    family words: vacation (n); vacant (adj)

11-1 JUST MOVE IT!

All fifteen words below have to do with how you move. Fill in the correct word in each blank below. Each word is only used once. Let's not hesitate. Just move it!

ascend	dodge	jog	scamper	stagger
creep	glide	plod	slink	strut
descend	hurdle	ramble	sprint	vacate

1. _____ to move or walk heavily and laboriously; trudge; to work steadily and monotonously

2. _____ to move or twist swiftly aside; to shift suddenly as to avoid something or someone; a trick used in evading or cheating

3. _____ to go up; to move upward; to proceed from a lower to a higher level or degree

4. _____ to move in a quiet or sneaking manner as from fear or guilt; sneak

5. _____ to leave (a room, house, etc.) uninhabited; to make vacant

6. _____ to move slowly and easily, as in skating; easy flow or movement

7. _____ to walk or stroll about idly, without any special goal; an aimless stroll

8. _____ to move unsteadily, as though about to collapse; to lose determination; to affect strongly with astonishment

9. _____ to walk in a vain, stiff, swaggering manner; swaggering gait or walk

10. _____ to move along at a slow, steady pace or trot; a slow, exercise run

11. _____ to move from a higher to a lower place; come down or go down

12. _____ to jump over (a barrier) as in a race; to overcome; frame-like barrier

13. _____ to run or go hurriedly or quickly

14. _____ to move along with the body close to the ground, as on hands and knees; annoying or disgusting person

15. _____ to run or race at full speed, especially for a short distance; short run or race at full speed

11-2   HOW WOULD YOU MOVE IF . . .?

Here are fifteen different scenes. Tell how you would move in each case by writing the word in the blank after each number. Each word is used only once.

ascend	dodge	jog	scamper	stagger
creep	glide	plod	slink	strut
descend	hurdle	ramble	sprint	vacate

How would you move if . . .

1. _____ you had to run at top speed?

2. _____ you were ready to faint from heat exhaustion?

3. _____ you were trying to make your way on foot through heavy snow?

4. _____ you were jumping over some boxes that were in your way?

5. _____ you were climbing down from the top of a mountain?

6. _____ you were trying to run quickly or hurriedly?

7. _____ you were on your hands and knees, close to the ground trying to go unnoticed?

8. _____ you were leaving a room in your house?

9. _____ you chose to move along at a slow, steady pace?

10. _____ you were walking proudly and showily after scoring the winning goal?

11. _____ you were moving across the ice at your local rink?

12. _____ a bicyclist was heading right toward you on the sidewalk?

13. _____ you were walking away after being embarrassed by your teacher or coach for doing something wrong?

14. _____ you were climbing up a mountain?

15. _____ you were walking through the local park at a leisurely pace?

11-3   NEWSPAPER CAPTIONS

Fifteen newspaper captions (without their pictures) are reprinted below. Fill in the appropriate word for each caption. Each word below is used only once.

ascend	dodge	jog	scamper	stagger
creep	glide	plod	slink	strut
descend	hurdle	ramble	sprint	vacate

1. Thousands of city residents _____ their way home through the congested city sidewalks.

2. Marathon runners take a leisurely _____ as they warm up before yesterday's grueling 26.2-mile event.

3. Embarrassed fan tries to _____ away from booing crowd after throwing a soda can at the third-base coach.

4. Spring is the perfect season for lovers to _____ through the city's beautiful parks to enjoy nature's pleasures.

5. Squirrels attempting to catch each other _____ up the tree.

6. King Stephen prepares to _____ the steps to greet the crowd below.

7. Commuters deftly _____ large puddles hoping to keep their shoes dry after a late afternoon rain shower.

8. Runners quickly _____ the Empire State Building steps making their up to the 102nd floor.

9. Mayor fails to _____ angry protestors outside City Hall yesterday.

10. Students _____ along classroom floor to avoid smoke in demonstration fire escape drill.

11. Championship skaters _____ across the ice to receive their medals.

12. Conceited professional wrestler shows how to _____ as he parades himself before cheering admirers.

13. Residents _____ their homes to get to safe ground before Hurricane Andrew's arrival.

14. George Tennet and Frankie Rosco _____ toward the tape in yesterday's 100-meter dash at the Armory.

15. Injured accident victims _____ away from this morning's head-on collision.

11-4 DON'T BE STAGGERING THROUGH THIS PUZZLE!

The fifteen words from Unit 11 are found in this puzzle. So are eleven words that can be formed from the word *staggering,* a form of one of Unit 11's words. Fill in the correct letters, and don't be staggering through this puzzle!

Across

4. *Winnie the Pooh* character
6. to walk or stroll about idly, without any special goal
7. a telephone has it; a finger could have one too
8. to run or go hurriedly or quickly
9. to move unsteadily, as though about to collapse
12. to move slowly and easily, as in skating
16. to move from a higher to a lower place
18. to walk in a vain, stiff, swaggering manner
20. to go up; to move upward

Down

1. money paid to an apartment owner each month
2. to move along at a slow, steady pace or trot
3. to leave a room or place uninhabited

4. a drop of water from the eye
5. really terrific
7. strong anger
8. to move in a quiet or sneaking manner as from fear or guilt
9. to run or race at full speed, especially for a short distance
10. alcoholic beverage
11. slang word for a substandard newspaper
12. they swing on hinges
13. to move or walk about heavily and laboriously; trudge
14. to move or twist swiftly aside; to shift suddenly as to avoid something or someone
15. to jump over (a barrier) as in a race
17. to move along with the body close to the ground, as on hands and knees
18. to droop
19. a label

Unit 12
WRITE ON!

WRITE ON!

1. **autobiography:** (n) the story of one's own life written by or dictated by oneself

    How could he have included such personal family information in his *autobiography*?

    family words: autobiographical (adj)

    Helpful Hint: *Autobiography* = "auto-" (self) + "bio-" (life) + "-graphy" (writing)

2. **biography:** (n) an account of a person's life, described by another; life story

    The author did a wonderful job in writing the noted politician's *biography*.

    family words: biographical

    Helpful Hint: *Biography* = "bio-" (life) + "-graphy" (writing)

3. **comedy:** (n) a play or motion picture with a more or less humorous treatment of characters and situations and a happy ending; novel, or any narrative, having a comic theme, tone, etc; an amusing or comic event or sequence of events

    Neil Simon, the famous playwright, included humorous, memorable characters in every *comedy* that he wrote.

    syn: farce, joke, burlesque; **ant:** tragedy, drama

    family words: comedic (adj); comedically (adv)

4. **drama:** (n) a literary composition that tells a story, usually of human conflict, by means of dialogue, to be performed by actors; now, specifically, any play that is not a comedy

    Hamlet, William Shakespeare's *drama*, is one of the world's most famous plays.

    syn: play, piece, pageant

    family words: dramatic (adj); dramatically (adv)

5. **elegy:** (n) any poem, song of lament (sorrow) and praise for the dead

    I cry each time I read the *elegy* that the poet wrote in honor of his deceased son.

    family words: elegiac (adj); elegist (n)

6. **epic:** (n) long narrative poem about the deeds of a traditional or historical hero or heroes; (adj) having the characteristics of an epic

    Homer's *Iliad* and *Odyssey* are examples of the *epic*.

    The Song of Roland is a famous French *epic* about Charlemagne.

    This palatial mansion has a dining room of *epic* proportions.

    syn: noble, grand, Homeric, legendary (adj)

    family words: epical (adj); epically (adv)

    Helpful Hint: EPIC, HEROIC, and GIGANTIC all mean large or huge!

7. **epigram:** (n) a short poem with a witty or satirical point. Ben Franklin's "There has never been a good war or a bad peace" is an example of an epigram.

    I am always amazed that something as short as an *epigram* can also have so much meaning.

    syn: aphorism, adage, saying, proverb, maxim

    family words: epigrammatic, epigrammatical (adj); epigrammatically (adv)

8. **essay:** (n) a short literary composition of an analytical, interpretative, or reflective kind, usually expressive of an author's outlook and personality; (v) to test the nature or quality of; to try out

    Our teacher expected us to turn in a 250-word *essay* on a specific literary topic each Monday morning.

    Do you think I should *essay* this path before the other members of the group do so?

    syn: article, paper (n); try, attempt, strive (v)

family words: essayist, essayer (n); essayistic (adj)

Helpful Hint: *Essay* comes from the French word *essayer*, meaning "to try." Thus, an *essay* is your try to convince another of your point of view.

9. **haiku:** (n) a Japanese verse with seventeen syllables. The verse consists of three unrhymed lines of five, seven, and five syllables, respectively, often on some subject of nature.

My greatest difficulty in writing a *haiku* is making sure that there are exactly seventeen syllables within the three lines.

10. **journal:** (n) a daily record of happenings, as a diary; daily newspaper; record of the transactions of a legislature, club, etc.; any newspaper or periodical, as one dealing with scientific or professional matters

I often record school happenings and my reactions to them in my *journal*.

My aunt reads her favorite medical *journal* each month.

syn: notebook, memoir

family words: journalist, journalism (n); journalistic (adj)

11. **limerick:** (n) a nonsense poem with five lines. The rhyme scheme is a-a-b-b-a.

Edward Lear popularized the form. An example of a limerick is the following:

> There was a young lady named Harris
>
> Whom nothing could ever embarrass
>
> Till the bath salts one day
>
> In the tub where she lay
>
> Turned out to be plaster of Paris.

Though the *limerick* is a nonsense poem, I find some sense within its five lines.

syn: jingle, rhyme, doggerel

Helpful Hint: Want the TRICK to writing a great LIMERICK? Five lines of nonsense! Now that makes sense!

12. **myth:** (n) a traditional story of unknown authorship, usually with a historical basis, but serving usually to explain some phenomenon of nature, man's origin, or the customs, institutions, religious rites, etc., of a people; myths usually involve the exploits of gods and heroes

For the ancients, a *myth* often explained the seeming unexplainable in nature.

syn: legend, fable, allegory; **ant:** fact

family words: mythic, mythical (adj)

13. **novel:** (n) a relatively long fictional prose narrative [examples of the novel include *The Adventures of Tom Sawyer* by Mark Twain and *Little Women* by Louisa May Alcott]; (adj) new and unusual, especially being the first of its kind

A *novel* by Charles Dickens usually contains at least three hundred pages.

My older brother taught me a *novel* way to perform that trick.

family words: novelist (n); novelistic (adj)

14. **short story:** (n) a kind of story shorter than a novel or novelette, developing a single central theme and limited in scope and number of characters

Though I often find it hard to sit down to read a novel, I can easily read a *short story* since it does not take so long.

15. **skit:** (n) a short piece of satirical or humorous writing; a short comic theatrical sketch

For our school's talent show, Larry and Frank performed a *skit* about two of our English teachers.

12-1   I'D LIKE TO READ

Mrs. Flowers, our town's librarian, has written down the most recent requests that the library's patrons have made to her. Using the words below, identify each type of work and write that word on the appropriate line next to the number. Then circle the letter in the answer indicated by the number after the sentence. Write all of these letters (in order) at the bottom of this page. If your answers are correct, these letters will tell you (in three words) what Mrs. Flowers does in her spare time.

autobiography	drama	epigram	journal	novel
biography	elegy	essay	limerick	short story
comedy	epic	haiku	myth	skit

1. _____ "Do you have a literary composition that tells a story of human conflict and has dialogue and actors in it?" **(2)**

2. _____ "Can you find me a short literary composition that may be analytical, interpretative, or reflective?" **(1)**

3. _____ "Could you please locate a short poem with a witty or satirical point?" **(6)**

4. _____ "Do you have a play or motion picture with a more or less humorous treatment of characters and situations and a happy ending?" **(5)**

5. _____ "Do you have a short, comic theatrical sketch?" **(1)**

6. _____ "May I please have a poem or song of lament and praise for the dead?" **(4)**

7. _____ "Will you help me locate a daily record of happenings similar to a diary?" **(4)**

8. _____ "May I ask to see a long narrative poem about the deeds of a traditional or historical hero or heroes?" **(1)**

9. _____ "Can I ask you to please show me where I may find a Japanese verse with seventeen syllables?" **(2)**

10. _____ "Perhaps you could direct me to a traditional story of unknown authorship, usually with a historical basis, that explains some phenomenon of nature, man's origin, or the customs of people?" **(3)**

11. _____ "Can you help me out by finding an account of a person's life, described by another?" **(1)**

12. _____ "Do you have the story of one's own life written or dictated by oneself?" **(4)**

13. _____ "May I request a relatively long fictional prose narrative?" **(2)**

14. _____ "Could you find a nonsense poem of five lines?" **(8)**

15. _____ "Would you see if you have a kind of story shorter than a novel that develops a central theme and is limited in scope and number of characters?" **(1)**

_____

_____

12-2 LEGENDS AMONGST US

Today you will meet with five legendary American figures—if you correctly match the words in Column A with their definitions in Column B. Write the corresponding three-letter answer next to each word from Unit 12. Then transfer those forty-five letters (in consecutive order) to the bottom of this page. These will spell out the names of five legendary American figures. Do all of this correctly—and be legendary yourself!

Column A

1. _____ autobiography
2. _____ biography
3. _____ comedy
4. _____ drama
5. _____ elegy
6. _____ epic
7. _____ epigram
8. _____ essay
9. _____ haiku
10. _____ journal
11. _____ limerick
12. _____ myth
13. _____ novel
14. _____ short story
15. _____ skit

Column B

aja. a nonsense poem with five lines

ane. a Japanese verse with seventeen syllables

bet. a short poem with a witty or satirical point

car. an account of a person's life, described by another; life story

ill. a short piece of humorous or satirical writing; a short, comic theatrical sketch

joh. a literary composition that tells a story of human conflict, by means of dialogue, to be performed by actors

kit. the story of one's life written by or dictated by oneself

nhe. any poem or song of lament and praise for the dead

nry. a long narrative poem about the deeds of a traditional or historical hero or heroes

osb. a kind of story shorter than a novel or novelette that develops a central theme and limits the characters in both number and scope

pec. a relatively long prose narrative

sac. a daily record of happenings, as a diary; daily newspaper

son. a play or motion picture with a more or less humorous treatment of characters and situations and a happy ending

tyz. a short literary composition that may be analytical, interpretative, or reflective

wea. a traditional story of unknown authorship designed to explain some phenomenon of nature, man's origin, or the customs of people

_____

_____

Name: _____ Date: _____ Period: _____

12-3 LITERARY CROSSWORD

In addition to the fifteen literature-based words that are found in Unit 12, the names of seven authors are answers in this Literary Crossword. The eight clues offer the name of a literary work, and you are asked to identify the work's author. Fill in the answers and enjoy this Literary Crossword!

Across

1. a relatively long fictional prose narrative
5. a short poem with a witty or satirical point
6. *James and the Giant Peach*
9. "The Pit and the Pendulum"
10. *Pygmalion*
11. nonsense talk
15. a long narrative poem about the deeds of a traditional or historical hero or heroes
17. a kind of story shorter than a novel or novelette, developing a central theme and limited in scope and number of characters
20. the story of one's own life written by or dictated by oneself
21. a daily record of happenings, as a diary; daily newspaper
22. a short literary composition of an analytical, interpretative, or reflective kind, usually expressive of an author's outlook or personality

Down

2. any poem or song of lament and praise for the dead
3. a literary composition that tells a story usually of human conflict, by means of dialogue, to be performed by actors
4. *Charlotte's Web*
7. a play or motion picture with a more or less humorous treatment of characters and situations and a happy ending; an amusing event or sequence of events
8. *Death of a Salesman*
10. *The Cat in the Hat*
12. a nonsense poem with five lines
13. an account of a person's life, described by another; life story
14. a short piece of satirical or humorous writing; a short, comic theatrical sketch
16. a traditional story of unknown authorship, usually with a historical basis, but serving usually to explain some phenomenon of nature, man's origin, or the customs of a people
18. a Japanese verse with seventeen syllables
19. *Where the Red Fern Grows*

12-4 REALLY RESEARCHING

Match the fifteen literary terms with the example provided for each one. Write the corresponding letter on the line after each number. One answer is already given to you. If your answers are correct, two literary terms will be found within your letters. Write those two terms at the bottom of this page.

X. autobiography	**H.** drama	**O.** biography
A. novel	**I.** epigram	**R.** haiku
B. comedy	**K.** essay	**S.** skit
C. short story	**L.** myth	**Y.** journal
F. epic	**N.** elegy	**Z.** limerick

1. ____ Vergil's *Aeneid*

2. ____ Daedelus and Icarus

3. ____ *The Adventures of Huckleberry Finn*

4. ____ Abbott and Costello's "Who's on First"

5. ____ *Twelve Angry Men*

6. ____ *The Importance of Being Earnest*

7. _A_ *The Autobiography of Ben Franklin*

8. ____ O. Henry's "The Ransom of Red Chief"

9. ____ Edward Hoagland's "The Courage of Turtles"

10. ____ "Experience is the name that everyone gives to his mistakes."

11. ____ Kojo's lines:
Night, and the moon!
My neighbor, playing on his flute-out of tune!

12. ____ *Ben Franklin: An American Life*

13. ____ Thomas Gray's most famous poem

14. ____ *Michigan Quarterly Review*

15. ____ There was a silly old man from Maine
Who never went out in the rain
He stayed indoors all day long
Writing silly words for his silly song
That silly old man from Maine.

_____

_____

Units 10–12   REVIEW TEST

Directions: Please circle the correct **synonym.** Then write the answer's corresponding letter on the line next to the question's number. Each question is worth four points.

1. ____ **bisect**   (a) to divide into three parts   (b) to cut off completely
(c) to divide into two equal parts

2. ____ **perpendicular**   (a) relationship between many numbers   (b) an abbreviation
(c) straight up and down

3. ____ **proportion**   (a) unnecessary   (b) equality between ratios
(c) quality common to all members of a species or class

4. ____ **hurdle**   (a) to overcome an obstacle   (b) to be defeated   (c) to haggle

5. ____ **scamper**   (a) to walk about laboriously   (b) to run or go hurriedly
(c) to respond to rudely

6. ____ **strut**   (a) to remove from office   (b) to calculate   (c) to show off

7. ____ **elegy**   (a) song of lament and praise for the dead   (b) an amusing or comic event
(c) daily record of happenings

8. ____ **limerick**   (a) a play that is not a comedy   (b) a nonsense poem of five lines
(c) a relatively long fictional prose piece

9. ____ **autobiography**   (a) an account of a person's life, described or written by another
(b) a long narrative poem   (c) the story of one's own life written or dictated by oneself

10. ____ **epigram**   (a) a short poem with a witty or satirical point   (b) a Japanese verse with
seventeen syllables   (c) a traditional story of unknown authorship

Directions: Please circle the correct **antonym.** Then write the answer's corresponding letter on the line next to the question's number. Each question is worth four points.

11. ____ **plod**   (a) to walk with heavy steps   (b) to think about carefully   (c) to glide

12. ____ **dodge**   (a) to avert   (b) to confront   (c) to memorize

13. ____ **slink**   (a) to move honestly and confidently   (b) to forget   (c) to go down the stairs

14. ____ **vacate**   (a) to occupy   (b) to leave   (c) to remain

15. ____ **ascend**   (a) to go upwards   (b) to recall   (c) to dismount

16. ____ **ramble**   (a) to jump   (b) to walk or talk purposefully   (c) to fight for a cause

17. ____ **stagger**   (a) to move unsteadily   (b) to move steadily   (c) to remove

18. ____ **descend**   (a) to go downwards   (b) to sift through   (c) to soar

19. ____ **jog**   (a) a marathon   (b) a hurdle   (c) a sprint

20. ____ **sprint**   (a) to run very slowly   (b) to mount   (c) to hasten

Units 10–12   REVIEW TEST (continued)

Directions: Please circle the word that correctly **completes** the sentence. Then write the answer's corresponding letter on the line next to the question's number. Each question is worth four points.

21. ____ Seven is ten _____ of seventy.
    (a) symbol   **(b) perpendicular**   **(c) percent**

22. ____ If you divide 8 into 40, the _____ is 5.
    (a) divisor   **(b) quotient**   **(c) dividend**

23. ____ My English teacher asked us to compose a(n) _____, a Japanese verse
    form with seventeen syllables.   **(a) haiku**   **(b) journal**   **(c) essay**

24. ____ In the expression "4 to the 2nd power," the number 2, placed to the right and above
    the number 4, is the _____.
    (a) property   **(b) exponent**   **(c) corresponding**

25. ____ My friend and I wrote and performed a two-person _____ that many
    audience members thought was hilarious.   **(a) elegy**   **(b) epic**   **(c) skit**

Unit 13

POPULAR SAT WORDS

POPULAR SAT WORDS

1. abduct: (v) to take (a person) away unlawfully and by force or fraud; kidnap

The criminals wanted to *abduct* the two bank tellers and take them to an undisclosed location.

syn: carry off, make off with, take away

family words: abductor, abduction (n)

Helpful Hint: *Abduct* comes from the word meaning "to lead away." An *abductor* "leads another away."

2. amiable: (adj) having a friendly and likeable disposition; good-natured

My neighbor is one of the most *amiable* people I know.

syn: genial, warm, kind, pleasant; **ant:** disagreeable, unpleasant, cold

family words: amiability (n); amiably (adv)

Helpful Hint: *Ami-* is French for "friend." Thus, *amiable* means "able to be friendly."

3. apprentice: (n) a person who is acquiring a trade, craft, or skill under specified conditions, usually as a member of a labor union; any learner or beginner; novice

Before he earned his plumber's license, Wally worked as an *apprentice* to the more experienced and skillful Brooklyn plumber, Mr. Jim Carrano.

syn: tyro, recruit; **ant:** expert, master, veteran, old hand

family words: apprenticeship

4. beret: (n) a flat, round cap of felt, wool, etc.

Many French men wear a *beret* as they ramble along the Parisian streets.

5. brutal: (adj) cruel and unfeeling; savage, violent, ruthless, etc.; very harsh or rigorous

With temperatures far below the freezing mark for the past three weeks, outside working conditions, to say the least, have been *brutal*.

syn: fierce, vicious, barbarous, intolerable; **ant:** gentle, humane, compassionate

family words: brutality (n); brutally (adv)

Helpful Hint: AL, the BRUTE, is BRUTAL—so cruel and unfeeling!

6. caption: (n) a heading or title, as of an article; a descriptive title or legend, as under an illustration; (v) to supply a caption for

This cartoonist always has a clever *caption* below his perceptive political cartoon.

We will need to *caption* this cartoon and still not take away from the drawing itself.

syn: head, superscription

7. current: (adj) now going on; now in progress; at the present time; contemporary; (n) flow of water or air, especially when strong or swift, in a definite direction; a general tendency or drift; course

I need to know the *current* temperature since I plan to go outside immediately.

The river's *current* was so strong that it carried us downstream in twenty minutes.

syn: present, prevalent, prevailing; **ant:** previous, bygone, past, outmoded, out-of-date, unfashionable

family words: currently (adv)

Helpful Hint: "Cur-" means *to run.* If it is *current,* whether it is water or news, it is *running.*

8. frenetic: (adj) frantic; frenzied

The factory manager was in a *frenetic* state as she rushed her workers to ship all the packages out by the six o'clock deadline.

syn: maniacal, raving, distraught, distracted; **ant:** calm, composed, serene, tranquil

family words: frenetical (adj); frenetically (adv)

Helpful Hint: FRENZIED and FRANTIC FRED was FRENETIC.

9. **frugal:** (adj) not wasteful; not spending freely or unnecessarily; thrifty; economical; inexpensive

   Whereas most of her siblings spend freely, Georgette is rather *frugal*.

   syn: saving, sparing, penny-pinching, close-fisted; **ant:** extravagant, prodigal, spendthrift, generous

   family words: frugality (n); frugally (adv)

   Helpful Hint: FRANCOIS, my FRUGAL FRENCH FRIEND, spent little and wasted nothing.

10. **perceive:** (v) to grasp mentally; to take note (of); to observe; to become aware

    I could not *perceive* that scientific explanation for the life of me!

    Look closely and see if you can *perceive* the deer in that part of the woods.

    syn: discern, behold, understand, apprehend, realize

    family words: perception, perceiver (n); perceivable (adj); perceivably (adv)

11. **perplex:** (v) to make (a person) uncertain, hesitant, or doubtful; to confuse; to puzzle; to make intricate or complicated

    Most difficult math problems *perplex* and frustrate me.

    syn: baffle, mix up, bewilder, dumbfound; **ant:** explain, solve, enlighten, reassure, clarify

    family words: perplexity (n); perplexing (adj); perplexingly (adv)

    Helpful Hint: How do you PERPLEX REX? Simply confuse him!

12. **ruthless:** (adj) pitiless; without compassion; without sorrow or grief

    The dictator's *ruthless* mistreatment of his subjects drew the anger of humane world leaders.

    syn: merciless, unmerciful, unpitying, heartless; **ant:** compassionate, pitying, sympathetic, softhearted

    family words: ruthlessness (n); ruthlessly (adv)

13. **subtle:** (adj) delicately skillful or clever; not direct or open; crafty; sly; delicately suggestive

    Our boss could either be *subtle* or direct in letting us know we could be better.

    syn: gentle, sensitive, refined; **ant:** gross, coarse, insensitive, dense

    family words: subtlety, subtleness (n); subtly (adv)

14. **tenure:** (n) the act or right of holding property, an office, position, etc.; the length of time, or the conditions under which, something is held

    Since my science teacher was recently granted *tenure*, she seems more relaxed about staying on as our teacher.

    syn: incumbency, occupancy

    family words: tenured (adj)

    Helpful Hint: "Ten-" means *to hold. Tenure* is "a hold" on something like an office or position. Do you have "a hold on" the word *tenure*?

15. **wheedle:** (v) to influence or persuade (a person) by flattery, soothing words, coaxing, etc.; to get (something) by coaxing or flattering

    We attempted to *wheedle* Mom and Dad into taking us to the movies by telling them what wonderful parents they are.

    syn: cajole, persuade

    family words: wheedler (n); wheedlingly (adv)

    Helpful Hint: Ever try to WHEEDLE the doctor from using the NEEDLE? It's impossible!

13-1   LET'S GO FISHING

Using the words from the list below, fill in the appropriate word by writing it in the correct space. Then write the letter of the word indicated on the line at the bottom of this page. Thus, for the first fill-in, you will use the fourth letter. Continue the same pattern. If your answers are correct, you will (consecutively) spell out four words associated with fishing.

abduct	beret	current	perceive	subtle
amiable	brutal	frenetic	perplex	tenure
apprentice	caption	frugal	ruthless	wheedle

1. My grandfather worked as an _____ to a carpenter during the 1940s. **(4)**

2. The pace of the game was not just fast; it was _____. **(3)**

3. Such a difficult math problem will generally _____ even the most astute student. **(6)**

4. Usually, _____ people will have many friends and acquaintances. **(6)**

5. The dictator employed _____ measures to force the people to submit to his tyranny. **(5)**

6. Because he was so _____, Ted was able to save much money over the past twenty years. **(3)**

7. Grandpa Murphy proudly wore his _____ as he sailed along the Seine River in 1990. **(3)**

8. Can you _____ how the magician is able to conceal so many objects without our seeing him put them out of our sight? **(5)**

9. The strange woman attempted to _____ the small child from his parents in the parking lot. **(5)**

10. What a funny _____ accompanied the cartoon in last night's newspaper! **(6)**

11. Though he proved to be too stubborn, we did our best to _____ Dad into taking us to the movies last Saturday evening. **(5)**

12. I need to know the _____ temperature, not yesterday's temperature. **(6)**

13. Maureen will receive _____ as an elementary teacher because she is so effective and well respected in the district. **(2)**

14. With the thermometer nearing 100 degrees, and the humidity also very unpleasant, the conditions for our triathlon were nothing less than _____. **(4)**

15. Trying not to be too obvious, we attempted to inform her in other _____ ways. **(1)**

_____

_____

13-2   THE FOURTH-OF-JULY SPECIAL

Match each word in Column A with its definition in Column B. Write the corresponding two-letter answer on the line next to the number in Column A. Write these letters at the bottom of this page. One is already done for you. If your answers are correct, you will spell out a name and the first three words of a song title associated with the Fourth of July. Make some fireworks here and answer them all correctly.

Column A

1. _____ abduct
2. _____ amiable
3. _____ apprentice
4. _____ beret
5. ___IP___ brutal
6. _____ caption
7. _____ current
8. _____ frenetic
9. _____ frugal
10. _____ perceive
11. _____ perplex
12. _____ ruthless
13. _____ subtle
14. _____ tenure
15. _____ wheedle

Column B

an. to make a person uncertain, hesitant, or doubtful; confuse; puzzle; to make intricate or complicated

as. frantic; frenzied

ds. pitiless; without compassion; without sorrow or grief

es. to influence or persuade (a person) by flattery, soothing words, coaxing, etc.; to get something by coaxing or flattering

hn. having a friendly and likeable disposition; good-natured

il. a flat, round, cap of felt, wool, etc.

ﾒﾞ. cruel and unfeeling; savage, violent, ruthless, etc.; very harsh or rigorous

ip. the act or right of holding property, an office, position, etc.; the length of time, or the conditions under which, something is held

jo. to take a person away unlawfully and by force or fraud; kidnap

ph. a person who is acquiring a trade, craft, or skill under specified conditions, usually as a member of a labor union; novice

rs. to grasp mentally; take note of; observe; to become aware

so. a heading or title, as of an article; a descriptive title or legend, as under an illustration

ta. not wasteful; not spending freely or unnecessarily; thrifty; economical; inexpensive

tr. delicately skillful or clever; not direct or open; crafty; sly; delicately suggestive

us. now going on; now in progress; at the present time; contemporary; flow of water or air, especially when strong or swift in a definite direction.

_____

_____

_____ Forever"

13-3   TO THE Nth DEGREE

How smart are you when it comes to knowing the words in this Magic Square? Perhaps you are smart "to the *n*th degree." Let's see. Match the words with their definitions, including the word *n*th, by writing the correct number in the appropriate box within the Magic Square. (One is done for you.) If your answers are correct, the rows, columns, and the two diagonals will all add up to the same number. So now off to the Nth degree of vocabulary skills you go!

A=	B=15	C=	D=
E=	F=	G=	H=
I=	J=	K=	L=
M=	N=	O=	P=

Magic Number:

_____

A. wheedle **E.** perplex **I.** apprentice **M.** tenure
B. frenetic **F.** amiable **J.** caption **N.** *n*th
C. brutal **G.** current **K.** beret **O.** subtle
D. frugal **H.** perceive **L.** abduct **P.** ruthless

1. to influence or persuade (a person) by flattery
2. to an indefinite degree or power; to an extreme
3. a descriptive title or legend, as under an illustration (or cartoon)
4. to make (a person) uncertain, hesitant, or doubtful; confuse; puzzle
5. now going on; now in progress; flow of water or air
6. to take (a person) away unlawfully and by force or fraud
7. pitiless; without compassion; without sorrow or grief
8. cruel and unfeeling; savage; violent
9. delicately skillful or clever; not direct or open; crafty; sly
10. not wasteful; not spending freely or unnecessarily; thrifty
11. to grasp mentally; take note (of); observe
12. a flat, round cap of felt, wool, etc.
13. a person who is acquiring a trade, craft, or skill under specified conditions, usually as a member of a labor union; any learner or beginner; novice
14. having a friendly and likeable disposition; good-natured
15. frantic; frenzied
16. the act or right of holding property, an office, position, etc.

13-4   BY A NOSE

Curious title? After you finish this activity, you might not think so. First, determine whether or not the definition next to each word is the same (S) or opposite (O) of the word itself. Thus, in number 1, the definition next to *abduct* is the *same*. Write S (for same) on the line next to the number 1. If the definition next to any word is the opposite, write O (for opposite) on the line next to the appropriate number. The question number is the number of points that that S or O is worth. Now add up all those numbers that have an S next to them. Then add up all those numbers that have an O next to them. If your answers are correct, you will find that the Opposites total 61, and the Sames total 59. So the Opposites will win by two points—or BY A NOSE!

1. ___ **abduct:** to take a person away unlawfully and by force

2. ___ **amiable:** evil-natured; having an unfriendly and unlikable disposition

3. ___ **apprentice:** experienced, learned worker

4. ___ **beret:** flat, round cap

5. ___ **brutal:** kind and sensitive; merciful

6. ___ **caption:** a descriptive title or legend under a cartoon

7. ___ **current:** old-fashioned; out-of-date; already passed

8. ___ **frenetic:** calm and relaxed; easygoing

9. ___ **frugal:** not wasteful; not spending freely or unnecessarily; thrifty

10. ___ **perceive:** to grasp mentally; take note of; observe

11. ___ **perplex:** to make (a person) certain; clarify; to simplify

12. ___ **ruthless:** showing pity; compassionate

13. ___ **subtle:** obvious; direct; open; very suggestive

14. ___ **tenure:** the act or right of holding property, office, or position

15. ___ **wheedle:** to influence or persuade (a person) by flattery, soothing words, or coaxing

The total of the O's is _____.

The total of the S's is _____.

Unit 14

WHAT WE'D LIKE SAID ABOUT US

WHAT WE'D LIKE SAID ABOUT US

1. **charitable:** (adj) kind and generous in giving money or other help to those in need; kind and forgiving in judging others

    The *charitable* woman worked many hours helping out at shelters and food banks.

    The police officer was *charitable* to the young driver when she spoke to him rather than issuing him a ticket.

    syn: (for "kind and generous") bountiful, benevolent (adj); (for "kind and forgiving") lenient, humane, tolerant (adj); **ant:** (for "kind and generous") stingy, miserly, penurious (adj); (for "kind and forgiving") intolerant, cruel, harsh, stern (adj)

    family words: charity (n); charitably (adv)

2. **congenial:** (adj) kindred; compatible; having the same tastes and temperament; friendly; sympathetic

    Always in a good mood and friendly to all the people he meets, Frank is one of the most *congenial* men I know.

    syn: (for "kindred") like, congruous (adj); (for "compatible") agreeable, amenable (adj); (for "friendly") pleasant, agreeable (adj); **ant:** (for "kindred") alien (adj); (for "friendly") uncongenial, unpleasant, cold

    family words: congeniality (n); congenially (adv)

3. **creative:** (adj) having or showing imagination and artistic or intellectual inventiveness

    Inventors and mystery writers share many of the same *creative* talents.

    syn: ingenious, resourceful, productive, prolific; **ant:** barren, sterile, unimaginative, not resourceful

    family words: creativity, creativeness (n); creatively (adv)

4. **diligent:** (adj) hardworking; industrious; persevering and careful in work; done with careful, steady effort

    You will do well in high school because you are so *diligent* in making sure all of your assignments are complete and correct.

    syn: painstaking, assiduous; **ant:** slothful, lazy, indolent

    family words: diligence (n); diligently (adv)

    Helpful Hint: The hardworking and persevering GENT was certainly DILIGENT.

5. **enthusiastic:** (adj) having an intense or eager interest; having a passion for

    Her mother's *enthusiastic* cheering helped her daughter's team win the cheerleading competition.

    syn: ardent, zealous, earnest; **ant:** indifferent, half-hearted, apathetic, cool

    family words: enthusiasm (n); enthusiastically (adv)

6. **genuine:** (adj) not counterfeit or artificial; real, true; authentic; sincere and frank

    After careful study, experts have revealed that this painting is *genuine* and not some secondhand reproduction.

    syn: legitimate; **ant:** spurious, bogus, counterfeit, fake

    family words: genuineness (n); genuinely (adv)

7. **humane:** (adj) having the best qualities of a human being; civilized, kind, tender, merciful, sympathetic

    This society's purpose is to ensure that all animals are treated in a *humane* way with respect and dignity.

    syn: compassionate, tender; **ant:** cruel, harsh

    family words: humaneness (n); humanely (adv)

WHAT WE'D LIKE SAID ABOUT US (continued)

8. **humorous:** (adj) funny; amusing; comical

    Juan is so *humorous* in our biology class that even Ms. Nocera, our teacher, laughs at his comedic comments.

    syn: witty, droll, jocular; **ant:** serious, grave, stern, doleful

    family words: humor (n); humorously (adv)

9. **insightful:** (adj) intuitive; having the ability to understand clearly the inner nature of things

    These detectives are so *insightful* that they will clearly understand why the criminal acted in such a manner.

    syn: perceptive, understanding, sagacious

    family words: insight (n); insightfully (adv)

    Helpful Hint: SIGHT, the ability to see, is found within the word INSIGHTFUL.

10. **intelligent:** (adj) having or showing an alert mind or high intelligence; bright, informed, clever; informed; wise

    Able to clearly explain some of the most complex properties of the universe, Stephen Hawking, the renowned physicist, is probably one of the most *intelligent* men I have met.

    syn: astute, quick, perspicacious; **ant:** stupid, obtuse, ignorant

    family words: intelligence (n); intelligently (adv)

11. **practical:** (adj) designed for use; workable; utilitarian

    Yvonne is able to apply the intricate, theoretical aspects of this concept in a very *practical* fashion.

    syn: pragmatic, realistic, down-to-earth; **ant:** unworkable, unfeasible, romantic

    family words: practicality (n); practically (adv)

12. **prompt:** (adj) quick to act or do what is required; ready; punctual

    Our chorus director wants all members to be *prompt* so that she can start the rehearsal at eight o'clock sharp.

    syn: (for "quick to act") rapid, quick, swift (adj); (for "punctual") on time; **ant:** (for "quick to act") slow (adj); (for "punctual") late, delayed, tardy (adj)

    family words: promptness (n); promptly (adv)

13. **reputable:** (adj) well thought of; respectable; having a good reputation

    Since his knee operation was going to be complicated, Lyle selected the most *reputable* surgeon he could find.

    syn: honorable, estimable, honored; **ant:** shady, corrupt, notorious

    family words: reputability (n); reputably (adv)

    Helpful Hint: A REPUTABLE person has a RESPECTED REPUTATION.

14. **respectful:** (adj) showing deference or dutiful regard

    Instead of acting rudely, the *respectful* boy did all he could to treat the visitor well.

    syn: obedient, reverent, courteous; **ant:** rude, disobedient, irreverent

    family words: respect (n, v); respectfully (adv)

    Helpful Hint: One who is RESPECTFUL is certainly FULL OF RESPECT.

15. **unassuming:** (adj) modest, retiring; not pretentious or forward

    Not one to brag about her accomplishments, my aunt, the newspaper's feature journalist, is both very talented and quite *unassuming*.

    syn: unpretentious, self-effacing, diffident; **ant:** pretentious, arrogant, conceited

    family words: unassumingly (adv)

14-1   END WITH JAMES BOND

Fill in the correct word from the list below in its appropriate space. Each word is used only once. Then circle the letters of the word as indicated by the numbers following the sentence. Thus, in number 1, you will circle letters 3 and 4 of the correct answer. Finally, write all those required-letter combinations at the bottom of the page (in order). If your answers are correct, you will have six four-letter words and one five-letter word that is James Bond's occupation. Go to it!

charitable	diligent	humane	intelligent	reputable
congenial	enthusiastic	humorous	practical	respectful
creative	genuine	insightful	prompt	unassuming

1. The television psychologist, an _____ doctor, can quickly assess and offer solutions to the problems brought before him. **(3,4)**

2. It is important that the television stations report on the work of the _____ people in business and not focus on those who lack respect in the business world. **(1,2)**

3. The grill that can be used both indoors and outdoors offers many other _____ accessories. **(5,6)**

4. The rich man showed how _____ he was through his generous donations. **(9,10)**

5. Since the bus will leave at exactly seven o'clock tomorrow morning, be _____ or you will be left behind. **(2,3)**

6. With an I.Q. of over 160, Samantha is the most _____ member of our class. **(3,4)**

7. This mystery novelist, who has written more than twenty suspenseful and intricate books, is one of the most _____ writers of our time. **(5,6)**

8. The art dealer assured us that this painting is a _____ Picasso, and not some bogus reproduction. **(6,7)**

9. Even after winning three major awards during the past four years, Evelyn remains very _____ . **(7,8)**

10. Most great, spirited coaches are quite _____ about teaching their individual sport to others. **(9,10)**

11. Jennifer's jokes are proof that she is a good joke teller and a very _____ person. **(3,4)**

12. Our primary classroom rule is that each person must be _____ of others by showing kindness and consideration at all times. **(4,5)**

13. Always serving the sick and poor, Mother Teresa of Calcutta, India, was an extraordinary example of a _____ human being. **(4)**

14. The two _____ friends enjoyed many of the same activities, including bowling, playing cards, and watching movies. **(4,5)**

15. This movie writer, a _____ worker, labored over her newest film both day and night for the past ten years. **(7,8)**

_____

_____

14-2   DON'T TELL THIS TO BABE RUTH OR MICHAEL JORDAN!

If the definition next to the boldfaced word is correct, circle the two letters under the YES column. If not, circle the two letters under the NO column. Then transfer the two-letter combinations to the bottom of this page. If your answers are correct, the letters will spell out a quote and the three initials of the quote's author. Once you correctly write the quote, you will certainly understand the activity's title.

	Yes	No	
1.	ev	te	**charitable:** kind and generous in giving money or help
2.	er	br	**congenial:** compatible; friendly; having the same tastes
3.	ss	yh	**creative:** unimaginative; not inventive
4.	fa	er	**diligent:** lazy; not exhibiting careful, steady effort
5.	on	ob	**enthusiastic:** dull; not showing strong interest for or toward
6.	ec	fe	**genuine:** real; true; authentic
7.	re	om	**humane:** uncivilized; unkind; unsympathetic
8.	hi	es	**humorous:** not funny; not amusing
9.	ab	rt	**insightful:** understanding clearly; intuitive
10.	sm	or	**intelligent:** stupid; dense
11.	gg	ea	**practical:** unworkable; not usable; not useful
12.	tl	li	**prompt:** on time; ready; quick to act or do
13.	wi	as	**reputable:** not respected; having a bad reputation
14.	tr	so	**respectful:** showing regard or deference
15.	te	we	**unassuming:** proud; forward; pretentious

_____

_____

_____

14-3   ILLUSTRATIVE EXAMPLES

The actions of fifteen people are illustrated below. Circle the two adjectives that apply to each person's actions—and those actions alone. Be ready to tell why you have selected those two adjectives to describe each action.

1. Molly raised over $10,000 in two months for the poor in her community. **(a) enthusiastic and charitable OR (b) genuine and unassuming**

2. Georgia can fix many appliances. **(a) respectful and prompt OR (b) insightful and practical**

3. Stephanie tells you exactly what she is feeling. **(a) unassuming and diligent OR (b) insightful and genuine**

4. Colleen attended an Ivy League college and is now a cardiologist. **(a) diligent and intelligent OR (b) humorous and charitable**

5. Jimmy has never been late for a meeting in the past five years. **(a) diligent and prompt OR (b) enthusiastic and unassuming**

6. Yvonne volunteers at soup kitchens and homeless shelters. **(a) practical and prompt OR (b) humane and charitable**

7. Patsy does not like to show off or be in the spotlight. **(a) unassuming and genuine OR (b) humorous and congenial**

8. Kenneth has many friends. **(a) practical and intelligent OR (b) reputable and congenial**

9. Moe likes to tell jokes and laugh. **(a) reputable and practical OR (b) creative and humorous**

10. Craig can really figure out problems quickly. **(a) intelligent and insightful OR (b) genuine and congenial**

11. Johnnie has been voted the Most Respected in Our Community. **(a) creative and prompt OR (b) humane and reputable**

12. Martina designs websites, writes comedies, and has patented a machine. **(a) intelligent and creative OR (b) insightful and respectful**

13. Laurene always treats people with regard and concern. **(a) respectful and humane OR (b) enthusiastic and diligent**

14. Kyle has not taken a vacation in six years. All that time he has worked on his new invention. **(a) diligent and creative OR (b) genuine and unassuming**

15. Janine, who works as a missionary in a poor country, donates most of her money to the needy. **(a) respectful and congenial OR (b) humane and charitable**

14-4 AND NOW FOR THE ONE NOUN FORM

Fill in the correct answer for each clue below. Fifteen of the sixteen answers are adjectives. There is only one answer that is in the noun form. Fill that one in too! Good luck!!

Across

1. funny; amusing
3. hard-working; industrious; persevering and careful in work
5. designed for use; workable
6. having or showing imagination and artistic or intellectual inventiveness
10. noun form of the adjective *reputable*
11. intuitive; having the ability to understand clearly the inner nature of things
13. showing deference or dutiful regard
14. kind and generous in giving money or other help to those in need; kind and forgiving in judging others

Down

2. modest; retiring; not pretentious or forward
4. bright; informed; clever; wise
5. quick to act or do what is required; ready; punctual
6. compatible; friendly; sympathetic
7. having an intense or eager interest; having a passion for
8. not counterfeit or artificial; real; true; authentic
9. well thought of; respectable
12. civilized; kind; tender; merciful

Unit 15
TO A DEGREE

TO A DEGREE

1. **drought:** (n) a prolonged period of dry weather; lack of rain; a prolonged or serious shortage or deficiency

   The *drought* has made it very difficult to grow crops on the formerly arable land.

   This city's professional sports teams have certainly had a *drought* on winning major championships, not having won one in thirty years!

   family words: droughty (adj)

   Helpful Hint: A DROUGHT is WITHOUT rain.

2. **epidemic:** (n) the rapid spread of a disease; (adj) widespread

   Had vaccinations been used during that century, the *epidemic* that killed thousands of people would not have occurred.

   Discussions about the famous trial were *epidemic*; everywhere you went, people were talking about this trial!

   syn: plague, outbreak, endemic (n); prevalent, rife, rampant (adj); **ant:** limited, contained, isolated (adj)

   family words: epidemical (adj); epidemically (adv)

3. **feeble:** (adj) weak and frail; not strong; without force or effectiveness

   Sadly, this geriatric patient has lost her strength and has become *feeble* and unable to make her way around the home.

   syn: infirm, ailing, debilitated; **ant:** strong, vigorous, healthy, robust

   family words: feebleness (n); feebly (adv)

4. **gorged:** (v) swallowed greedily

   Trained to eat as a lady would eat, the debutante never *gorged* herself on any food, including her favorite food, filet mignon.

   syn: stuffed, overate, gulped

   Helpful Hint: GEORGE, who GORGED himself on the delectable seafood assortment, had a hard time getting up from the table because he was so full.

5. **infinite:** (adj) without an end; never ending

   Since the possible methods of solving this problem are *infinite,* we can take our time and select the best from all these choices.

   syn: immeasurable, limitless, boundless; **ant:** finite, limited, measurable

   family words: infinity, infiniteness (n); infinitely (adv)

   Helpful Hint: INFINITE and FINITE are opposites. *Finite* means "with an end." *Infinite* means "without end."

6. **intermittent:** (adj) stopping and starting at intervals; pausing from time to time

   The *intermittent* rain delayed the start of our town's parade for two hours.

   syn: discontinuous, irregular, occasional; **ant:** continuous, incessant, perpetual

   family words: intermittence (n); intermittently (adv)

7. **marginal:** (adj) borderline; limited; minimal

   Even though the researcher had labored for many years trying to find the cure for the disease, she had made only *marginal* gains in her work.

   syn: unimportant, insignificant, minor; **ant:** primary, crucial

   family words: marginality (n); marginally (adv)

8. **monopoly:** (n) exclusive control of a commodity or service in a given market, or control that makes possible the fixing of prices and the virtual elimination of free competition; exclusive possession or control of something

Not wanting one company to have a *monopoly* on the market, the government ensures that there is free enterprise so that many companies can compete.

syn: control, dominate, corner; **ant:** share, compete

family words: monopolize (v)

Helpful Hint: "Mono-" means *one.* "Poly-" means *many* or *much. Monopoly* means that one has *many* or *much!*

9. **multitude:** (n) a large number of persons or things, esp. when gathered together or considered as a unit; host; myriad; the masses

That infamous, large rock concert will be remembered for many things, including the wild activities of the *multitude* of young people in attendance.

syn: crowd, throng, horde

family words: multitudinous (adj)

Helpful Hint: "Multi-" means *many.* A MULTITUDE has MANY.

10. **numerous:** (adj) consisting of many persons or things; very many

The chorus director requested the audience's vocal participation *numerous* times throughout the concert.

syn: abundant, countless, plentiful; **ant:** scant, sparse, few, scarce

family words: numerousness (n); numerously (adv)

11. **puny:** (adj) of inferior size, strength, or importance; weak; slight

The *puny* wrestler was no match for his massive opponent.

syn: small, insignificant, undersized; **ant:** large, sizable, considerable, weighty

Helpful Hint: PUNY, meaning *small,* is a small word. HUMONGOUS, meaning *large,* is a large word. PUNY and HUMONGOUS are opposites.

12. **quench:** (v) to extinguish; to put out; to overcome; to subdue; to suppress; to satisfy

Each day the farm worker would drink several gallons of water to *quench* his thirst.

syn: quell, quash, appease, abate; **ant:** light, kindle, whet, increase

family words: quencher (n); quenchable, quenchless (adj)

13. **substantial:** (adj) of having substance; real; actual; true; not imaginary; strong; solid; firm; important; considerable

Lately, my uncle's stocks, instead of moving along modestly, have made *substantial* gains.

syn: generous, firm, sturdy, sound; **ant:** flimsy, fragile, frail, meager

family words: substantiality (n); substantially (adv)

14. **temperate:** (adj) moderate in one's actions, speech, etc.; self-restrained; neither very hot nor very cold

Jason is always quite *temperate* in his actions, never becoming too excited or too passive.

Those who live in the *Temperate* Zones do not experience the Frigid Zone's extremely cold temperatures or the Torrid Zone's excruciatingly hot temperatures.

syn: mild, pleasant, agreeable, conservative; **ant:** extreme, passionate, impetuous

family words: temperateness (n); temperately (adv)

Helpful Hint: TEMPER means "to balance." TEMPERATE means "balanced" (or in check).

15. **trickle:** (n) a slow, small flow; (v) to flow slowly in a thin stream or fall in drops; to move slowly

Before the storm had gained its real strength, the raindrops had begun to *trickle* down the car windows.

syn: drop, leak, drip, seepage (n); dribble, leak, seep (v)

Helpful Hint: It is no TRICK that TRICKLE (small, slow flow) is an opposite of TEEM (heavy flow).

15-1   PLACING THEM IN

Fifteen words are waiting for you to place them into their proper spaces. Each word is used only once. Let's get started!

drought	gorged	marginal	numerous	substantial
epidemic	infinite	monopoly	puny	temperate
feeble	intermittent	multitude	quench	trickle

1. The contestant _____ himself with hot dogs in the "All You Can Eat" contests held last weekend.

2. Unfortunately, her many hours of practice only had a _____ effect on her performance in the tournament.

3. The marathon runner drank several cups of water to _____ her thirst during the 26.2-mile race.

4. Because the weather here is never too hot or too cold, it is located in an area appropriately named the _____ Zone.

5. Throughout the afternoon we listened to the rain _____ into the bucket.

6. A(n) _____ of ants was found underneath our porch steps.

7. In contrast to last summer's _____, we have had nothing but rain these past few weeks.

8. There are a(n) _____ number of possibilities of how we may solve this problem.

9. The government did not want one company to have a(n) _____ on the railroads in the country.

10. Luckily, the rain was both light and _____, and we did not have to cancel our picnic.

11. After making _____ mistakes in his essay, the student decided to start over rather than make so many corrections.

12. The athlete's new diet made a _____ difference in both her weight and her appearance.

13. Nobody wants to become old and _____, unable to perform life's daily routines.

14. Obviously, this _____ wrestler was no match for his exceptionally strong opponent.

15. The _____ that Europe experienced many years ago killed many people.

15-2   WHERE DID THE WORD *NUMBER* GO?

Each of the words from Unit 15 and a word (or two) found in each word's definition (we will call them the "associated" words) are found in the list below AND in the word-find puzzle. Oddly, although the word *multitude* is listed here, its associated word, *number*, is missing. Circle the fifteen Unit 15 words and their associated words that are found in the list below. Then, on a separate piece of paper, match the words with their associated words. Each word is used only once. Have fun!

borderline	flow	many	puny
considerable	frail	marginal	quench
disease	gorged	moderate	satisfy
drought	greedily	monopoly	substantial
epidemic	infinite	multitude	temperate
exclusive	intermittent	no end	trickle
feeble	intervals	numerous	weak
			weather

```
m d m o n o p o l y w e a k k e n g s f
n a i n t o e x c l u s i v e p u o t m
s n n n j e e d r o u g h t f i m r w l
b u b y t m m n s a t i s f y d e g j z
q o b w i e p p d f l o w w p e r e v h
x y r s n d r w e a t h e r m m o d m q
v p f d t x t m v r y l f m j i u m u p
p b f h e a c t i d a g h o k c s a l y
g z e c r r n r r t i t r d v p z r t q
z d e c v j l t d i t s e e k g g g i u
v f b w a m d i i s c e e r e p q i t e
r k l m l n c x n a x k n a r d j n u n
p w e q s g r x f e l z l t s x i a d c
r n c o n s i d e r a b l e f e d l e h
i n i f i n i t e f r a i l p u n y y h
```

15-3   TRIPLE THE NUMBER

Only five of these fifteen analogies are synonyms. Their corresponding numbers total 30. The corresponding numbers of the ten antonyms total 90—triple the synonyms' total. Write the letter S for synonym and A for antonym on the appropriate lines next to their corresponding numbers.

1. ____ substantial : considerable

2. ____ puny : large and strong

3. ____ intermittent : constant

4. ____ temperate : severe

5. ____ quench : to satisfy

6. ____ trickle : slow, small flow

7. ____ gorged : swallowed greedily

8. ____ drought : wet weather

9. ____ multitude : small number of persons or things

10. ____ numerous : small number

11. ____ epidemic : rapid spread of a disease

12. ____ monopoly : shared possession or control

13. ____ infinite : having a definite end

14. ____ feeble : strong

15. ____ marginal : of high quality

S total = _____

A total = _____

15-4   HEY! SOME LETTERS ARE MISSING!

Unfortunately, half the letters from the words in Unit 15 are missing. Fill in the missing letters and make them complete!

1. __ r __ u __ h __: a prolonged period of dry weather

2. __ p __ d __ m __ c: the rapid spread of a disease

3. __ e __ b __ e: weak and frail

4. __ o __ g __ d: swallowed greedily

5. __ n __ i __ i __ e: without an end; never ending

6. __ n __ e __ m __ t __ e __ t: stopping and starting at intervals; pausing from time to time

7. __ a __ g __ n __ l: borderline

8. __ o __ o __ o __ y: exclusive possession or control of something

9. __ u __ t __ t __ d __: a large number of persons or things

10. __ u __ e __ o __ s: very many

11. __ u __ y: of inferior size; weak

12. __ u __ n __ h: to satisfy

13. __ u __ s __ a __ t __ a __: considerable

14. __ e __ p __ r __ t __: moderate

15. __ r __ c __ l __: a slow, small flow

Name: _____ Date: _____ Period: _____ Score: _____ %

Units 13–15   REVIEW TEST

Directions: Please circle the correct **synonym.** Then write the answer's corresponding letter on the line next to the question's number. Each question is worth four points.

1. ____ **drought** (a) prolonged period of dry weather (b) musical composition (c) former farmer

2. ____ **epidemic** (a) old story (b) experiment (c) rapid spread of disease

3. ____ **monopoly** (a) democracy (b) fragrance (c) excessive control of a community or service in a given market

4. ____ **beret** (a) flat, round cap (b) French boat (c) halo

5. ____ **frenetic** (a) tranquil (b) frenzied (c) observant

6. ____ **tenure** (a) a teacher's salary (b) the length of time that something is held (c) person who collects money

7. ____ **apprentice** (a) veteran (b) soloist (c) novice

8. ____ **enthusiastic** (a) having an intense or eager interest (b) considerable (c) satisfactory

9. ____ **practical** (a) compatible (b) energetic (c) workable

10. ____ **insightful** (a) spendthrift (b) having the ability to clearly understand the inner nature of things (c) merciful

Directions: Please circle the correct **antonym.** Then write the answer's corresponding letter on the line next to the question's number. Each question is worth four points.

11. ____ **frugal** (a) pleasant (b) prodigal (c) very friendly

12. ____ **temperate** (a) mild (b) compassionate (c) passionate

13. ____ **quench** (a) increase (b) inflict (c) undo

14. ____ **prompt** (a) tardy (b) on time (c) early

15. ____ **feeble** (a) healthy (b) weak (c) forgetful

16. ____ **current** (a) prevalent (b) bygone (c) delicate

17. ____ **subtle** (a) clever (b) insensitive (c) baffling

18. ____ **congenial** (a) friendly (b) same (c) unpleasant

19. ____ **humane** (a) kind (b) cruel (c) obedient

20. ____ **reputable** (a) corrupt (b) friendly (c) ruthless

Units 13–15   REVIEW TEST (continued)

Directions: Please circle the word that correctly **completes** the sentence. Then write the answer's corresponding letter on the line next to the question's number. Each question is worth four points.

21. _____ The cartoonist's hysterical _____ included only three words!
    (a) epidemic   (b) caption   (c) tenure

22. _____ Rather than only giving her workers a single reminder, the boss had to speak to them _____ times.   **(a) numerous   (b) frugal   (c) amiable**

23. _____ We tried extremely hard to _____ Dad into taking us to the amusement park last week.   **(a) wheedle   (b) perceive   (c) abduct**

24. _____ After the dolphin had _____ himself on the fish given to him, we did not think that he could get up and jump as high as he did.
    (a) trickled   (b) quenched   (c) gorged

25. _____ These _____ sounds coming from the dark forest lack a consistent cadence.   **(a) intermittent   (b) ruthless   (c) perplexed**

Unit 16

ALL TYPES OF PEOPLE

ALL TYPES OF PEOPLE

1. **amateur:** (n) a person who engages in some art, science, sport, etc., for the pleasure of it rather than for money; nonprofessional; person who does something without professional skill; (adj) of or done by amateur or amateurs; amateurish

   Though the professional photographers submitted their best pictures, the contest winner was an *amateur* photographer.

   His *amateur* skills were a stark contrast to those of the professionals in the same contest.

   syn: hobbyist, dabbler (n); **ant:** professional, expert, master, specialist (n)

   family words: amateurishness (n); amateurishly (adv)

2. **assassin:** (n) one who kills someone of importance

   The Warren Commission researched whether Lee Harvey Oswald was the sole *assassin* of President John F. Kennedy.

   syn: executioner, hit-man, murderer, sniper

   family words: assassinate (v); assassinator (n)

3. **bachelor:** (n) an unmarried man

   Rather than marry, Uncle Henry decided to remain a *bachelor* for the rest of his life.

   family words: bachelorhood, bachelorship (n)

4. **bursar:** (n) a treasurer at a college or similar institution

   My older sister met with the *bursar* to discuss the tuition payment plan.

5. **cynic:** (n) one who is critical of society; one who believes that people are motivated in all their actions only by selfishness; one who is sarcastic or sneering; one who denies the sincerity of people's motives and actions

   Only a *cynic* would believe that the man had ulterior motives when he helped the older couple into their car.

   syn: skeptic, pessimist; **ant:** enthusiast, optimist, supporter

   family words: cynicism (n); cynical (adj); cynically (adv)

6. **dupe:** (n) one who is easily fooled; (v) to deceive by trickery; to fool or cheat

   These bullies made a *dupe* out of the new student in our school by selling him an elevator pass—though we do not have an elevator in our school!

   The dishonest financial manager was able to *dupe* the family out of a considerable sum of money.

   syn: victim, sucker, fall-guy (n); trick, hoodwink, deceive (v)

   family words: duper (n); dupable (adj)

7. **feminist:** (n) one who strives for equality for women

   An ardent *feminist,* my sister strives for equal rights and opportunities for women.

   family words: feminism (n); feministic (adj)

8. **journalist:** (n) one whose occupation consists of gathering, writing, editing, and publishing the news

   Bob Woodward, a *journalist,* did extensive investigative reporting concerning the break-in at the Watergate Hotel in Washington, DC.

   syn: newsman, newswoman, reporter, correspondent

   family words: journalism (n); journalistic (adj)

ALL TYPES OF PEOPLE (continued)

9. miser: (n) one who is stingy

Who would ever think that the free-spending guy could have a brother who was a *miser*?

syn: skinflint, hoarder, usurer; **ant:** prodigal, wastrel, spendthrift

family words: miserly (adv)

10. nomad: (n) member of a tribe or group with no permanent home

The performer said that he felt like a *nomad* as he traveled from town to town with the circus.

syn: wanderer, rover, migrant; **ant:** resident

family words: nomadic (adj)

Helpful Hint: A NOmad has NO place to call home.

11. orator: (n) an eloquent public speaker

Abraham Lincoln's Gettysburg Address proved that he was a talented *orator*.

syn: lecturer, rhetorician, sermonizer

family words: oratorical (adj)

12. orthodontist: (n) a dentist whose specialty is straightening teeth

Since this tooth feels a little sore, I will visit my *orthodontist* to have my braces adjusted.

family words: orthodontics (n); orthodontic (adj)

Helpful Hint: *Orthodontist* = "ortho-" (to straighten) + "don't-" (teeth) + "-ist" (one who does)

13. traitor: (n) one who betrays his or her country, a cause, or a friend

The government will punish this *traitor* who gave away confidential files to the enemy.

syn: turncoat, renegade, deserter; **ant:** loyalist

family words: traitorousness (n); traitorous (adj); traitorously (adv)

Helpful Hint: TRAITOR and BETRAYER sound alike. They also mean the same—to switch sides in a battle or cause.

14. tyrant: (n) a cruel, obsessive ruler

Those who advocate humane treatment of each human being do not look favorably on the actions of this *tyrant,* who mistreats and even kills his citizens.

syn: despot, dictator, autocrat

family words: tyranny (n); tyrannical (adj); tyrannically (adv)

Helpful Hint: A TYRANT never TIRES from treating people cruelly.

15. virtuoso: (n) one who displays great technical skill in some fine art

The famous *virtuoso* sang that beautiful aria in last night's opera.

syn: master, genius, wizard, artiste; **ant:** amateur

16-1   WHO SAID IT?

Write the name of the type of person who probably said each quote below. Each is used only once.

amateur	bursar	feminist	nomad	traitor
assassin	cynic	journalist	orator	tyrant
bachelor	dupe	miser	orthodontist	virtuoso

1. _____ "Tomorrow I plan to deliver the best speech of my life!"

2. _____ "I seldom trust anybody!"

3. _____ "I will not be fooled again!"

4. _____ "You will do as I say or pay the price!"

5. _____ "I have yet to meet the right woman to call my wife!"

6. _____ "I will give you a receipt for your tuition payment."

7. _____ "Let's see if you need braces."

8. _____ "Why should women not be given equal rights?"

9. _____ "I do not like to spend my money."

10. _____ "They say I have great talent for playing the piano."

11. _____ "They called me a hired killer."

12. _____ "Where shall we set up our next camp?"

13. _____ "Read my interesting story in today's newspaper."

14. _____ "I will show loyalty to my country's enemy."

15. _____ "I do not get paid for playing baseball on this nonprofessional team."

Name: _____ Date: _____ Period: _____

16-2   ALL SORTS OF PEOPLE

Here are twenty people waiting for you to correctly identify them. Place the correct letters within the crossword puzzle and make these twenty happy. Good luck!

Across

9. One lacking the skill of a professional
10. One who displays great technical skill in some fine art
11. Short for "constable on patrol"
12. Dentist whose specialty is straightening teeth
16. One who betrays his or her country, a cause, or a friend
17. Short form of "detective"

Down

1. College official responsible for collecting tuition
2. Short form of "veterinarian"
3. One who is easily fooled
4. Unmarried man
5. One who strives for equality for women
6. One who greedily saves his or her money
7. Member of a tribe or group with no permanent home
8. One who usually writes for a newspaper or magazine
9. One who kills someone of importance
11. One who believes that all people are motivated by selfishness
12. An eloquent public speaker
13. A cruel, obsessive ruler
14. Short form of "cab driver"
15. Short form of "professor"

16-3 POLITICALLY SPEAKING

Fill in the correct answers in these fifteen blanks. Each word is used only once. Then circle the number letter as indicated after the sentence. Thus, in number 1, you should circle the fifth letter. Transfer all the circled letters (consecutively) to the bottom of the page. If you have correctly filled in the correct words and circled the correct letter in each word, you have spelled out two people associated with politics.

amateur	bursar	feminist	nomad	traitor
assassin	cynic	journalist	orator	tyrant
bachelor	duping	miser	orthodontist	virtuoso

1. The hired _____ felt no guilt after murdering the country's leader. **(5)**

2. My friend is a(n) _____ photographer who, although he has tried very hard, has not sold any of his photographs. **(5)**

3. Only a(n) _____ would believe that the kind woman's deeds were done for a selfish reason. **(3)**

4. People would often travel very far to listen to the wisdom of the _____. **(3)**

5. Authorities captured the _____, who said that he hated his native country and would do anything to destroy it. **(5)**

6. My _____ told me that I would get my braces off in a few months. **(5)**

7. Democratic countries do not want to see another _____ take over that country. **(3)**

8. Rude people enjoyed _____ the guy who was easily deceived. **(6)**

9. Never having married during his lifetime, the _____ said that he had no regrets that he had lived alone his entire life. **(7)**

10. We listened to the violin _____, who entertained the audience for more than two hours. **(1)**

11. The newspaper reporter interviewed the _____, who spoke fervently about women's rights. **(2)**

12. I heard about the _____ who was so cheap that he died a wealthy man. **(5)**

13. A(n) _____ crossed the desert in search of another new place to live for that time. **(1)**

14. As she reported on the war in that foreign country, the _____ witnessed many horrible atrocities. **(2)**

15. We gave our tuition payment to the _____ yesterday. **(3)**

_____

_____

16-4   HAVE YOU SEEN THE . . .?

Select the words from the columns below to fill in the blank before each description. Each word is used only once.

amateur	bursar	feminist	nomad	traitor
assassin	cynic	journalist	orator	tyrant
bachelor	duping	miser	orthodontist	virtuoso

Have you seen the . . .

1. _____ woman who is responsible for accepting our tuition payments each semester?

2. _____ lady who has devoted her life to women's rights?

3. _____ leader who gets pleasure from torturing his citizens?

4. _____ man who was hired to shoot and kill the country's leader?

5. _____ lady who gave away secret government papers to the enemy?

6. _____ man who has never married?

7. _____ woman whose article about New Zealand appeared in the weekly national magazine?

8. _____ guy who would like to play professionally but does not quite have the talent to do so?

9. _____ talented musician who recently played at Carnegie Hall in New York City?

10. _____ unfortunate person who is easily deceived by those who like to take advantage of people?

11. _____ stingy man who was very cheap and seldom spent any money?

12. _____ older man who wanders across the desert with no home to call his own?

13. _____ dentist who straightens teeth?

14. _____ sarcastic person who distrusts people and says that most people are basically selfish?

15. _____ well-spoken woman who delivered a stirring speech about animal rights?

Unit 17

AN INTERESTING COMBINATION OF WORDS

AN INTERESTING COMBINATION OF WORDS

1. absurd: (adj) so clearly untrue or unreasonable as to be laughable or ridiculous

Thinking you can run a mile in under three minutes is *absurd*!

syn: silly, irrational, foolish

family words: absurdness, absurdity (n); absurdly (adv)

2. arable: (adj) suitable for plowing, hence for producing crops

These *arable* acres of land will produce many crops over the next few years.

family words: arability (n)

3. bibliography: (n) a list of sources of information on a given subject, period, etc., or of the literary works of a given author, publisher, etc.; a list of the books, articles, etc., used or referred to by an author

Fortunately, I was able to find a great *bibliography* that included many books that helped me find useful information on my assigned topic.

family words: bibliographic, bibliographical (adj); bibliographically (adv)

Helpful Hint: *Bibliography* (a list of books) = "biblio-" (book) + "-graphy" (to write)

4. commiserate: (v) to condole (to express sympathy) or sympathize (with)

I attended the memorial ceremony to *commiserate* with the deceased man's family.

family words: commiseration (n); commiserative (adj); commiseratively (adv)

Helpful Hint: *Commiserate* (share pity or sympathy) = "com-" (with) + "miserate" (to show pity)

5. deceive: (v) to make (a person) believe what is not true; to delude; to mislead; to deliberately mislead

Rather than *deceive* the police authorities, the suspected criminal showed them exactly where he had hidden the stolen items.

syn: misinform, defraud, cheat

family words: deceiver (n); deceivable (adj); deceivingly (adv)

6. fatal: (adj) important in its outcome; fateful; decisive; resulting in death; very destructive; disastrous

The foreign country's president's decision to enter the war proved *fatal* for many of his countrymen who were killed in battle.

syn: deadly, mortal, lethal, pernicious

family words: fatalness, fatalism, fatalist (n); fatalistic (adj); fatalistically (adv)

7. foster: (v) to bring up with care; rear; to help to grow or develop; to stimulate; (adj) having the standing of a specified member of the family, though not by birth or adoption, and giving, receiving, or sharing the care appropriate to that standing

My parents try to *foster* a sense of independence in each of us.

Adopted when he was only seven months old, Reggie is my *foster* brother.

syn: raise, nurture, cultivate; **ant:** neglect, hamper, abandon

family words: fosterer (n)

8. glimmer: (v) to give a faint, flickering light; to appear or be seen faintly or dimly; (n) a faint, flickering light

We will look for the light that will *glimmer* at midnight.

There is still a *glimmer* of hope that he will find the watch that he lost at the playground.

syn: sparkle, twinkle, glitter (v, n)

9. meticulous: (adj) extremely or excessively careful about details; finicky

Ted is so *meticulous* about keeping his car clean that we have to clean off the bottoms of our shoes before we get into his prized auto.

syn: painstaking, punctilious, fastidious; **ant:** careless, slovenly, negligent

family words: meticulousness (n); meticulously (adv)

10. **publicize:** (v) to give publicity to; to draw public attention to

> To attract as many runners as possible, the race officials decided to *publicize* the event in several different media, including television, radio, and newspapers.

syn: air, advertise, promulgate; **ant:** conceal, hide, cover up

family words: publicity (n)

Helpful Hint: When you PUBLICize, you present it to the PUBLIC.

11. **rave:** (v) to talk incoherently or wildly, as in a delirious or demented state; to talk with great or excessive enthusiasm (about); to rage or roar, as a storm; (n) an extremely or excessively enthusiastic praise or approval; (adj) enthusiastic, glowing

> The critic had to *rave* about the stunning performance of the two lead characters in last night's play.

> The *rave* about the musician's performance was justified since it was one of the best concerts that I had ever attended.

> This play received *rave* reviews, and its star was nominated for prestigious awards.

syn: babble, rant, prattle (v); tribute, accolade (n); poor (adj); **ant:** disparage, censure, detract (v)

family words: raver (n)

12. **restrict:** (v) to keep within certain limits; to put certain limitations on; to confine

> Knowing that it might hurt her business, the restaurant owner was forced to *restrict* smokers from smoking inside the building.

syn: limit, circumscribe, restrain; **ant:** loose, loosen, free

family words: restriction (n); restricted (v, adj); restrictively (adv)

13. **rustic:** (n) a country person, esp. one regarded as unsophisticated, simple, or awkward; (adj) of or living in the country, as distinguished from cities or towns; lacking refinement, elegance, polish, or sophistication

> Compared to the sophisticated city resident, the *rustic* was quite simple and unrefined.

> The family's *rustic* cabin provided a wonderful haven from the hectic pace of the city.

syn: rural (n); countrified, agrarian, bucolic (adj); **ant:** sophisticated, citified (adj)

family words: rusticity (n); rustically (adv)

Helpful Hint: RUSTIC RUSS enjoys the country setting.

14. **serpentine:** (adj) of or like a serpent; coiled or twisted; winding; (n) something that twists or coils like a snake

> The *serpentine* line for the movie wound around the corner and down the next block.

> During the parade honoring the champions, we threw down the *serpentine* that unrolled as it made its way to the ground.

syn: winding, zigzag, snaking; **ant:** straight, unswerving

Helpful Hint: See the coiling SERPENT (snake) in SERPENTine.

15. **subdue:** (v) to bring into subjection; to conquer; to control; to make less intense; to reduce; to diminish

> The stronger army was easily able to *subdue* its less capable adversary in just a few days.

syn: (for "to bring into subjection") defeat, overcome, overpower (v); (for "to make less") soften, mute, lessen (v); **ant:** (for "to bring into subjection") lose, succumb, capitulate (v); for "to make less") increase, intensify, augment (v)

family words: subduer (n)

Helpful Hint: "Sub-" means *under* or *less than*. To *subdue* anything means to "make it less."

17-1   COMING OR GOING THERE LATE

Fill in the blanks with the words below. Then circle the last letter of each word. The last letters of six consecutive words make up a hyphenated two-word expression for a late-night or all-night commercial airline flight on which your eyes could become bloodshot. At the bottom of the page, indicate which six consecutive answers' last letters spell out this type of flight.

absurd	commiserate	foster	publicize	rustic
arable	deceive	glimmer	rave	serpentine
bibliography	fatal	meticulous	restrict	subdue

1. Please do not try to _____ me; be honest with me and we can make progress in this matter.

2. In the bottom of the last inning, there was a _____ of hope that our team could still win the game.

3. Do you think you want to _____ that embarrassing information and have even more people know about it?

4. It is _____ to think that you can run that fast when you first wake up in the morning!

5. Is there any way that the zookeeper can _____ that angry animal before people get hurt?

6. Have you found a _____ to help you locate the books you will need for your research project?

7. Never shy about voicing their opinions, the fans at Wrigley Field love to _____ about their Cubs.

8. My dad and mom decided to purchase a _____ cabin, far from the noise and pollution of the major city.

9. Two people were killed in that horrible, _____ accident that took place on the highway.

10. Sandra's aunt is so _____ that she has everything in the house in perfect order without a spot of dirt to be found anywhere.

11. How do the children expect us to _____ healthy habits when we smoke and do not exercise?

12. Far from looking straight and orderly, the _____ line wound around the cars in the parking lot.

13. For safety's sake, the town officials had to _____ people from swimming at the town beach when lifeguards were not on duty.

14. _____ land is uncommon after the weeks of no rain that we recently experienced.

15. I certainly _____ with you after your recent family loss.

17-2 PEOPLE WILL NOT BE MAD AT US THIS TIME

Twenty-three words have been hidden in this word-find puzzle. Yet, four of the words you are asked to find are right there in the activity's title. So, playing on the word *publicize,* one of the words from this unit, see if you can locate the eight publications, all magazine titles, and the fifteen words from Unit 17. The words are found horizontally, vertically, and diagonally. Get into shape and find these twenty-three words. Good luck!

```
t  g  w  g  r  z  d  k  b  r  p  x  n  m  q  j  s  k  b  t
b  r  b  w  f  x  h  b  j  r  p  z  m  h  y  v  v  j  i  c
z  f  c  j  k  r  y  y  w  l  u  w  y  f  k  m  f  m  b  m
p  k  d  c  p  d  e  q  j  c  b  l  k  j  w  e  r  n  l  y
k  l  s  o  c  m  x  s  m  t  l  z  j  s  k  t  y  t  i  v
m  k  g  m  y  k  y  p  t  g  i  m  s  t  g  i  f  k  o  p
p  z  l  m  t  n  f  z  h  r  c  q  f  r  z  c  f  t  g  z
f  n  i  i  m  t  j  m  s  r  i  t  o  p  k  u  y  n  r  q
a  l  m  s  t  j  u  h  a  e  z  c  s  d  e  l  j  y  a  l
t  i  m  e  a  b  s  u  r  d  e  s  t  e  b  o  n  y  p  d
a  y  e  r  x  y  u  m  a  b  h  h  e  c  d  u  p  m  h  s
l  c  r  a  g  b  b  o  b  o  m  a  r  e  l  s  c  l  y  c
k  l  z  t  l  q  d  n  l  o  d  p  z  i  q  y  s  w  e  x
r  a  v  e  x  c  u  e  e  k  h  e  w  v  r  u  s  t  i  c
j  q  l  n  n  y  e  y  g  s  e  r  p  e  n  t  i  n  e  r
```

absurd	fatal	people	serpentine
arable	foster	publicize	shape
bibliography	glimmer	rave	subdue
commiserate	mad	redbook	time
deceive	meticulous	restrict	us
ebony	money	rustic	

17-3   WHO SAID WHAT?

We have fifteen quotes from fifteen different people all ready to be matched. On the line next to the quote's number, write the corresponding Group One letter of the person who said that. On the blank in the quote itself, write the word from Group Two that most appropriately makes sense in the sentence. Each item from Group One and each item from Group Two is used only once. Let's go and match them all up!

Group One

A. artist	**F.** hardware store clerk	**N.** publicist
B. astronomer	**G.** librarian	**O.** real estate agent
C. construction foreman	**H.** news anchor	**P.** salesperson
D. farmer	**I.** newspaper editor	**Q.** scientist
E. funeral director	**J.** police chief	**R.** teacher

Group Two

absurd	commiserate	foster	publicize	rustic
arable	deceive	glimmer	rave	serpentine
bibliography	fatal	meticulous	restrict	subdue

1. ____ "I want to _____ a greater awareness of cancer. We can do this through print ads and radio and television commercials that explain how we can defeat this deadly disease."

2. ____ "Do not be _____! That is just silly reasoning. Our company's architect knows exactly how to design such a building."

3. ____ "I will need to _____ these colors since they appear much too bright for my tastes."

4. ____ "I _____ with you over the loss of your beloved spouse."

5. ____ "Tonight, we begin our broadcast with the _____ fire that took the lives of three people."

6. ____ "Have you found a _____ that might help you to find more information about this project?"

7. ____ "If you look very closely through your telescope, you can see the _____ of light just beyond that spot in the heavens."

8. ____ "Please do not think that I am trying to _____ you. This machine will work efficiently for the next twenty years—or we will refund you money."

9. ____ "I never expected anything to grow on this plot of land since anybody can tell that it is not _____."

10. ____ "I could easily see you fishing by the lake just outside your _____ home, far away from the hustle and bustle of the suburbs and city."

11. ____ "Because the governor's motorcade will be coming along Main Street, we will _____ any motorists from driving their cars near that street."

12. ____ "This tool has _____ qualities that allow it to make its way through any set of curved pipes."

13. ____ "I will ask you to be more _____ in doing your homework assignments since I will not accept any more sloppy papers from you."

14. ____ "I have observed that when this particular monkey was not given a banana, he did not _____ and act angrily as the other monkeys did."

15. ____ "_____ the team's victory in tomorrow morning's edition. It is a very big deal in this small town!"

17-4 ALL FIFTEEN

Included in this Magic Square is a fifteen-letter science word. This word includes one letter from each of the Unit 17 words. Match each word with its definition by writing the correct number in the appropriate Magic Square box. (One is done for you.) If your answers are correct, the rows, columns, and two diagonals will add up to the same number.

A=	B=6	C=	D=
E=	F=	G=	H=
I=	J=	K=	L=
M=	N=	O=	P=

Magic Number:

_____

A. meticulous   **E.** publicize   **I.** foster   **M.** rustic
B. restrict   **F.** commiserate   **J.** rave   **N.** absurd
C. bibliography   **G.** arable   **K.** fatal   **O.** electropositive
D. deceive   **H.** subdue   **L.** serpentine   **P.** glimmer

1. to condole (to express sympathy) or sympathize (with)
2. to bring up with care; rear; to help grow and develop
3. capable of acting as a positive electrode; having a positive electric charge
4. to make (a person) believe what is not true; delude; mislead
5. a country person, esp. one regarded as unsophisticated and simple; of or living in the country
6. to keep within certain limits; put certain limitations on
7. to bring into subjection; conquer; to make less intense; reduce
8. important in its outcome; fateful; decisive; very destructive; disastrous
9. list of sources of information on a given subject, period, etc., or of the literary works of a given author or publisher
10. to give a faint, flickering light; to appear or be seen faintly or dimly; a faint, flickering light
11. to talk incoherently or wildly, as in a delirious state; to talk with great or excessive enthusiasm about; to rage or roar, as a storm
12. to give publicity to; draw public attention to
13. coiled or twisted; winding; something that coils or twists like a snake
14. suitable for plowing, hence for producing crops
15. extremely or excessively careful about details; finicky
16. so clearly untrue or unreasonable as to be laughable or ridiculous

Unit 18

ALL IN THE FAMILY

ALL IN THE FAMILY

1. adoption: (n) taking another into one's own family by legal process and raising him or her as one's own child; taking and using as one's own

For some families who want to raise others' children, *adoption* is a viable option.

syn: utilization, appropriation

family words: adopt (v); adoptive (adj)

2. akin: (adj) related through a common ancestor; having similar qualities; similar

Since our ancestors are the same people, we are *akin* to each other.

The laughter of the older brother is *akin* to that of the younger brother.

syn: (for "related through") kin, kindred (adj); (for "having similar qualities") alike, comparable, analogous (adj); **ant:** (for "related through") unrelated, unconnected (adj); (for "having similar qualities") different, dissimilar (adj)

Helpful Hint: AKIN and a KIN are both related. These KIN are AKIN to each other!

3. clan: (n) social group bearing the same family name and having a common ancestor; a group of; clique; set

All 256 members of the *clan* had come from six different states for the large reunion.

syn: tribe, family, kin, commune

family words: clannish (adj)

4. fraternal: (adj) characteristic of a brother; brotherly; designating twins having hereditary characteristics not necessarily the same

His *fraternal* feelings toward his three brothers were very obvious.

syn: familial

family words: fraternalism, fraternity (n); fraternally (adv)

Helpful Hint: FRATernal, FRATernity, and FRATernize all begin with "frat-," meaning brother. They are FRAT brothers!

5. generation: (n) average period (about thirty years) between the birth of one generation and that of the next single stage or degree in the succession of natural descent (father, son, and grandson are three generations); origination

This *generation* of soldiers appreciates the bravery and perseverance of the previous *generation's* soldiers.

family words: generate (v); generational (adj)

6. heritage: (n) birthright; something handed down from one's ancestors or the past, such as property, a characteristic; culture or tradition

Part of his family's *heritage* included a large tract of land near the James River, several mansions, and a relative who had been a state senator.

syn: patrimony, legacy, estate

Helpful Hint: When you think of the word HERITAGE think of the word INHERIT because that's exactly what you do when your *heritage* is passed down to you!

7. kin: (n) relatives; family; kinfolk; kindred

Most of Emily Dickinson's immediate *kin* had lived in the vicinity of Amherst, Massachusetts.

family words: kinship (n)

8. **lineage:** (n) direct descent from an ancestor; ancestry; family

 Her *lineage* can be traced back to the Virginia region of 1730 or so.

 syn: derivation, parentage, genealogy

 Helpful Hint: The word LINE is in the word LINEage. Your family LINE is your LINEage!

9. **maternal:** (adj) of, like, or characteristic of a mother or motherhood; motherly

 When trouble began, Paula's *maternal* instincts were evident as she immediately soothed and protected the two smaller children from danger.

 family words: maternally (adv)

 Helpful Hint: Many words beginning with "mater-" or "matr-" have to do with *mother*.

10. **matriarch:** (n) a mother who rules her family or tribe; a highly respected elderly woman

 Grandmother Elda, still robust at 102 years old, is the Miller family's *matriarch*.

 family words: matriarchy (n); matriarchal (adj)

11. **paternal:** (adj) of, like, or characteristic of a father; fatherly

 Mr. Dodson's five children admired his *paternal* qualities, including his strong work ethic, perseverance, and diligence.

 family words: paternalism, paternity (n); paternally (adv)

 Helpful Hint: Many words beginning with "pater-" or "patr-" have to do with *father*.

12. **patriarch:** (n) the father and ruler of a family or tribe; a man of great age or dignity

 Grandpappy Igor, a rugged, former farmer, is the 92-year-old *patriarch* of our family.

 family words: patriarchy (n); patriarchal (adj)

13. **relative:** (adj) related to each other; relevant, connected with; comparative; (n) person connected to another by blood or marriage

 In this argument, apples and oranges are quite different, not *relative*.

 Each *relative* on my dad's side of the family will attend the annual holiday party at my aunt's house.

 syn: (for "related to each other") pertinent, relating to, regarding (adj); (for "comparative") variable, dependent (adj); relation, kin (n); **ant:** (for "related to each other") irrelevant, unrelated, separate, inapplicable; (for "comparative") invariable, independent (adj)

 family words: relativity (n); relatively (adv)

14. **sibling:** (n) one of two or more persons born of the same parents, or sometimes, having one parent in common; brother or sister

 My oldest *sibling* is my twenty-four-year-old brother.

15. **spouse:** (n) partner in marriage; one's husband or wife

 My dad always says that Mom is the world's best *spouse*.

 family words: spousal (adj)

 Helpful Hint: Generally, a SPOUSE lives in the same HOUSE.

18-1   IT'S A FAMILY AFFAIR

All fifteen words below deal with family in one way or another. Write the appropriate word in each blank to complete each sentence. Each word is used only once. Make your family proud and correctly complete these sentences!

adoption	fraternal	kin	matriarch	relative
akin	generation	lineage	paternal	siblings
clan	heritage	maternal	patriarch	spouse

1. Two weeks after his birth, the child was put up for _____.

2. When Emily became a mother, she took on many of the _____ qualities taught to her by her mother.

3. In social studies class we studied the migration habits of the _____ that traveled through this part of Europe.

4. My father could not have asked for a better _____ than my mother.

5. Cousin Al is the favorite of all my _____ that includes over two hundred relatives.

6. Grandpa Giovanni is the _____ of the Milletello family.

7. My grandmother, who died when she was nearly 100 years old, could adapt to each new _____ of ideas and habits.

8. This photograph is much _____ to the one my aunt took thirty years ago.

9. Our family tree clearly depicts the _____ of the Soldine family for the past 175 years.

10. I try to send each _____, including all my cousins, aunts and uncles, a birthday card.

11. My brother and I share many _____ characteristics including our artistic tastes and abilities.

12. Part of Hank's _____ included ownership of a city apartment, a farm, and inheriting nearly half a million dollars.

13. Marcia's three _____ include two younger brothers and a sister who is three years older than she.

14. My dad's _____ qualities include patience and compassion.

15. Nana Louise, our family's beloved _____, is both friendly and funny.

Copyright © 2004 by John Wiley & Sons, Inc.

18-2   DOUBLE-LETTER WORDS

Match up the fifteen family words in Column A with their definitions in Column B. Write the two-letter combination on the line after the appropriate Column A number. Then write the two-letter combinations (in order) at the bottom of this page. Then separate the letters to form five six-letter words. Te*rr*ific!

Column A

1. _____ adoption

2. _____ akin

3. _____ clan

4. _____ fraternal

5. _____ generation

6. _____ heritage

7. _____ kin

8. _____ lineage

9. _____ maternal

10. _____ matriarch

11. _____ paternal

12. _____ patriarch

13. _____ relative

14. _____ sibling

15. _____ spouse

Column B

ar. partner in marriage

ba. related to each other

bb. related through a common ancestor

bu. a mother who rules her family or tribe; a highly respected elderly woman

cu. ancestry; direct descent from an ancestor

et. the father and ruler of a family or tribe; a man of great age or dignity

fl. characteristic of a brother; brotherly

fy. birthright; something handed down from an ancestor

it. social group bearing the same family name and having a common ancestor

ll. characteristic of a father; fatherly

ra. to take into one's own family by legal process

uf. origination; production; average period of years between the parent and the children

um. characteristic of a mother; motherly

va. relatives; family; kindred

za. one of two or more persons born of the same parents

_____

_____

_____

18-3   NO FEUDING WITHIN THE FAMILY HERE

Let us not get under each other's skin here in this activity all about family names. If you do it correctly, there will be no arguing, and everybody will be happy. Use each word below only once. Write the correct word on the line next to its appropriate number. Thus, there will be no feuding!

adoption	fraternal	kin	matriarch	relative
akin	generation	lineage	paternal	sibling
clan	heritage	maternal	patriarch	spouse

1. _____ characteristic of a father

2. _____ characteristic of a mother

3. _____ characteristic of a brother

4. _____ social group bearing the same name and having a common ancestor

5. _____ a highly respected elderly woman

6. _____ a father and ruler of a family tribe; a man of great age or dignity

7. _____ brother or sister but not aunt or uncle

8. _____ relatives; family; kinfolk

9. _____ brother or sister or aunt or uncle

10. _____ husband or wife

11. _____ birthright; something handed down from one's ancestors

12. _____ ancestry; family; direct descent from an ancestor

13. _____ origination; production

14. _____ to take into one's own family through the legal process

15. _____ having similar qualities; related through a common ancestor

18-4   HEADLINES

Fifteen headlines have been cut out of the local newspaper. Unfortunately, a word has been ripped from each headline. Help to complete each headline by writing in the correct word from the list below. Each word is used only one time. The family certainly thanks you for all your cut-and-paste efforts here!

adoption	fraternal	kin	matriarch	relative
akin	generations	lineage	paternal	sibling
clan	heritage	maternal	patriarchs	spouse's

1. NEXT OF _____ INHERITS MILLIONS OF DOLLARS

2. _____ INSTINCTS PAY OFF AS MOTHER RESCUES HER CHILD

3. BROTHERS REUNITED TWENTY YEARS AFTER _____ BY SEPARATE FAMILIES

4. HUSBAND APPLAUDS _____ EFFORTS AS HOMEMAKER OF THE YEAR

5. APPRECIATIVE SON CITES FATHER'S _____ INSTINCTS AS KEYS TO HIS SUCCESS IN LIFE

6. STUDIES _____ TO ONE ANOTHER SHARE SCIENCE AWARDS

7. MRS. GAVIGAN, FAMILY'S _____, DIED YESTERDAY

8. TWO HUNDRED FAMILY _____ ATTEND JOE AND TINA'S WEDDING

9. ABRAHAM, ONE OF THE BIBLE'S MOST FAMOUS _____, IS SUBJECT OF TONIGHT'S MEETING

10. PRESIDENT'S BROTHER CITED AS PRESIDENT'S MOST INFLUENTIAL _____

11. _____ TWINS BORN THIS MORNING IN CAB

12. RECORDS OF 300 MEMBERS OF ANCIENT _____ FOUND NEAR RIVER

13. MEMBERS OF OLD AND YOUNG _____ ATTEND MUSIC FESTIVAL

14. SON INHERITS FINANCIAL FORTUNE AS PART OF _____

15. HISTORIAN FINDS FAMILY _____ DATES BACK NEARLY THREE CENTURIES

Units 16–18   REVIEW TEST

Directions: Please circle the correct **synonym.** Then write the answer's corresponding letter on the line next to the question's number. Each question is worth four points.

1. ____ **amateur**   (a) reserve player   (b) person who does something without a professional's skill   (c) collector of funds at a college

2. ____ **cynic**   (a) novelist   (b) guide   (c) one who is critical of society

3. ____ **tyrant**   (a) cruel, obsessive ruler   (b) one who leads in a democracy   (c) a temperate leader

4. ____ **bibliography**   (a) a list of books   (b) a drama   (c) an editor's corrections

5. ____ **glimmer**   (a) to appear or be seen faintly or dimly   (b) to raise a question or complaint   (c) to totally believe in

6. ____ **adoption**   (a) to record in a journal   (b) to take into one's own family by legal process and raise as one's own child   (c) to publicize and sell

7. ____ **maternal**   (a) fatherly   (b) brotherly   (c) motherly

8. ____ **fraternal**   (a) motherly   (b) brotherly   (c) fatherly

9. ____ **spouse**   (a) child   (b) uncle   (c) partner in marriage

10. ____ **journalist**   (a) one who writes plays   (b) one who records compact discs   (c) one whose occupation consists of gathering, writing, editing, and publishing the news

Directions: Please circle the correct **antonym.** Then write the answer's corresponding letter on the line next to the question's number. Each question is worth four points.

11. ____ **virtuoso**   (a) instrument   (b) amateur   (c) bachelor

12. ____ **foster**   (a) neglect   (b) deceive   (c) recall

13. ____ **publicize**   (a) to record in a newspaper or magazine   (b) to refer to   (c) to conceal

14. ____ **rustic**   (a) sophisticated   (b) meticulous   (c) immature

15. ____ **akin**   (a) dissimilar   (b) similar   (c) dwarfish

16. ____ **rave**   (a) to talk wildly   (b) to censure   (c) to cheer

17. ____ **subdue**   (a) to bring into subjection   (b) to capitulate   (c) to bring up for discussion

18. ____ **restrict**   (a) to punish   (b) to set limits upon   (c) to loosen

19. ____ **nomad**   (a) resident   (b) wanderer   (c) tyrant

20. ____ **miser**   (a) prodigal   (b) cheapskate   (c) professor

Units 16–18   REVIEW TEST (continued)

Directions: Please circle the word that correctly **completes** the sentence. Then write the answer's corresponding letter on the line next to the question's number. Each question is worth four points.

21. ____ The speech team's most renowned _____ received three awards in the final tournament.   **(a) orator**   **(b) orthodontist**   **(c) tyrant**

22. ____ My sister, a college sophomore, received a letter from the _____ informing her that she still owed $200 for this semester's tuition.
    (a) cynic   **(b) bursar**   **(c) amateur**

23. ____ The owner of the antique car took _____ care of her prized auto, making sure that it was always spotlessly clean.   **(a) arable**   **(b) fatal**   **(c) meticulous**

24. ____ The family's _____ was 96-year-old Great-Grandpa Maloney, a former lawyer and judge.   **(a) generation**   **(b) heritage**   **(c) patriarch**

25. ____ Although she had several brothers and sisters, her favorite _____ was her oldest sister, Jeanne.   **(a) sibling**   **(b) lineage**   **(c) matriarch**

Words, Words, Words!

Unit 19

SKILLED— OR NOT SO SKILLED

SKILLED—OR NOT SO SKILLED

1. **adroit:** (adj) skillful in a physical or mental way; clever; expert; dexterous

   The *adroit* mechanic quickly figured out why my sister's car was stalling so frequently.

   syn: deft, handy, proficient; **ant:** inept, clumsy, maladroit

   family words: adroitness (n); adroitly (adv)

2. **anarchist:** (n) a person who believes in or advocates anarchy or the complete absence of government; one into political disorder and lawlessness

   The *anarchist* was preaching the merits of why citizens should overthrow the "immoral government whose leaders serve only themselves."

   family words: anarchy, anarchism (n); anarchistic (adj)

   Helpful Hint: *Anarchist* = "an-" (away from) + "-archy" (head or leader). Thus, *anarchy* means *to go away from* or *get rid of* the head or leader (of a government).

3. **astute:** (adj) having or showing a clever or shrewd mind; cunning; crafty; wily

   Thinking that he was buying a "discounted" video camera wrapped in a decorative box from two guys on the city street, the young man, who was obviously not that *astute,* later found out that he had purchased a brick for $70.

   syn: intelligent, sagacious; **ant:** obtuse, dull, slow

   family words: astuteness (n); astutely (adv)

4. **competent:** (adj) well qualified; capable; fit; sufficient; adequate; able

   Though Hank was *competent* enough to perform the assignment, the committee preferred the other candidate, who was truly more capable.

   syn: proficient; **ant**: incompetent, inept, unskilled

   family words: competence, competency (n); competently (adv)

   Helpful Hint: Because you are COMPETEnt, you are ABLE to COMPETE.

5. **crafty:** (adj) subtly deceitful; sly; cunning; artful

   Fagin, a *crafty* character in *Oliver Twist* by Charles Dickens, forced children to "pick a pocket or two" and give him the stolen items.

   syn: guileful, duplicitous; **ant:** guileless

   family words: craftiness, craft (n); craft (v); craftily (adv)

6. **crass:** (adj) grossly stupid or dull; tasteless, insensitive, or coarse; money-grubbing, blatantly materialistic

   On today's *crass* television program, people performed demeaning actions, such as eating worms, in hopes of winning money or prizes.

   syn: unrefined, rough, indelicate; **ant:** fine, refined, sensitive

   family words: crassness (n); crassly (adv)

7. **endowed:** (v) provided with some talent, quality, etc.; gave money or property so as to provide an income for the support of a college, hospital, etc.

   Nature *endowed* Kamisha with great athletic abilities.

   Arturo *endowed* his former college with a gift of $25,000,000.

   syn: furnished, equipped, gifted

   family words: endowment (n)

8. **exemplary:** (adj) serving as a model or example; worth imitating; serving as a warning or deterrent; illustrative

   The musician's *exemplary* work ethic, attention to detail, and willingness to experiment should inspire all music students.

syn: commendable, admirable, estimable, representative; **ant:** reprehensible, regrettable, wretched

family words: exemplarily (adv)

9. **expertise:** (n) the skill, knowledge, judgment of an expert

   We hired this attorney because her *expertise* in business law is outstanding.

   syn: know-how, mastery, command

   family words: expertness (n)

   Helpful Hint: An EXPERT has EXPERTise.

10. **imaginative:** (adj) having, using, or showing imagination; having great creative powers; given to imagining

    Interior decorators usually have strong *imaginative* powers since they have to be creative in designing rooms.

    syn: inventive, original, productive; **ant:** practical, pragmatic, uninventive

    family words: imagination (n); imagine (v); imaginable (adj); imaginatively (adv)

    Helpful Hint: You are IMAGINATIVE if you have a good IMAGINATION.

11. **inept:** (adj) not suitable to the purpose; unfit; clumsy or bungling; inefficient

    Unfortunately, the politician's *inept* handling of the questions during the interview probably cost him the election.

    syn: inappropriate, improper, awkward; **ant:** suitable, fit, proper

    family words: ineptness, ineptitude (n); ineptly (adv)

    Helpful Hint: INEPT (unfit) and ADEPT (fit) are opposites.

12. **insufficient:** (adj) not enough; inadequate; not sufficient

    Unfortunately, her efforts to gain the necessary number of votes to change the law were *insufficient.*

    syn: deficient, scanty, meager; **ant:** sufficient, enough, adequate, ample

    family words: insufficiently (adv)

    Helpful Hint: *Insufficient* = "In-" (not) + "-sufficient" (enough)

13. **masterful:** (adj) having or showing the ability of an expert; expert; masterly; fond of acting the part of a master

    His *masterful* knowledge of many different subjects contributed to his winning the television quiz program's grand prize.

    syn: accomplished, commanding; **ant:** amateurish, unskilled, incompetent

    family words: masterfully (adv)

    Helpful Hint: The suffix "–ful" means *full of* or *like.* Thus, if you are *masterful,* you are like a *master* of any skill—very, very good!

14. **outcast:** (n) a person or thing cast out or rejected, as by society

    Because of a sin that she had committed, Hester Prynne, the female protagonist in Nathaniel Hawthorne's *The Scarlet Letter,* was an *outcast* from her Boston community.

    syn: exile, displaced person, persona non grata

    Helpful Hint: An OUTCAST is CAST OUT of a group or community.

15. **skillful:** (adj) having or showing skill; accomplished; expert

    The ambassador's *skillful* handling of the disagreement between the two countries prevented an even larger crisis.

    syn: adept, competent, practiced, adroit; **ant:** clumsy, bungling, inept, awkward

    family words: skill, skillfulness (n); skillfully (adv)

    Helpful Hint: *Skillful* = "skill-" (good ability) + "-ful" (full of)

19-1   BE AN EXEMPLARY STUDENT

You can call yourself an *exemplary* (one of this activity's answers) student if you can fill in all fifteen of these words below correctly. Each word is used only once. So start on your way to being that *exemplary* student!

adroit	competent	endowed	imaginative	masterful
anarchist	crafty	exemplary	inept	outcast
astute	crass	expertise	insufficient	skillful

1. The football player is so physically _____ that he looks like a Greek god.

2. For several years, the _____ and his associates plotted the overthrow of the neighboring country's government.

3. The company's officials felt that he was _____ enough to manage both of the Ohio offices.

4. Our behavior with the substitute teacher was so _____ that our regular teacher rewarded us with no homework the following two nights.

5. A _____ thief, the man had stolen many expensive pieces of jewelry and eluded police authorities for several months.

6. The rogue's behavior was so _____ that we questioned whether or not he had any manners at all.

7. When the new student had been in the school for only three weeks, he said he had never felt like an _____ since he had made many friends in a short time.

8. Our judo instructor possessed _____ in several martial arts.

9. Because Sylvia had a _____ command of song writing, we asked her to write the music for our graduation ceremony.

10. _____ in solving crossword puzzles, Mike also solved many other types of brain teasers.

11. Her outstanding _____ powers were apparent in the plays, poems, and novels that she wrote.

12. Brenda's _____ problem-solving abilities were obvious when she correctly answered five consecutive challenging math problems.

13. This month's rainfall was _____ to make up for the water needed to replenish our county's reservoirs.

14. My dad, a _____ truck driver, deftly maneuvered the rig into a very tight parking spot.

15. The official's _____ manner of dealing with the disgruntled crowd cost him many votes in the next election.

19-2 POSITIVE AND NEGATIVE WORDS

For each boldfaced word that is correctly defined, circle the two-letter combination in the *YES* column. For each boldfaced word that is incorrectly defined, circle the two-letter combination in the *NO* column. Then write each two-letter combination (in order) on its appropriate *YES* or *NO* line at the bottom of the page. If your answers are correct, you will spell out two positive words from the *YES* column and two negative words from the *NO* column.

	Yes	**No**	
1.	ab	st	**adroit:** clever; expert
2.	ra	do	**anarchist:** person who believes in the continuation of the existing government
3.	so	ig	**astute:** cunning; crafty; wily
4.	hl	ub	**competent:** inadequately qualified; insufficient
5.	po	tf	**crafty:** dull-witted; honest
6.	lu	rr	**crass:** unrefined; crude
7.	te	id	**endowed:** provided with some talent or quality; provided income for a hospital or college
8.	eg	ul	**exemplary:** not serving as a model or example
9.	ro	ly	**expertise:** lack of skill, knowledge, or judgment
10.	ly	gu	**imaginative:** having great creative powers
11.	su	bb	**insufficient:** inadequate; not suitable for the purpose
12.	st	if	**inept:** suited for the purpose; fit; efficient
13.	re	op	**masterful:** expert; skillful; masterly
14.	ly	io	**outcast:** person or things cast out or rejected, as by society; rejected
15.	no	fy	**skillful:** unaccomplished; inept

YES: _____

NO: _____

19-3   WHICH DOES NOT BELONG—AND WHY?

For numbers 1 through 10, circle the two words that are NOT synonyms of the boldfaced word. For numbers 11 through 15, circle the description that is NOT a synonym of the boldfaced word. Be ready to explain why you circled what you did.

1. **adroit**	clever	dexterous	not enough	untalented
2. **astute**	clumsy	cunning	wily	dull
3. **competent**	fit	incapable	sufficient	inadequate
4. **crafty**	sly	unskilled	cunning	illustrative
5. **crass**	unrefined	late	crude	fruitful
6. **exemplary**	model	illustrative	forgetful	uneventful
7. **inept**	unsuitable	fit	unfit	efficient
8. **insufficient**	imaginative	efficient	not sufficient	inadequate
9. **masterful**	great skill	expert	unable	competent
10. **skillful**	expert	inefficient	incompetent	accomplished

11. **anarchist:** one who advocates political disorder OR one who advocates political continuity

12. **endowed:** provided with some talent or quality OR lacking talent or quality

13. **expertise:** skill and knowledge of an expert OR lacking skill and knowledge

14. **imaginative:** having great creative powers OR lacking creative powers

15. **outcast:** accepted OR rejected

19-4   INVENTORS AND INVENTIONS

Since many of the words in Unit 19 deal with skillful people, we dedicate this crossword to those smart people called inventors. In addition to the fifteen words from Unit 19, four inventors are also answers in this crossword puzzle. Fill in your answers and, as these four scientists did, show your expertise!

Across

1. cunning; crafty; wily
2. serving as a model or example; illustrative
4. skillful in a physical or mental way; clever; dexterous
6. subtly deceitful; artful
9. well qualified; capable; fit; sufficient
12. not suitable to the purpose; unfit; clumsy
14. grossly stupid or dull; tasteless, insensitive, or coarse
15. not enough; inadequate
16. inventor of a sewing machine
17. accomplished; expert

Down

1. a person who believes in or advocates the complete absence of government
2. provided with some talent or quality
3. he developed wireless telegraphy
5. person or thing rejected, as by society; rejected
7. having great creative powers
8. the skill or knowledge of an expert
10. expert; skill; having or showing the ability of an expert
11. inventor of the cotton gin
13. inventor of the phonograph, microphone, and the incandescent lamp

Unit 20

HERE, THERE, AND EVERYWHERE

HERE, THERE, AND EVERYWHERE

1. **abound:** (v) to be plentiful; to exist in large numbers or amounts; to be filled

    A feeling of good spirits in our country will *abound* when the current crisis ends.

    syn: thrive, flourish, proliferate

    family words: abundant

    Helpful Hint: When stars ABOUND, they are ALL AROUND.

2. **accessible:** (adj) easy to approach or enter; obtainable; easily understood

    The politician knew that in order to win the upcoming election she had to make herself more *accessible* to the voters.

    syn: (for "easy to approach or enter") friendly, approachable, available (adj); (for "obtainable") within reach, nearby, at hand, possible (adj); **ant:** (for "easy to approach or enter") forbidding, standoffish, aloof, unavailable (adj); (for "obtainable") unattainable, impossible

    family words: accessibility (n); accessibly (adv)

3. **clutter:** (n) a number of things scattered in disorder; jumble; (v) to put into

    Since Dad wanted to park the car inside our garage, he asked us to remove the *clutter.*

    It is easier for many of us to *clutter* a room rather than to put everything away.

    syn: mess, litter, disarray (n); litter, mess (v); **ant:** neatness, tidiness, orderliness (n); neaten, tidy, untangle (v)

4. **copious:** (adj) very plentiful; abundant; wordy; full of information

    Wanting to know all she could about the new scientific procedure, Theresa took *copious* notes during the professor's lecture.

    syn: ample, superabundant, bountiful, replete; **ant:** scanty, scant, meager

    family words: copiousness (n); copiously (adv)

5. **cosmopolitan:** (adj) common or representative of all or many parts of the world; not national or local; at home in all countries or places; having a worldwide distribution, as some plants or animals; (n) a cosmopolitan person or thing; cosmopolite

    Juanita's *cosmopolitan* interests included going to the theaters, museums, and other cultural city attractions.

    He was truly a *cosmopolitan* since he rejected anything having to do with rural existence.

    syn: international, urban, urbane, sophisticated (adj); **ant:** provincial, local, small-town, narrow (adj)

    family words: cosmopolitanism, cosmopolite (n)

    Helpful Hint: "Cosmos-" means *world. Cosmopolitan* means *worldly* or *sophisticated*.

6. **domestic:** (adj) having to do with home or housekeeping; of the house or family; made or produced in the home country; native; (n) a servant for the home, as a maid or cook

    His *domestic* duties included doing the wash, cleaning the rooms, and cooking every meal for the family.

    Grandma Murphy had worked as a *domestic* for a wealthy family.

    syn: household, familial (adj); **ant:** foreign, exotic, alien (adj)

    family words: domesticity (n); domesticate (v); domestically (adv)

7. **legendary:** (adj) based on, of, or presented in legends; remarkable; extraordinary; well-known; famous

    The Rolling Stones, the *legendary* rock and roll band, have done thousands of appearances over the years.

    syn: traditional, mythical, epic, familial; **ant:** historical, factual, actual

family words: legend (n)

Helpful Hint: A LEGEND is LEGENDary.

8. **longevity:** (n) long life; great span of life; length or duration of a life

My aunt was given the company's "*Longevity* Award" since she had worked for the same company for fifty-three years!

syn: permanence, durability, endurance

Helpful Hint: LONGevity means a LONG time.

9. **plague:** (n) contagious epidemic that is deadly; calamity; scourge; anything that affects or troubles; (v) to afflict with a plague; to vex; to harass; to torment; to trouble

In the early 1330s, an outbreak of deadly bubonic *plague* occurred in China.

The selfish way that he had treated his younger brother continued to emotionally *plague* the middle-aged man.

syn: pestilence, pandemic, outbreak (n); distress, torment, disturb (v)

family words: plaguer (n); plaguy, plaguey (adj)

10. **proximity:** (n) state or quality of being near; nearness in time, space

We stay in *proximity* of the lifeguard's flag whenever we go swimming in the ocean.

syn: closeness, adjacency, approximation; **ant:** distance, remoteness, gap

family words: approximate (v); proximately (adv); proximate (adj)

Helpful Hint: If it is in PROXIMITY, it is APPROXIMATE or near.

11. **random:** (adj) lacking aim or method; purposeless; not uniform

Since there was no set selection process, these audience members were chosen in a *random* fashion.

syn: chance, casual, haphazard, accidental; **ant:** intentional, planned, designed, purposeful

family words: randomness (n); randomly (adv)

12. **teem:** (v) to be full; to pour; to abound; to swarm

After twenty minutes of light rain, it began to *teem*, and we were quickly soaked.

syn: overflow, crowd; **ant:** empty, vacate

Helpful Hint: Two thousand TEENS TEEMED out onto the field after the World Cup victory. Now, that's a lot!

13. **tether:** (n) a rope or chain fastened to an animal to keep it within certain bounds; the limit of one's abilities, resources, etc.; (v) to fasten or confine with a tether

Before entering the store, Mr. Thomas used a *tether* to tie his dog to the pole.

The owner had to *tether* his dog to the pole while he picked up some milk in the store.

syn: restraint, check, bridle, rope, leash (n); restrain (v)

14. **trek:** (n) journey; migration; a short trip on foot; (v) to travel slowly and laboriously

The four-hour journey seemed more like a *trek* than a friendly nature walk.

Instead of flying to the mountain lodge, the hikers decided to *trek* across the steep terrain.

syn: travel, migration, expedition (n)

family words: trekker (n)

15. **waif:** (n) a person without home or friends, esp. a homeless child; a stray animal

Author Charles Dickens had a special place in his heart for the *waif,* that child who lacked parents and a home to call his or her own.

syn: urchin

20-1   YOUR MOTHER IS WHAT KIND OF AN ENGINEER?

What a question! Yet the answer is right before your eyes! For each of these fifteen sentences, fill in the correct word from the list below. Write the answer on the appropriate line. Then you will assuredly know what kind of engineer your mother is!

abound	copious	legendary	proximity	tether
accessible	cosmopolitan	longevity	random	trek
clutter	domestic	plague	teem	waif

1. My mother, a homemaker, jokingly refers to herself as a _____ engineer.

2. We were in close enough _____ to watch the Fourth of July fireworks display.

3. The three of us made the _____ from Ninth Avenue to First Avenue in less than an hour.

4. All of the Little League team members were selected in a _____ fashion, disregarding the set pattern of years past.

5. The homeless and parentless _____ roamed London's streets seeking comfort from the cold.

6. The family could not find the package within the _____ piled in that section of the basement.

7. During most holiday seasons, many people are generally happy, and good feelings _____ .

8. Owners of the fancy restaurant made the entrance more _____ to the elderly patrons by installing ramps and elevators.

9. Dean Smith, the _____ coach of the North Carolina Tarheels men's basketball team, is the winningest Division I basketball coach.

10. A true _____ , James Farley has visited over fifty countries during his business career.

11. The _____ that beset London in the 1590s killed many citizens.

12. The perceptive, experienced store manager ordered a _____ number of gas grills to satisfy the customers who took advantage of the holiday sale.

13. My sister had predicted that the pool would _____ with swimmers during the abnormally hot weekend.

14. Having given forty years of service to the company, Mr. Collins was honored for his _____ .

15. Our neighbor tried to _____ his boat to the dock during the storm.

20-2   ADVERBS GALORE!

Circle the correct definition's two-letter answer for each word. Then write those two letters on the line next to the appropriate number. Write the two-letter answers (in order) at the bottom of the page. If all of your answers are correct, you will spell out six adverbs.

1. ____ **abound** (ar) decreasing (ve) exist in large numbers (gi) rebuilt

2. ____ **accessible** (ry) easy to approach (po) hard to approach (re) cannot be approached

3. ____ **clutter** (an) similar (se) jumble (to) narrow

4. ____ **copious** (oo) crooked (pe) hard to do (ld) abundant

5. ____ **cosmopolitan** (om) not national or local (ss) native to (tt) travel

6. ____ **domestic** (es) forgetful (fe) productive (do) of the house or family

7. ____ **legendary** (in) fractured (wn) extraordinary (po) very smart

8. ____ **longevity** (be) long life (st) want (rr) recent

9. ____ **plague** (te) settle (sy) nuisance (lo) calamity

10. ____ **proximity** (ws) closeness (ee) benign (fo) medical

11. ____ **random** (at) drawing (br) color (ob) not uniform

12. ____ **teem** (el) to be full (ef) organization (pp) snow

13. ____ **tether** (ro) ball (se) pole (at) rope or chain

14. ____ **trek** (ed) migration (do) relief (wi) ancient

15. ____ **waif** (ly) stray animal (lo) gravel (or) cracker

_____

_____

_____

20-3 MAKING YOUR WAY AROUND ANALOGIES

You will not think that this activity's title is that silly once you have answered all fifteen analogies correctly. Write the correct letter in each blank. If your answers are correct, you will have formed a fifteen-letter word. At the bottom of this page, tell how that fifteen-letter word connects to the activity's title.

1. ___ **plague : calamity** (c) dock : pier (d) shoe : sock (e) rainbow : storm

2. ___ **clutter : disorder** (h) fragrance : stench (i) pen : writing utensil (j) wrench : saw

3. ___ **abound : few** (p) accumulate : many (q) recall : several (r) reduce : more

4. ___ **legendary : remarkable** (c) humorous : funny (d) wealthy : poor (e) unknown : famous

5. ___ **teem : to be full** (s) discard : to keep (t) believe : to deny (u) mature : to age

6. ___ **cosmopolitan : worldly** (k) naïve : sophisticated (l) familiar : current
   (m) revere : esteemed

7. ___ **tether : fasten** (m) close : open (n) send : transmit (o) cover : release

8. ___ **proximity : closeness** (a) intelligence : smartness (b) height : weight (c) depth : length

9. ___ **accessible : obtain** (u) memorable : ignore (v) audible : hear (w) plentiful : change

10. ___ **longevity : long life** (h) meekness : pride (i) convenience : ease (j) brightness : dullness

11. ___ **waif : home** (g) hut : elegance (h) mansion : expense (i) camera : lens

12. ___ **random : plan** (y) successful : flaw (z) grateful : unknown (a) flimsy : durability

13. ___ **trek : journey** (s) school : teacher (t) loafer : footwear (u) elevator : people

14. ___ **copious : plentiful** (d) memorable : solid (e) dire : important (f) bashful : forward

15. ___ **domestic : housekeeping** (d) mechanical : machines (e) arid : snow
    (f) athletic : transportation

_____

_____

_____

Name: _____ Date: _____ Period: _____

20-4   HOW SIMPLE!

The only word that you are asked to match with its opposite that is not a Unit 20 word is the word *intricate*. Its opposite is *simple*. So this activity's title is appropriate! Match each word with its opposite by writing the correct number in the appropriate Magic Square box. (One is done for you.) If your answers are correct, the rows, columns, and two diagonals add up to the same number. Now make it simple!

A=	B=3	C=	D=
E=	F=	G=	H=
I=	J=	K=	L=
M=	N=	O=	P=

Magic Number:

_____

A. intricate	**E.** longevity	**I.** cosmopolitan	**M.** trek
B. proximity	**F.** accessible	**J.** abound	**N.** domestic
C. clutter	**G.** plague	**K.** teem	**O.** copious
D. waif	**H.** legendary	**L.** random	**P.** tether

1. unremarkable
2. simple
3. great distance
4. period of great health and wellness
5. exist in small numbers
6. sparse
7. untie
8. local; insular; unsophisticated
9. lack; want; to drizzle
10. civic; public; personal; private
11. to walk easily
12. planned
13. short life; short span of life
14. child without home and parents
15. arrangement; array; order
16. hard to approach; difficult to obtain entrance to

Unit 21

SMART—OR NOT SO SMART

SMART—OR NOT SO SMART

1. **acute:** (adj) having a sharp point; keen or quick of mind; shrewd

   Jessica's *acute* mind helped her to solve the problem twice as fast as any other student.

   syn: clever, discerning, perceptive; **ant:** dull, stupid, unaware, insensitive

   family words: acuteness (n); acutely (adv)

   Helpful Hint: An ACUTE angle is sharp. If you are ACUTE, you are also sharp—mentally!

2. **brilliant:** (adj) having or showing keen intelligence, great talent, or skill

   My *brilliant* lab partner won the award as the county's highest academic achiever.

   syn: brainy, intellectual, quick-witted, gifted; **ant:** unintelligent, dull, untalented, clumsy

   family words: brilliance (n); brilliantly (adv)

3. **buffoon:** (n) a person who is always clowning and trying to be funny; clown

   The college president did not expect any graduating senior to behave as a *buffoon* would behave at the graduation ceremony.

   syn: zany, comedian, jester, jokester

   family words: buffoonery (n); buffoonish (adj)

   Helpful Hint: A BUFFOON and a GOON are both silly in the afternoon!

4. **dense:** (adj) slow to understand; thick

   These *dense* students had trouble understanding the intricate scientific formulas.

   The *dense* forest made it difficult for the researchers to make good time as they attempted to reach their destination by dusk.

   syn: dull, unintelligent, slow, dimwitted; **ant:** quick, alert, sensitive, perceptive

   family words: density, denseness (n); densely (adv)

5. **impostor:** (n) a person who deceives or cheats others, especially by pretending to be someone or something that he or she is not

   Jamey played the role of the *impostor* when he made up false excuses for leaving his college friend.

   syn: pretender, impersonator, deceiver, trickster

6. **incisive:** (adj) sharp; keen; penetrating; cutting into

   Although we listened to several hours of debate regarding the controversial topic, the most *incisive* comments came from my teacher, Mr. Franz.

   syn: acute, clear-cut, trenchant; **ant:** dull, dense, superficial, vague, bland

   family words: incisiveness (n); incisively (adv)

7. **inventive:** (adj) skilled in inventing; creative

   The *inventive* practical joker fooled many people with his stunts.

   syn: ingenious, imaginative, fertile; **ant:** imitative, unimaginative, trite

   family words: inventiveness (n); invent (v)

   Helpful Hint: If you are INVENTive, you can INVENT ideas, stories, or even solutions well.

8. **judicious:** (adj) having, applying, or showing sound judgment; wise and careful

   Mother said to my older sister, "Please be *judicious* and drive attentively and safely."

   syn: prudent, enlightened, sensible; **ant:** unreasonable, foolish, silly, imprudent

   family words: judiciousness (n); judiciously (adv)

9. **prodigy:** (adj) a person, thing, or act so extraordinary as to inspire wonder, especially a child of highly unusual talent or genius

> The four-year-old *prodigy* was able to quickly compute complicated arithmetic problems without using a pencil or calculator.

syn: phenomenon, wonder, sensation, rarity

10. **quack:** (n) an untrained person who practices medicine fraudulently; any person who pretends to have knowledge or skill that he or she does not have in a particular field; charlatan; sound made by a duck

> Because our regular family doctor was on vacation, my mother was forced to take me to another doctor, a much lesser skilled doctor who is sarcastically known as "The *Quack.*"

> The duck's *quack* became annoying after the first hour.

syn: fraud, fake, impostor, dissembler

family words: quackery (n); quackish (adj); quackishly (adv)

11. **rational:** (adj) derived from reasoning; showing reason; not foolish or silly; sensible

> Rather than approaching the situation illogically, Ben used a more *rational* method.

syn: sane, reasonable, sound, clear-headed; **ant:** irrational, insane, unreasonable, dazed

family words: rationality, rationalization (n); rationalize (v); rationally (adv)

12. **sage:** (n) a very wise man, especially an elderly man widely respected for his wisdom, experience, and judgment; a type of plant; (adj) wise, discerning, judicious; showing wisdom and good judgment

> The *sage* predicted that my older sister would marry a millionaire and live in an exclusive section of Beverly Hills, California.

> Maureen took a photo of the *sage* growing near our neighbor's fence.

A *sage,* more experienced teacher gave the young, inexperienced teacher wise advice regarding classroom management techniques.

syn: pundit, intellectual, savant; **ant:** simpleton, ignoramus, dolt, fool

family words: sagacity (n); sagely (adv)

Helpful Hint: Because she is so smart, this SAGE knows what is on every PAGE.

13. **savvy:** (n) shrewdness or understanding; know-how; (v) to understand or get the idea

> The *savvy* police officer knew exactly where to obtain information about the suspected burglar.

syn: confidence, sense, knowledge, ability

Helpful Hint: *Savvy* comes from the French word for "to know." Thus, if you are *savvy,* you *know* and have good understanding.

14. **vigilant:** (adj) staying watchful and alert to danger or trouble

> Due to some recent on-campus attacks, we were instructed to be *vigilant* whenever we walked around campus after dark.

syn: wary, alert, cautious, circumspect; **ant:** unwary, careless, preoccupied, blind

family words: vigilance (n); vigilantly (adv)

15. **witty:** (adj) having, showing, or characterized by wit; cleverly amusing; having sharp, amusing cleverness

> His *witty* remarks made all of us laugh at the somewhat unpleasant situation.

syn: humorous, jocular, ingenious, alert; **ant:** stupid, slow, dull, obtuse

family words: wittiness (n); wittily (adv)

Helpful Hint: WIT is a good sense of humor. Thus, WITTY means humorous.

21-1   DO YOU HAVE THE SMARTS?

Fill in each blank with the correct word. Each word is used only once. If you have correctly filled in all the correct words, you certainly "do have the smarts." Show us your wit!

acute	dense	inventive	quack	savvy
brilliant	impostor	judicious	rational	vigilant
buffoon	incisive	prodigy	sage	witty

1. The child _____ could speak three languages and play three musical instruments before she turned five.

2. We read about the group members who visited the Indian _____ to learn about life's mysteries.

3. Our cautious police were even more _____ after the string of robberies occurred in the neighboring towns.

4. In troubled times it is important that we remain _____ and not do anything foolish or insensible.

5. Audience members were laughing hysterically at the comic's _____ remarks about living in a big city.

6. My grandfather's business _____ helped him to become a wealthy corporation leader.

7. Only a _____ would do something as childish and silly as that.

8. The _____ was able to deceive and cheat many people out of thousands of dollars.

9. Our debater's _____ remarks awed the judges, who selected her as the tournament's best debater.

10. We expected _____ decisions from our leaders, court officials, police, and teachers.

11. Geraldo's _____ mathematical ability enabled him to solve the most intricate problems in a few minutes.

12. Only a man as _____ as Thomas Edison could have created so many useful products such as the universal stock ticker, phonograph, and motion picture camera.

13. After the doctor prescribed the wrong medicine for the third time, my uncle referred to him as the county _____

14. Scoring perfectly on all state and national standardized examinations, Aaron was acclaimed as one of the most _____ students in the country.

15. Unfortunately, the man was too _____ and could not understand even the most basic concepts of the subject.

Name: _____ Date: _____ Period: _____

21-2   DO YOU HAVE THE SKILL?

Match the fifteen words in Column A with their appropriate *same* or *opposite* definition in Column B. Write the two-letter answer on the correct line next to the number. Thus, for word number 14, *vigilant,* match it up with "ma. not watching carefully; not paying attention (opposite)" since the definition given for *vigilant* is the opposite meaning of *vigilant*. Write all the two-letter combinations (in order) at the bottom of this page. If your answers are all correct, you will spell out four words that are synonyms of the word *skill*. So then you will, as the title suggests, "have the skill"!

Column A	Column B
1. _____ acute	**bi.** slow of mind (*opposite*)
2. _____ brilliant	**ea.** the real thing (*opposite*)
3. _____ buffoon	**er.** charlatan (*same*)
4. _____ dense	**ex.** slow of mind (*opposite*)
5. _____ impostor	**is.** slow to understand (*same*)
6. _____ incisive	**li.** not creative (*opposite*)
7. _____ inventive	**ma.** extraordinary talent (*same*)
8. _____ judicious	~~ma.~~ not watching carefully; not paying attention (*opposite*)
9. _____ prodigy	**nd.** not funny; not amusing (*opposite*)
10. _____ rational	**om.** shrewdness or understanding (*same*)
11. _____ quack	**pe.** showing keen intelligence (*same*)
12. _____ sage	**rt.** clown (*same*)
13. _____ savvy	**st.** not foolish or silly; sensible (*same*)
14. __ma__ vigilant	**ty.** showing sound judgment (*same*)
15. _____ witty	**yc.** wise person (*same*)

_____

_____

_____

21-3 EXPANDING YOUR VOCABULARY

Here you will match the fifteen words in Column A with their two synonyms from Column B. Write the correct number next to the letter in Column A. If your answers are correct, the numbers in Group One (A-E), Group Two (F-J), and Group Three (K-L) will each add up to 40. Use your dictionary if necessary.

Column A

A. _____ acute

B. _____ brilliant

C. _____ buffoon

D. _____ dense

E. _____ impostor

F. _____ incisive

G. _____ inventive

H. _____ judicious

I. _____ prodigy

J. _____ quack

K. _____ rational

L. _____ sage

M. _____ savvy

N. _____ vigilant

O. _____ witty

Column B

1. incisive; cutting

2. crisp; penetrating

3. level-headed; prudent

4. ingenious; innovative

5. savant; scholar

6. learned; erudite

7. crafty; foxy

8. zany; harlequin

9. fair; objective

10. wonder; unusually talented child

11. open-eyed; circumspect

12. block-headed; doltish

13. phony; faker

14. jocular; amusing

15. medical charlatan; incompetent practitioner

Group One (A, B, C, D, and E): _____ + _____ + _____ + _____ + _____ = _____

Group Two (F, G, H, I, and J): _____ + _____ + _____ + _____ + _____ = _____

Group Three (K, L, M, N, and O): _____ + _____ + _____ + _____ + _____ = _____

21-4 WORLD CAPITALS

Nine capital cities are some of the answers found in this crossword puzzle. Fill in the correct letters of these twenty-four clues and become a world crossword master!

Across

1. person who deceives or cheats others
6. wise person
7. clown
8. slow to understand
9. showing reason; not foolish or silly
12. Peru's capital
14. Cuba's capital
18. having a sharp point; keen or quick of mind
19. India's capital (New _____)
20. Venezuela's capital
22. creative
23. Ireland's capital

Down

2. extraordinary person, especially a young, talented child
3. Canada's capital
4. Norway's capital
5. Austria's capital
7. showing keen intelligence
10. keen; penetrating; acute
11. Greece's capital
13. shrewdness or understanding; know-how
15. watchful; alert to danger or trouble
16. having or showing sound judgment; wise and careful
17. medical fraud
21. cleverly amusing

Units 19–21   REVIEW TEST

Directions: Please circle the correct **synonym.** Then write the answer's corresponding letter on the line next to the question's number. Each question is worth four points.

1. ____ **impostor**   (a) person who wants to overthrow the existing government   (b) butter
(c) person who deceives or cheats others, especially by pretending to be someone or
something else

2. ____ **crass**   (a) remarkable   (b) grossly stupid or dull   (c) lacking aim or method

3. ____ **abound**   (a) to approach quietly   (b) to exist in large numbers   (c) to fasten or confine

4. ____ **judicious**   (a) wise and careful   (b) not uniform   (c) slow to understand

5. ____ **trek**   (a) to travel slowly and laboriously   (b) to be efficient   (c) to be full

6. ____ **tether**   (a) to cast out of a community   (b) to tie with a rope or another fastener
(c) to provide emotional support

7. ____ **endowed**   (a) inspired wonder and amazement   (b) very plentiful   (c) gave money to
an institution to provide support

8. ____ **buffoon**   (a) person without a home or friends   (b) person who deceives others
(c) clown

9. ____ **crafty**   (a) stupid   (b) cunning   (c) not enough

10. ____ **astute**   (a) having a clever mind   (b) somewhat qualified   (c) serving as a model or
example

Directions: Please circle the correct **antonym.** Then write the answer's corresponding letter on the line next to the question's number. Each question is worth four points.

11. ____ **clutter**   (a) neaten   (b) serving as an example   (c) jumble

12. ____ **adroit**   (a) expert   (b) clumsy   (c) forgetful

13. ____ **teem**   (a) remarkable   (b) lacking aim or method   (c) vacate

14. ____ **insufficient**   (a) adequate   (b) showing keen intelligence   (c) showing reason

15. ____ **witty**   (a) cleverly amusing   (b) obtuse   (c) hard to translate

16. ____ **inventive**   (a) creative   (b) costly   (c) unimaginative

17. ____ **rational**   (a) impossible   (b) unreliable   (c) unreasonable

18. ____ **proximity**   (a) remoteness   (b) journey   (c) great skill or knowledge

19. ____ **acute**   (a) worth imitating   (b) unaware   (c) having a worldwide distribution

20. ____ **competent**   (a) unskilled   (b) provided with talent   (c) gigantic

Units 19–21   REVIEW TEST (continued)

Directions: Please circle the word that correctly **completes** the sentence. Then write the answer's corresponding letter on the line next to the question's number. Each question is worth four points.

21. ____ Having no home or parents, the eight-year-old _____ wandered the lonely streets.   **(a) anarchist   (b) impostor   (c) waif**

22. ____ Since he was so _____ , it took him a long time to read and comprehend these social studies chapters.   **(a) expertise   (b) dense   (c) crafty**

23. ____ When the _____ appeared on the television quiz show, she answered every question correctly and earned over one million dollars.
    (a) sage   (b) outcast   (c) domestic

24. ____ Because the _____ played the piano so beautifully, his third-grade classmates listened in amazement.   **(a) legendary   (b) plague   (c) prodigy**

25. ____ My science teacher's _____ communication skills are the envy of all the other teachers in our building.   **(a) exemplary   (b) random   (c) inept**

Unit 22

A BIT
DIFFERENT

A BIT DIFFERENT

1. adolescent: (n) a teenaged person

Even though she was an *adolescent,* Heidi felt that her parents treated her as if she were an infant.

syn: youth, juvenile, youngster

family words: adolescence (n)

2. convict: (n) a person found guilty of a crime and sentenced by a court; a person serving a sentence in prison; (v) to prove (a person) guilty; to judge and find guilty of an offense

The *convict* was given ten years in the state penitentiary for armed robbery.

This evidence pointed to the suspect's guilt, so the jury found it easy to *convict* him.

syn: criminal, prisoner, inmate, delinquent

family words: conviction (n)

3. despot: (n) an absolute ruler; king with unlimited powers; autocrat; anyone in charge who acts like a tyrant

Ensuring that nobody would usurp his throne, the *despot* ordered the beatings of many of his country's people who had spoken out against him.

syn: tyrant, oppressor, dictator, authoritarian; **ant:** democrat, egalitarian, humanitarian

family words: despotism (n); despotic, despotical (adj); despotically (adv)

4. eerie: (adj) strange; odd; weird

My friends and I were scared by the *eerie* sound of the trapped animal.

syn: frightening, unearthly, bizarre, ghostly

family words: eeriness (n); eerily (adv)

Helpful Hint: Is it not EERIE that the word EERIE has only five letters, three of them being the letter E?

5. fanatic: (adj) unreasonably enthusiastic; overly zealous; (n) a person whose extreme zeal (intense enthusiasm) goes beyond what is reasonable

With a room full of Boston Bruins' memorabilia, including seven autographed hockey shirts and a thick book full of players' autographs, Georgette is certainly a *fanatic* when it comes to hockey and her Bruins.

syn: zealous, extreme (adj); enthusiast, zealot, extremist (n)

family words: fanaticism (n); fanatical (adj); fanatically (adv)

Helpful Hint: The word FAN is a smaller version of the word FANatic.

6. fugitive: (adj) fleeing, apt to flee, or having fled, as from danger, justice, etc.; passing quickly away; fleeting; (n) person who flees, or has fled, from danger, justice, etc.; a fleeting or elusive thing

Unfortunately, his *fugitive* actions went undetected by police authorities.

His *fugitive* thoughts of being elected senator were recorded in his biography.

Hoping to capture the *fugitive,* law enforcement officials displayed his photo in the region's post offices, stores, and newspapers.

syn: shifting, evanescent (adj); runaway, deserter, renegade, refugee, outlaw (n); **ant:** permanent, constant, enduring (adj)

7. lame duck: (n) an elected official whose term extends beyond the time of the election at which he or she was not reelected

After his defeat in the November election, the governor, a *lame duck,* knew that she would not be able to effect much change in the remaining months of her term.

8. maestro: (n) a master in any art; esp. a great composer, conductor, or teacher of music

My music teacher, who for many years has been considered a *maestro,* performed a memorable violin solo.

A BIT DIFFERENT (continued)

syn: artist, craftsman, impresario; **ant:** tyro, amateur, beginner

Helpful Hint: MAESTRO is the Italian word for MASTER.

9. **maverick:** (n) an unbranded animal, especially a strayed calf; a person who takes an independent stand, as in politics, refusing to conform to that of a party or group

    The *maverick,* again apart from his herd, was roaming in the valley.

    Often doing his "own thing" instead of going along with the rest of society, the *maverick* found that conforming to the accepted societal standards was not for him.

    syn: independent, nonconformist, outsider, eccentric

10. **parasite:** (n) a person who lives at the expense of another or others without making any useful contribution or return; hanger-on; in biology, a plant or animal that lives in an organism of another species from which it derives sustenance or protection without benefit to, and usually with harmful effects on, the host

    Never contributing to another's well-being, the *parasite* took advantage of all those around.

    syn: freeloader, scrounger, dependent, leech

    family words: parasitism (n); parasitic (adj)

    Helpful Hint: "Para-" means *next to.* That's exactly where a *parasite* is, next to the one he or she is living off—and giving nothing in return!

11. **serf:** (n) a person in feudal (period during medieval times in Europe) servitude, bound to his master's land and transferred with it to a new owner; any person who is oppressed and without freedom

    Tired and unappreciated, the *serf* hoped that his master would not force him to work long hours on the estate's lands.

    Helpful Hint: A SERF had no time to SURF because his master had him toiling in the fields all day.

12. **turncoat:** (n) a person who goes over to the opposite side or party; traitor

    A reward of several million dollars was offered for anyone who contributed to locating the *turncoat* who had turned over secret documents to the enemy.

    syn: renegade, defector, betrayer, double-dealer

13. **wanton:** (adj) undisciplined; unrestrained; recklessly or arrogantly ignoring justice, decency, morality, etc.; (n) a wanton person or thing

    The convict's *wanton* disregard for the jail's rules earned him many hours of solitary confinement.

    The lifestyle of this *wanton,* especially his more obvious destructive habits, is not to be copied.

    syn: (for "undisciplined") wayward, willful, irresponsible (adj); (for "unrestrained") extravagant, wild (adj); libertine, profligate (n)

    family words: wantonness (n); wantonly (adv)

14. **xenophobe:** (n) one who has fear or hatred of strangers or foreigners or of anything foreign or strange

    The *xenophobe,* with his fear and hatred of any foreign person or thing, is really denying himself many potentially interesting and memorable experiences.

    family words: xenophobia (n); xenophobic (adj)

15. **zany:** (n) clown or buffoon; silly or foolish person; simpleton; (adj) of or characteristic of a zany; comical in an extravagantly ludicrous manner; foolish or crazy

    The *zany* entertained the youngsters with his silly actions and tricks.

    My uncles enjoy watching the trio's *zany* antics, including pie throwing and shoving.

    syn: fool, jester (n); ludicrous, clownish, funny, hilarious (adj)

    family words: zaniness (n); zanily (adv)

22-1   A TRAITOR, A CRIMINAL, AND THE REST

Yes, in this fill-in activity, you will meet some very suspicious people. There is a traitor, a criminal, and other less-than-admirable souls. Yet, there is also a master and a really intense person as well. Fill in each blank and, unlike some of these characters, keep on the straight and narrow.

adolescent	eerie	lame duck	parasite	wanton
convict	fanatic	maestro	serf	xenophobe
despot	fugitive	maverick	turncoat	zany

1. Do you not think that a _____ is very narrow-minded when it comes to meeting and accepting foreign people?

2. The _____ approached the podium to lead the orchestra in a stirring rendition of that lively musical piece.

3. Though I am still an _____, my parents treat me as though I am older.

4. The protestors displayed _____ disregard for the wishes of the police on duty at the large assembly.

5. Since he went against his own country in the American Revolutionary War, Benedict Arnold is a prime example of a _____.

6. The _____ mayor could not enact many new changes since he had few followers after his election defeat.

7. A _____ from the law for the past nine years, the man was finally apprehended when he was shopping in a convenience store along a minor highway.

8. The concept of being ruled by a _____ is so foreign to U.S. citizens that they will even try to unseat such a ruler in a foreign land.

9. This _____ has spent the last fifteen years in solitary confinement in the state penitentiary.

10. The fact that she always wants to copy our homework assignments and never do her own is proof that she is a _____.

11. Not conforming to any of the organization's rules, Hector was regarded as a _____.

12. My father laughs hysterically when watching the _____ antics of the comedy team known as The Three Stooges.

13. The _____ sounds coming from the woods outside my bedroom last night around midnight scared me.

14. During medieval times, the primary worker in the master's fields was called the _____.

15. When it came to rooting for his favorite sports teams, Ken was nothing less than a _____.

22-2 FINDING THE COUNTRIES

You will not have to use an atlas to find countries today. Simply match these fifteen words in Column A with their definitions in Column B. Write each two-letter corresponding answer from Column B on its appropriate line next to the Column A number. Then transfer those fifteen two-letter answers (in order) to the bottom of the page and you will spell out the names of the six countries. Happy travels!

Column A

1. _____ adolescent

2. _____ convict

3. _____ despot

4. _____ eerie

5. _____ fanatic

6. _____ fugitive

7. _____ lame duck

8. _____ maestro

9. _____ maverick

10. _____ parasite

11. _____ serf

12. _____ turncoat

13. _____ wanton

14. _____ xenophobe

15. _____ zany

Column B

az. an elected official whose term extends beyond the time of the election that he or she lost

br. person who flees from justice

dl. undisciplined; unrestrained

eg. a teenaged person

ha. traitor

hi. strange; odd; weird

ib. one who fears or hates strangers

il. master in any art

me. one who lives off another or others and gives nothing in return

na. overly zealous

nc. person in feudal servitude under the command of a master

tc. absolute ruler; king with unlimited powers

ya. silly or foolish person; simpleton

ye. person who takes an independent stand, refusing to conform to that of a party or group

yp. person serving a sentence in prison

_____

_____

_____

22-3   PEOPLE AND WHAT THEY SAID

Using the fifteen people below, write the person's name next to his or her quote. Although quote number 15 describes a situation, the other fourteen describe the person. Each name is used only once.

adolescent	eerie	lame duck	parasite	wanton
convict	fanatic	maestro	serf	xenophobe
despot	fugitive	maverick	turncoat	zany

1. _____ "I have seen over 500 sporting events in the past two years alone!"

2. _____ "I will conduct the symphony orchestra for the next two months."

3. _____ "Jail is no place to be. I wish I had obeyed the law."

4. _____ "I can live off others and not have to do much myself."

5. _____ "I have always done it my way despite what others do."

6. _____ "I always like to act in a silly, buffoonish way."

7. _____ "I do not want anyone who is originally from another country living anywhere near me."

8. _____ "I will never be caught by the authorities. I have been on the loose for more than three years now."

9. _____ "So what if I have spent over three thousand dollars on useless items? I just love to spend."

10. _____ "I want to be treated more like an adult than as a little kid!"

11. _____ "With only two more months in office, I doubt if I will be able to get any new laws passed."

12. _____ "My master commands me to work the fields for many hours each day."

13. _____ "I will severely punish those who do not follow my orders every day."

14. _____ "I have given much information to my country's enemies."

15. _____ "That bird's unusual sound really freaks me out."

22-4   WHERE DID THE WORD *MAESTRO* COME FROM?

Have you ever wondered where the word *maestro* originated? This Magic Square will tell you! Insert the correct number next to the appropriate letter. If your answers are correct, the rows, columns, and two diagonals will add up to the same number. If that happens, consider yourself a maestro!

A=	B=1	C=	D=
E=	F=	G=	H=
I=	J=	K=	L=
M=	N=	O=	P=

Magic Number:

_____

A. fugitive	**E.** maverick	**I.** adolescent	**M.** turncoat
B. fanatic	**F.** maestro	**J.** Italy	**N.** wanton
C. xenophobe	**G.** convict	**K.** zany	**O.** eerie
D. despot	**H.** serf	**L.** lame duck	**P.** parasite

1. a person whose extreme zeal goes beyond what is reasonable
2. a person serving a sentence in prison
3. a clown or buffoon; a silly or foolish person
4. undisciplined; unrestrained; one who recklessly ignores justice, decency, or morality
5. traitor
6. an elected official whose term extends beyond the time of the election at which he or she was not reelected
7. a person in feudal servitude, bound to his master's land and transferred with it to a new owner
8. a person who flees, or has fled, from danger or justice
9. a person who lives at the expense of another or others
10. a teenaged person
11. a person who takes an independent stand
12. an absolute ruler; king with unlimited powers
13. one who has fear or hatred of strangers
14. a master in any art
15. the origin of the word *maestro*
16. strange; odd; weird

Unit 23

HOW (OR NOT HOW) TO SAY IT

HOW (OR NOT HOW) TO SAY IT

1. **conversant:** (adj) familiar or acquainted (with), esp. as a result of study or experience; versed (in)

   Since Francesco is so *conversant* with botany, we asked him to be our guest speaker for the plants' portion of our program.

   syn: skilled, practiced, erudite; **ant:** unfamiliar, incapable

   family words: conversance, conversancy (n); conversantly (adv)

2. **curt:** (adj) brief, esp. to the point of rudeness; terse or brusque; blunt

   The student's *curt* response to the principal's question was quite unlike his usual pleasant and congenial answers.

   syn: concise, succinct, crisp; **ant:** long, extended, drawn-out

   family words: curtness (n); curtly (adv)

3. **debate:** (v) to discuss opposing reasons; to argue; to take part in a formal discussion or a contest in which opposing sides of a question are argued; (n) discussion or consideration of opposing reasons; argument about or deliberation on a question

   My neighbor and my father will often *debate* the merits of this fertilizer or that brand of grass seed.

   The forty-minute *debate* on the question of allowing women the right to participate in this tournament was certainly controversial.

   syn: dispute, discuss, quarrel (v)

   family words: debater (n)

4. **dialogue:** (n) a talking together; conversation; interchange and discussion of ideas, esp. when open and frank, as in seeking mutual understanding or harmony; a literary work in the form of a conversation on a single topic; the passages of talk in a play, story, etc.; (v) to hold a conversation; to express in dialogue

   Arthur Miller, a famous playwright, created *dialogue* that truly captured the verbal exchanges of everyday people.

   The two disagreeing parties *dialogued* about the issues that were preventing a resolution to the problem.

   syn: repartee, chat, exchange

   family words: dialogist (n)

5. **digress:** (v) to turn aside; esp. to depart temporarily from the main subject in talking or writing; to ramble

   Our guest speaker would often *digress* from her speech to include an anecdote related to the point she was making.

   Unfortunately, because the speaker continued to *digress*, his listeners became bored and confused.

   family words: digression, digressiveness (n); digressively (adv)

   Helpful Hint: "-Gress" means *to move*. "Di-" means *two*. So if you *digress*, you verbally *move in two directions*.

6. **disclaim:** (v) to give up or renounce any claim to or connection with; to refuse to acknowledge or admit; to repudiate; to make a disclaimer

    In a bold manner, the suspect *disclaimed* any responsibility for the fire that destroyed the company's main building.

    syn: deny, decline, reject; **ant:** affirm, accept, consent

    family words: disclaimer, disclamation (n)

    Helpful Hint: "Dis-" means *away from. Claim* means that it belongs to you. Thus, to *disclaim* is to give up all ownership of or connection to a thing or action.

7. **dissuade:** (v) to turn (a person) aside (from a course, etc.) by persuasion or advice

    Although we tried to *dissuade* her from going out with the guy who looks for trouble, she would not be convinced by our reasons.

    syn: discourage, disincline, avert; **ant:** encourage, assure, inspire

    family words: dissuader (n)

8. **feud:** (n) a bitter, long-continued, and deadly quarrel, esp. between clans or families; land held from a feudal lord in return for service; (v) to carry on a feud; quarrel

    The bloody *feud* between the Montagues and the Capulets was depicted in William Shakespeare's *Romeo and Juliet.*

    Rather than trying to reach an agreement, the gangs chose to *feud.*

    syn: conflict, hostility, schism (n); contend, fight, war (v); **ant:** agreement, peace, harmony, concord (n); agree, concur, cooperate (v)

    family words: feudalism (n); feudal, feudalist (adj)

9. **forthright:** (adj) outspoken; frank; direct; straightforward

    The candidate's *forthright* approach to solving the county's fiscal problems turned off some of the more conservative people at "Meet the Candidates Night."

    syn: candid, blunt; **ant:** devious, indirect, veiled

    family words: forthrightness (n); forthrightly (adv)

10. **interrupt:** (v) to break into or in upon (a discussion, train of thought, etc.); to break in upon (a person) who is speaking, working, etc.; to stop or hinder; to make a break in the continuity of; to cut off; to obstruct

    My thoughts were *interrupted* when the fire alarm sounded.

    The television announcer stated, "We *interrupt* this program to bring you an important message from the National Weather Service."

    syn: disturb, interfere, intercept

    family words: interruption, interrupter (n); interruptive (adv)

11. **mediate:** (v) to be in an intermediate position or location; to be an intermediary or conciliator between persons or sides; to settle by mediation

   Our gym teacher tried to *mediate* the loud disagreement between the rival volleyball teams.

   syn: reconcile, intervene, referee, moderate

   family words: mediator, mediation (n)

   Helpful Hint: "Med-" means *in the middle.* If you *mediate,* you are in the *middle,* trying to bring both sides (parties, people) more toward the middle or toward a greater understanding or agreement.

12. **paraphrase:** (n) a rewording of the meaning expressed in something spoken or written; a free reworking of a musical text or composition; (v) to compose or express in paraphrase

   The *paraphrase* of the woman's lengthy statement was sufficient enough to give us her plan's main ideas.

   Instead of reading the character's entire speech word for word, I *paraphrased* his thoughts.

   syn: summary, synopsis (n); reword, rephrase, restate (v)

   family words: paraphraser (n)

13. **quibble:** (v) to evade the truth of the point in discussion by hedging; to hedge; to nit-pick; to equivocate; (n) evasion of the main point as by emphasizing some petty detail; petty objection or criticism

   Let us not *quibble* about such a small issue when there are much more important concerns for our club.

   Do you think that his *quibble* is important enough to discuss when we have all these other really key issues to talk about tonight?

   syn: equivocate (v); equivocation, cavil, evasion (n)

   family words: quibbler (n)

14. **retort:** (v) to turn (an insult, epithet, deed, etc.) back upon the person from whom it came; to answer (an argument, etc.) in kind; to say in reply or response; (n) a quick, sharp, or witty reply, esp. one that turns the words of the previous speaker back on that speaker; the act or practice of making such reply

   When questioned about his involvement in the scandal, the suspect quickly *retorted,* "Hey, my hands are clean!"

   Although the man's question was clever, Jerry's *retort* was even more entertaining.

   syn: respond, answer (v); rejoinder, riposte, comeback (n)

15. **verbose:** (adj) using or containing too many words; wordy; long-winded

   The professor's brief responses were quite unlike the *verbose* answers of our former instructor.

   syn: gabby, circumlocutory; **ant:** concise, laconic, direct, terse

   family words: verbosity, verboseness (n); verbosely (adv)

23-1 IT'S NOT THAT GREEK TO YOU!

The fifteen words from Unit 23 are this crossword puzzle's answers. So are six letters from the Greek alphabet. Write your answers in the appropriate spaces. If you do so correctly, you will see that it's not that Greek to you!

Across

1. to turn aside; to depart temporarily from the main subject of talking or writing
5. ninth letter of the Greek alphabet
6. to bring about conciliation
10. last letter of the Greek alphabet
14. versed in; familiar with as a result of study or experience
15. second letter of the Greek alphabet
16. to give up any connection with; to refuse to admit or acknowledge; repudiate
17. fourth letter of the Greek alphabet
18. using or containing too many words; wordy; long-winded

Down

1. a talking together; passages of talk in a play or story
2. third letter of the Greek alphabet
3. outspoken; frank; direct
4. quick, sharp, or witty reply
5. to break into or in on a discussion; to break in on a person who is speaking
7. to discuss opposing reasons; argument about or deliberation on a question
8. first letter of the Greek alphabet
9. rewording of the meaning expressed in something spoken or written
11. to hedge; to equivocate; to nit-pick
12. to turn a person aside from a course of action by advice or persuasion
13. a bitter, long-continued, and deadly quarrel, esp. between clans or families; quarrel
14. brief, esp. to the point of rudeness; terse or brusque; blunt

23-2   U-R THAT CLEVER!

Match up the words from Column A with their definitions in Column B. Write the corresponding three-letter answers on the line next to the correct Column A word. Then transfer those answers (in order) to the back of this sheet. If your answers are correct, you will spell nine words, all containing the "ur" combination. Thus, if you spell out these nine "ur" words, U-R that clever!

Column A

1. _____ conversant

2. _____ curt

3. _____ debate

4. _____ dialogue

5. _____ digress

6. _____ disclaim

7. _____ dissuade

8. _____ feud

9. _____ forthright

10. _____ interrupt

11. _____ mediate

12. _____ paraphrase

13. _____ quibble

14. _____ retort

15. _____ verbose

Column B

abr. familiar and acquainted with; versed in

agr. outspoken; frank; direct

bur. to turn an insult back on the person from whom it came; a quick, sharp, or witty reply

dru. to settle by mediation; to bring about by conciliation

eru. to evade the truth of the point in discussion by hedging; to nit-pick; to equivocate

fru. to discuss opposing reasons; argue; to take part in a formal discussion

gal. a talking together; conversation; to hold a conversation

idp. a rewording of the meaning expressed in something spoken or written

lap. using or containing too many words; wordy; long-winded

rub. a bitter, long-continued, and deadly quarrel, esp. between clans and families

ser. to turn aside, esp. to depart temporarily from the main subject in talking or writing; ramble

umr. to give up or renounce any connection with; repudiate

unt. to break into or in on a discussion; stop or hinder

upt. brief, esp. to the point of rudeness; terse or brusque; blunt

uta. to turn (a person) aside from a course of action by persuasion or advice

23-3   THIS IS SO EASY!

Select the correct answer for these fifteen analogies. Write the letter on the line next to the analogy. Then write all fifteen letters (in order) at the bottom of this page. If your answers are correct, you will spell out a fifteen-letter word that means *so easy,* as the activity's title says it should be!

1. ___ **conversant : familiar with**   (u) ambidextrous : skilled   (b) zany : sophisticated
(e) boastful: humble

2. ___ **curt : long-winded**   (e) counterfeit : false   (l) bulky : small   (r) normal : typical

3. ___ **debate : formal discussion**   (f) anecdote : dramatic presentation
(o) mendicant : wealthy person   (t) pun : play on words

4. ___ **dialogue : conversation**   (s) xenophobe : lover of foreigners   (r) metropolis : large city
(t) autobiography : dialogue

5. ___ **digress : to stay on the main subject**   (a) ascend : to go down   (d) strut : to walk in
a proud manner   (i) pilfer : to steal

6. ___ **disclaim : to refuse to acknowledge or admit**   (o) usurp : to give up power to another
(c) hoard : to accumulate and hide   (k) interrogate : to answer rudely

7. ___ **dissuade : to persuade a person to a different course of action**   (c) snare : to set free
(t) detest : to admire greatly   (o) oppress : to trouble

8. ___ **feud : love affair**   (n) babble : coherent, sensible speech   (m) orator : an eloquent
public speaker   (s) tyrant : cruel, obsessive ruler

9. ___ **forthright : not direct; not straightforward**   (b) feeble : weak and frail
(e) arable : suitable to producing crops   (v) judicious : unwise; not careful

10. ___ **interrupt : to break into or on; to stop or hinder**   (w) deceive : to treat honestly
(u) mumble : to speak coherently   (e) expose : to reveal

11. ___ **mediate : to be an intermediary or conciliator**   (n) blurt : to say suddenly
(p) annihilate : to construct; to build up   (u) elude : to capture

12. ___ **paraphrase : rewording of the meaning expressed in something spoken or written**
(b) surplus : scarcity   (i) dupe : one who is easily fooled   (c) offspring : ancestor

13. ___ **quibble : to evade the truth by hedging; to nit-pick**   (e) dwindle : to decrease in
size or amount   (v) scamper : to walk slowly   (h) wheedle : to dissuade

14. ___ **retort : sharp, witty reply**   (a) trek : money exchange   (w) mutation : continuation of
an existing condition   (n) dividend : the number or quantity to be divided

15. ___ **verbose : terse**   (t) ruthless : exhibiting pity   (g) massive : big and solid
(r) meticulous : excessive about details

23-4   A VERY SILLY POEM

The blanks in this silly poem should be filled in with the words from Unit 23. Yes, the poem's lines do rhyme. Because they do, we have placed a restriction on you and your classmates. We have not included a word bank. Instead, take another look at Unit 23's words, and then begin filling in the poem's blanks. We hope the silliness of this poem will not take away your poetry appreciation. Good luck!

My sister wrote a silly _____ (1)
Between a person and a frog.
Though I really tried to _____ (2)
Her mind was already made.
I thought it quite rude
If I were to start a _____ (3)
So rather than _____ (4)
On a candy, I started to nibble.
I had chosen not to be _____ (5)
For I knew my words could hurt.
Why should I with my sister _____ (6)
Knowing that the outcome would not be great?
My mother would want to _____ (7);
That, too, would not be too great!
Of the literary work, my sister would not _____ (8)
Knowing quite well she would get the blame.
She was very _____ (9)
Though she would not want to fight.
Yes, I tried to be a good sport
And chose not to give a nasty _____ (10).
To me, frog conversations lack intent;
Of them, I am not _____ (11).
On this topic I will not _____ (12).
Since I could create more of a mess
I will certainly not _____ (13).
Though I truly might be abrupt
For this poem, there will be no craze
And no one will use it for _____ (14).
Why? Hey, everybody knows!
This poem is very, very _____ (15)!

Unit 24

GONE!

GONE!

1. **abdicate:** (v) to give up formally (a high office, a throne, authority); to surrender or repudiate (a right, responsibility)

    Knowing that he was in immediate danger, the despot *abdicated* his position in order to save his own life.

    syn: renounce, resign, relinquish

    family words: abdicator, abdication (n)

    Helpful Hint: "Ab-" means *away from.* Know the prefix "ab-." Do not run away from it!

2. **abstain:** (v) to hold oneself back; to voluntarily do without; to refrain from

    The doctor told the man to *abstain* from sweets if he wanted to lose weight.

    syn: forbear, desist, decline, resist

    family words: abstention, abstainer (n)

3. **annihilate:** (v) to destroy completely; to put out of existence; to demolish; to conquer decisively; to crush

    Because the coach knew that his team could *annihilate* its opponent, he only played his reserve players.

    syn: exterminate, extinguish, eradicate

    family words: annihilator, annihilation (n); annihilative (adj)

4. **depression:** (n) low spirits; gloominess; dejection; sadness; a decrease in force

    Immediately after losing her sons in the tragic accident, the saddened mother went into a deep *depression.*

    After several years of financial good times, the national economy's *depression* was caused by several different factors.

    syn: (for "low spirits, gloominess") melancholy, despondency, torpor; **ant:** (for "low spirits, gloominess") cheerfulness, optimism, hopefulness

    family words: depress (v); depressive, depressed (adj)

5. **dismantle:** (v) to strip of covering; to strip of furniture, equipment, means of defense; to take apart

    After the play's final performance, the stage workers had to *dismantle* the set and store all the equipment.

    family words: dismantlement, dismantler (n)

    Helpful Hint: *Dismantle* once meant to "take off one's cloak."

6. **dissolve:** (v) to make or become liquid; to melt; to break up; to disunite; to decompose; to disintegrate

    His hopes of winning the election quickly began to *dissolve* when he saw his opponent's strong support.

    syn: evaporate, end, dematerialize; **ant:** solidify, congeal, unite, consolidate

    family words: dissolver (n); dissolvable, dissolvent (adj)

7. **eject:** (v) to throw out; to cast out; to expel; to emit; to discharge; to drive out; to evict

    The referee *ejected* the fighting players from the game.

    syn: dismiss, banish

    family words: ejection, ejector (n); ejective, ejectable (adj)

    Helpful Hint: *Eject* = "e-" (away from) + "-ject" (to throw)

GONE! (continued)

8. elude: (v) to avoid or escape from by quickness, cunning, etc.; to evade; to escape from detection, notice, or understanding

Because the runner was so swift and agile, she was able to *elude* her opponents in the game of tag.

syn: shun, avoid, flee, circumvent

family words: elusion, elusiveness (n); elusive (adj); elusively (adv)

9. erode: (v) to eat into; to wear away; to disintegrate; to cause to deteriorate, decay, or vanish

The strong waves that *eroded* the beach's shoreline caused much erosion.

syn: consume, abrade

family words: erosion (n); erodible, erosive (adj)

10. kleptomaniac: (n) one who has an abnormal, persistent impulse or tendency to steal, not prompted by need

Several small items, each worth very little, were found in the *kleptomaniac's* pockets.

family words: kleptomania

Helpful Hint: The prefix "klepto-" means *thief.*

11. lack: (n) the fact or condition of not having enough; shortage; deficiency; complete absence; (v) to be in need; to fall short; to be wanting or missing

The poor country's *lack* of food caused starvation and death.

If you do not save your money wisely, you will *lack* the funds needed to purchase the car.

syn: deficiency, insufficiency (n); miss, need, require (v); **ant:** surplus, extra, plethora (n)

12. penury: (n) lack of money, property, or necessities; extreme poverty; destitution

The young boy could not understand how a town could have such wealth on one side of the railroad tracks and such *penury* on the other side.

family words: penuriousness (n); penurious (adj)

Helpful Hint: Say the following sentence five times (fast): PENURY is POVERTY, and POVERTY is PENURY.

13. porous: (adj) full of tiny openings through which fluids, light, or air may pass

This *porous* container will certainly not be able to hold water.

syn: absorbent; **ant:** nonporous, solid

family words: porousness, porosity (n); porously (adv)

14. purge: (v) to cleanse or rid of impurities, foreign matter, or undesirable elements; to cleanse of guilt, sin, or ceremonial defilement; to empty; (n) the act of purging; that which purges

The older man hoped that his prayers would *purge* away his sins.

This dictator's *purge* of political enemies began by placing them all in a cold and remote portion of the country.

syn: eliminate, remove, banish (v); annihilation, extermination

family words: purger, purgation (n); purgative (adj)

15. ransack: (v) to search thoroughly; to examine every part of in searching; to search through for plunder; to pillage; to rob

I *ransacked* my bedroom looking for the misplaced notebook.

Burglars *ransacked* the wealthy woman's home hoping to find money and jewels.

syn: scour, rifle, rummage (v)

family words: ransacker (n)

24-1   TWO AT A TIME

Use the words below to fill in the fifteen blanks. Each word is used only once. Then identify the two letters as indicated by the numbers found after each sentence. Write those letters on the line before each sentence. Finally, write those letters (in order) at the bottom of the page. If your answers are correct, you will spell out eight four-letter words. So, other than number 15, take the letters two at a time and start to spell out these words.

abdicate	depression	eject	kleptomaniac	porous
abstain	dismantle	elude	lack	purge
annihilate	dissolve	erode	penury	ransack

1. _____ Unfortunately, since the material was _____, it would not hold any water. **(1,2)**

2. _____ The police arrested the _____ after they found several stolen items in her purse. **(2,3)**

3. _____ That country's leader decided to _____ the throne after seeing the political unrest that was going on. **(5,6)**

4. _____ We had never witnessed such _____ as when we went to help the needy in that part of our state. **(1,2)**

5. _____ The scientists decided to _____ the container of its germs. **(1,2)**

6. _____ The recent _____ of rain caused the soil to be hard, making it very difficult to grow vegetables. **(3,4)**

7. _____ Workers had to _____ the rides and booths after the last night of the carnival. **(8,9)**

8. _____ Sports reporters were saying that our football team would _____ our rival in the annual Thanksgiving Day game. **(1,2)**

9. _____ Several criminals were able to cleverly _____ police authorities at the local restaurant last night. **(2,3)**

10. _____ Her grandmother had fallen into a mental _____ after she lost her husband of fifty years. **(4,5)**

11. _____ We were able to _____ that solid in just a few minutes and leave hardly a trace in the sink. **(4,5)**

12. _____ Looters had planned to _____ the corner home, but, acting on a tip, our town police officers were able to prevent this possible robbery. **(6,7)**

13. _____ During that religious time, we _____ from eating sweets, and, as an added benefit, we also lose a few extra pounds. **(4,5)**

14. _____ The umpire threatened to _____ the players if they continued to physically bully each other. **(4,5)**

15. _____ Since battery acid will _____ this clothing material, you must be very careful if you want to wear that shirt again. **(2,3,4,5)**

_____

_____

24-2   WATER, WATER EVERYWHERE

This activity invites you into the world of opposites. Match each word in Column A with its opposite in Column B. Write the corresponding two-letter answer on the line before the Column A word. Then write the letters (in order) at the bottom of this page. If your answers are correct, you will spell out six bodies of water.

Column A

1. _____ abdicate
2. _____ abstain
3. _____ annihilate
4. _____ depression
5. _____ dismantle
6. _____ dissolve
7. _____ eject
8. _____ elude
9. _____ erode
10. _____ kleptomaniac
11. _____ lack
12. _____ penury
13. _____ porous
14. _____ purge
15. _____ ransack

Column B

am. restore; return; recoup; repair

ca. claim; defend; hold; maintain

ea. take in; accept; establish; confirm

er. donor

iv. ripen; freshen; renew; restore; cleanse

lb. construct; build; renew; restore; create

na. indulge; take in

nd. wealth; luxury; abundance

nr. seek; invite; allure; entice

oc. appear; unite; integrate; become solid

ok. equip; appoint; outfit

po. abundance; plenty; fullness; satiation

re. to dirty; to sully; to foul; to soil

ro. buoyancy; elation

st. airtight; having no holes; impenetrable

_____

_____

_____

24-3   "-URY" IS IN

In addition to the fifteen words found in Unit 24, seven other words that end in "-ury," as in the word *penury,* are answers in this crossword puzzle. What a luxury for you to fill in all twenty-two answers! So bury those answers within this puzzle, and no jury would find fault with your actions. Good luck!

Across

2. low spirits; gloominess
6. violent anger; wild rage; violence; fierceness
7. full of tiny openings through which fluids, light, or air may pass
9. shortage; deficiency; to be in need
10. the art or practice of lending money at a rate that is excessive or unlawfully high
11. to destroy completely; put out of existence; demolish
13. to eat into; wear away; disintegrate
16. telling of a lie while under lawful oath
17. to give up a high office or throne or authority lawfully; to surrender a right or responsibility
19. one who has an abnormal, persistent impulse or tendency to steal, not prompted by need
20. lavishness; opulence; treat

Down

1. those who decide a person's fate in court
2. to make or become liquid; melt; to break up; disunite
3. to throw out; cast out; expel; emit; discharge
4. physical harm or damage to a person; an offense against a person's feelings
5. to place a dead body into the earth; to hide something in the ground
8. to cleanse or rid of impurities; to empty; to cleanse of guilt or sin
11. to hold oneself back; voluntarily do without; refrain from
12. to avoid or escape from by quickness, cunning, or the like; to escape from detection
14. to search thoroughly; examine every part of in searching; to search through for plunder
15. to strip of covering; to take apart; to strip of furniture or equipment
18. lack of money, property, or necessities; extreme poverty

24-4   COUNT ON IT TO BE ONE OF THE FIRST

One of the words in this Magic Square is one of the oldest types of counting machines. Match that word with its definition, and do the same for the other fifteen words below. If your answers are correct, all the rows, columns, and the two diagonals will add up to the same number.

A=	B=13	C=	D=
E=	F=	G=	H=
I=	J=	K=	L=
M=	N=	O=	P=

Magic Number:

_____

A. erode	**E.** abacus	**I.** eject	**M.** dismantle
B. lack	**F.** abdicate	**J.** porous	**N.** elude
C. dissolve	**G.** penury	**K.** purge	**O.** abstain
D. depression	**H.** annihilate	**L.** kleptomaniac	**P.** ransack

1. to make or become liquid
2. full of tiny openings through which water, air, or other things may pass
3. to surrender a right or responsibility; to formally give up a high office, throne, or authority
4. refrain from; voluntarily do without
5. to search through for plunder; pillage; rob; to search thoroughly
6. a frame with beads or balls that can be slid on wires or in slots, for doing or teaching arithmetic
7. to throw out; cast out; expel; to drive out
8. gloominess; low spirits; dejection; sadness
9. to strip of covering; to strip of equipment or furniture; to take apart
10. to destroy completely; to conquer decisively; crush
11. one who has an abnormal, persistent impulse or tendency to steal, not prompted by need
12. to cause to deteriorate, decay, or vanish; wear away; disintegrate
13. the condition of not having enough; shortage; deficiency
14. to cleanse or rid of impurities
15. poverty; extreme poverty; destitution
16. to escape from detection, notice, or understanding; to avoid or escape from by quickness or cunning

Units 22–24 REVIEW TEST

Directions: Please circle the correct **synonym**. Then write the answer's corresponding letter on the line next to the question's number. Each question is worth four points.

1. ____ **elude** (a) to turn aside by persuasion (b) to escape from detection (c) to see clearly

2. ____ **ransack** (a) to develop a plan (b) to examine every part of in searching (c) to cut off

3. ____ **digress** (a) to examine carefully (b) to depart temporarily from the main subject (c) to break into two equal parts

4. ____ **mediate** (a) to bring about by conciliation (b) to cleanse or rid of impurities (c) to steal in small quantities

5. ____ **abstain** (a) to voluntarily do without (b) to flee from someone or something (c) to be indecisive

6. ____ **turncoat** (a) designer (b) buffoon (c) traitor

7. ____ **eerie** (a) odd (b) simple (c) complex

8. ____ **serf** (a) person who is oppressed and without freedom (b) person who has mastered an art (c) person who has written an autobiography

9. ____ **convict** (a) person who designs book jackets (b) person who convinces others, often by flattery (c) person serving a sentence in prison

10. ____ **fugitive** (a) person who attends rock and roll concerts (b) person who flees from danger or justice (c) person who helps farmers

Directions: Please circle the correct **antonym**. Then write the answer's corresponding letter on the line next to the question's number. Each question is worth four points.

11. ____ **maestro** (a) master (b) beginner (c) standout

12. ____ **despot** (a) humanitarian (b) absolute ruler (c) onlooker

13. ____ **curt** (a) blunt (b) drawn-out (c) intelligent

14. ____ **dissuade** (a) discourage (b) encourage (c) remember

15. ____ **verbose** (a) concise (b) wordy (c) wonderful

16. ____ **conversant** (a) impure (b) pure (c) unfamiliar

17. ____ **porous** (a) not level (b) full of tiny openings (c) solid

18. ____ **lack** (a) surplus (b) mass (c) wordiness

19. ____ **depression** (a) low spirits (b) optimism (c) water

20. ____ **dissolve** (a) congeal (b) dematerialize (c) amaze

Units 22–24   REVIEW TEST (continued)

Directions: Please circle the word that correctly **completes** the sentence. Then write the answer's corresponding letter on the line next to the question's number. Each question is worth four points.

21. ____ With his biases, the _____ did not want to be included in the ceremony lauding the contributions of foreigners.   **(a) adolescent   (b) xenophobe   (c) convict**

22. ____ We need to _____ the positive and negative aspects of the proposed traffic changes.   **(a) debate   (b) ransack   (c) abstain**

23. ____ The suspect _____ any involvement in the burglary.
     (a) eroded   (b) ejected   (c) disclaimed

24. ____ Let us not _____ about this very unimportant aspect of the plan.
     (a) purge   (b) quibble   (c) interrupt

25. ____ Before we institute the proposed additions to the building, we definitely should _____ with all concerned parties.
     (a) dialogue   (b) annihilate   (c) dismantle

Unit 25

AGE

AGE

1. **anachronism:** (n) the representation of something as existing or occurring other than at its proper time, esp. earlier

   The movie director's including a laptop computer in the film depicting the late 1800s is obviously an *anachronism*.

   family words: anachronistic, anachronous (adj); anachronistically (adv)

   Helpful Hint: "Ana-" means *away from* or *out of*. "Chron-" means *time*. Thus, *anachronism* means *away from* or *out of* time.

2. **antique:** (adj) of ancient times; ancient; old; out-of-date; old-fashioned; (n) piece of furniture made in a former period

   This *antique* clock is now several centuries old.

   We bid $3,000 for the *antique* hoping that we could then place the old chair in our den.

   syn: relic, artifact, fossil (n); **ant:** new, modern

   family words: antiqueness, antiquity (n); antiquely (adv)

3. **archaic:** (adj) belonging to an earlier period; ancient; antiquated; old-fashioned

   Many teens feel that their parents' way of thinking is *archaic* rather than modern.

   syn: outdated, obsolete; **ant:** modern, recent, current

   family words: archaism, archaist (n); archaistic (adj); archaically (adv)

   Helpful Hint: "Arch-" means the *first of its kind*. Thus, if it is *archaic,* it is old!

4. **callow:** (adj) young and inexperienced; immature; still lacking the feathers needed for flying

   Callow workers usually need the guidance of an older, more experienced, and more knowledgeable mentor.

   The *callow* bird could only watch as the other flock members flew in and out of the birdhouses.

   syn: youthful, unseasoned, green; **ant:** experienced, mature

   family words: callowness (n)

5. **contemporary:** (adj) living or happening in the same period of time; of about the same age; modern; (n) a person living in the same period as another or others

   My mom prefers antique furniture to *contemporary* furniture.

   Christopher Marlowe was Shakespeare's *contemporary,* since both lived in the late 1500s.

   syn: simultaneous, synchronous, current (adj); **ant:** old-fashioned, out-of-date, historical (adj)

   family words: contemporaneousness (n); contemporize (v); contemporaneous (adj); contemporaneously (adv)

   Helpful Hint: "Con-" means *with*. "Temp-" means *time*. Thus, *contemporary* means *with time* or *modern*.

6. **crone:** (n) an ugly, withered old woman; hag

   The young children were frightened when they saw and heard the *crone* on the porch.

7. **extinct:** (adj) no longer in existence or use; having no living descendant

   Since there are no dinosaurs on earth, we have no memories of this *extinct* beast that once ruled the earth.

   syn: dead, defunct, nonexistent; **ant:** living, thriving, flourishing

   family words: extinction (n); extinctive (adj)

8. **fledgling:** (n) a young, inexperienced person; a young bird who has just grown the feathers necessary to fly; (adj) new; beginning

   Having now worked only seven months on the magazine's staff, Jim was still a *fledgling* when contrasted to the older, more experienced writers.

   The *fledgling* waited for its mother's assistance before attempting to fly from the nest.

AGE (continued)

Working along with his more experienced miner, our *fledgling* worker quickly learned how to do the job.

syn: novice, beginner, neophyte; **ant:** veteran, professional, master

9. **geriatric:** (adj) the branch of medicine that deals with the diseases and problems of old age

   In stark contrast to her work with newborns, Connie Lynn is now working in the hospital's *geriatric* unit.

10. **innovate:** (v) to introduce new methods or devices

    While designers and inventors *innovate,* historians record.

    family words: innovation, innovator (n); innovative, innovational (adj)

    Helpful Hint: "Nov-" means *new.*

11. **novice:** (n) a person on probation in a religious group or order before taking vows; neophyte; apprentice; beginner

    The *novice* met with the more experienced nuns to ask their advice on certain issues.

    You would expect that the *novice* actor, not the very experienced actor, would make such a silly mistake.

    syn: trainee, apprentice; **ant:** veteran, expert

    Helpful Hint: "Nov-" means *new.*

12. **obsolete:** (adj) no longer in use or practice; discarded; no longer in fashion; out-of-date; passé

    Do not think that asking a father's approval to marry his daughter is an *obsolete* thing to do because I know that my brother did exactly that just last month!

    syn: outmoded, archaic; **ant:** current, up-to-date, modern

    family words: obsoleteness, obsolescence (n); obsolescent (adj); obsolesce (v)

13. **regenerate:** (v) to cause to be spiritually reborn; to cause to be completely reformed or improved

    Some of the members of our church have become complacent in their duty to aid others in the community, so our pastor wants to *regenerate* their interest in helping the poor.

    syn: reform, rehabilitate, remedy; **ant:** lower, defile, demolish

    family words: regeneration, regenerator, regeneracy (n)

    Helpful Hint: "Generate" means *to start.* "Re-" means *again.* Thus, to *regenerate* means *to start again.*

14. **renovate:** (v) to make sound or fresh again, as though new; to clean up; to replace worn and broken parts in, repair

    Neighborhood residents want to *renovate* the littered and neglected park so that their children can make good use of the area again.

    syn: refurbish, modernize, renew, remodel

    family words: renovation, renovator (n); renovative (adj)

    Helpful Hint: "Nov-" means *new.*

15. **veteran:** (adj) experienced; practiced; (n) an old, experienced soldier, one who served in time of war; any person who has served in the armed services; a person of long experience in some occupation or position

    The *veteran* educator was able to give good practical advice to the new teachers.

    Many *veterans* attended the memorial service for their deceased fellow soldiers.

    The nurse, a *veteran* of thirty years at the local hospital, was given a special service award at last week's ceremony.

    syn: adept, seasoned (adj); master, pro, expert (n); **ant:** green, inexperienced, raw (adj); beginner, apprentice (n)

25-1   THE LAST LETTERS

Use the words below to fill in the fifteen blanks. Each word is used only once. If all your answers are correct, the last letter of each word (in order) will spell out five three-letter words. Write those words at the bottom of the page.

anachronism	callow	extinct	innovate	regenerate
antiue	contemporary	fledgling	novice	renovate
archaic	crone	geriatric	obsolete	veteran

1. Having a tape recorder included in a movie set in the early days of Rome is an example of a(n) _____.

2. Using such an _____ tool instead of this modern implement to help plow this field is senseless.

3. Unlike his more experienced comrades, the _____ soldier did not understand some of the basic methods of warfare training.

4. We saw that the _____ was incapable of leaving its nest since it was very, very young.

5. The new mayor wanted to _____ new transportation routes throughout the city.

6. Can we _____ the spirit of the team after we have had such a tough losing streak?

7. His _____ classroom management techniques did not go over well in this modern time.

8. My grandmother and mother purchased an expensive _____ that will be placed in our living room next to the piano.

9. The club members could hear the loud, incessant complaints coming from the _____ in the adjacent room.

10. One of my friends told me that his relative had been a _____ of Babe Ruth's during the 1920s.

11. The interior designer had some ideas on how to _____ our dining room without costing too much money.

12. This twelve-year _____ of the professional team in our city had a statue erected for him outside the arena.

13. If we are not more careful, this bird may soon become _____ and become only a memory.

14. The _____ police officer learned her job in a few months, thanks to her more experienced associates.

15. Patients in this _____ ward always talk about the "good old days" when they were youths living in the city.

_____

_____

25-2 STARTING FRESH

Since the theme of Unit 25 deals with age, this crossword puzzle does the same. In addition to the fifteen words from the unit, there are four other clues, the word *newcomer,* for which you are to fill in synonyms for *novice.* Fill in those four and the other fifteen answers and you, like the *newcomer,* started fresh and ended even better!

Across

4. to cause to be completely reformed or improved; to cause to be spiritually reborn
6. of ancient times; ancient; old; out-of-date
7. belonging to an earlier period; ancient; antiquated; old-fashioned
11. a person on probation in a religious group or order before taking vows; neophyte
13. a young, inexperienced person; a young bird who has just grown feathers necessary to fly
14. newcomer
16. newcomer
17. no longer in practice or use; discarded; no longer in fashion
18. living or happening in the same period of time; of about the same age; modern

Down

1. to make sound or fresh again, as though new; clean up; replace warn and broken parts in
2. young and inexperienced; immature; still lacking the feathers for flying
3. the branch of medicine that deals with the diseases and problems of old age
5. no longer in existence or use; having no living descendent
6. the representation of something as existing or occurring other than at its proper time, esp. earlier
8. an ugly, withered old woman; hag
9. introduce new methods or devices
10. newcomer
12. experienced; an old, experienced soldier, esp. one who served in time of war; any person who has served in the armed forces; person of long experience in some occupation or position
15. newcomer

25-3   ONE HUNDRED YEARS AND COUNTING

A person who is at least eighty years old is an octogenarian. One who is at least ninety years old is a nonagenarian. Do you know what a person who is at least one hundred years old is called? If so, that will help you in today's Magic Square. Match these sixteen words and then write the correct number in each box. If your answers are correct, the rows, columns, and two diagonals will add up to the same number.

A=	B=6	C=	D=
E=	F=	G=	H=
I=	J=	K=	L=
M=	N=	O=	P=

Magic Number:

_____

A. anachronism	**E.** antique	**I.** renovate	**M.** novice
B. crone	**F.** contemporary	**J.** regenerate	**N.** archaic
C. geriatric	**G.** callow	**K.** veteran	**O.** centenarian
D. innovate	**H.** extinct	**L.** fledgling	**P.** obsolete

1. belonging to an earlier period; ancient; antiquated
2. young and inexperienced; immature
3. a young, inexperienced person; a young bird who has just grown feathers necessary to fly
4. the representation of something as existing or occurring other than at its proper time, esp. earlier
5. a person of long experience in some occupation or position; experienced; practiced; an old, experienced soldier
6. an ugly, withered old woman; hag
7. neophyte; apprentice; beginner; a person on probation in a religious group or order before taking vows
8. no longer in existence or use; having no living descendent
9. of ancient times; old; out-of-date; old-fashioned
10. no longer in use or practice; discarded; no longer in fashion; out-of-date; passe
11. the branch of medicine that deals with the diseases and problems of old age
12. to cause to be completely reformed or improved; to cause to be spiritually reborn
13. introduce new methods or devices
14. to make sound or fresh again, as though new; clean up; replace worn or broken parts in
15. living or happening in the same period of time; of or about the same age; modern
16. a person at least one hundred years old

Name: _____ Date: _____ Period: _____

25-4   PONCE DE LEON'S SEARCH

The words below all deal with age in one form or another. Most people would love to find the same thing that Ponce de Leon, the explorer, searched for hundreds of years ago, namely the Fountain of Youth. So start with the Fountain of Youth and Ponce de Leon, and then match up the other fifteen words in the Magic Square. If your answers are correct, the rows, columns, and the two diagonals will add up to the same number. Good luck!

A=	B=11	C=	D=
E=	F=	G=	H=
I=	J=	K=	L=
M=	N=	O=	P=

Magic Number:

_____

A. antique	**E.** crone	**I.** obsolete	**M.** geriatric
B. callow	**F.** veteran	**J.** novice	**N.** contemporary
C. anachronism	**G.** regenerate	**K.** extinct	**O.** Fountain of Youth
D. renovate	**H.** fledgling	**L.** archaic	**P.** innovate

1. the branch of medicine that focuses on older people
2. a soldier who fought in a war
3. a young bird that just grew its feathers
4. what Ponce de Leon thought would make him young again
5. type of thinking that is really outdated
6. a digital clock in a 1930s movie
7. a 1920s car in a 1990s movie
8. a religious order member who has not taken all her vows
9. an animal that has no descendents
10. what you might want to do to update your old-fashioned kitchen
11. the most inexperienced worker on the job
12. what the horse and buggy is when contrasted to the fast car
13. what two women who lived during the same time are to each other
14. what one calls the complaining, old hag
15. what an animal might do to its damaged body part
16. what inventors love to do

Copyright © 2004 by John Wiley & Sons, Inc.

Unit 26

WHO WANTS TO BE CALLED THAT?

WHO WANTS TO BE CALLED THAT?

1. **boastful:** (adj) inclined to brag; one who is vainly proud

    Few people can tolerate listening to *boastful* people bragging about themselves.

    syn: bragging, inflated, cocky; **ant:** modest, diffident, humble, self-effacing

    family words: boaster, boastfulness (n); boastfully (adv)

    Helpful Hint: One who is BOASTFUL is FULL of BOASTING.

2. **cross:** (adj) ill-tempered; cranky; irritable; (n) an upright post with a bar across it near the top; a mark (X) made as a signature by one who cannot write; (v) to make the sign of the cross over or upon; to lie across or intersect; to go from one side to another; to oppose

    Unless you enjoy people who are often cranky and irritable, you will usually not enjoy living with a *cross* person.

    The religious person prayed in front of the altar's *cross*.

    In olden days, the slaves would often sign their names by making a *cross* on the paper.

    It is not a good idea to *cross* an animal that is already very angry.

    syn: contrary, adverse, petulant (adj); crucifix (n); intersect (v); **ant:** agreeable, compliant (adj); assist (v)

3. **deceitful:** (adj) dishonest; representing what is known to be false as true

    Honest people do not imitate the actions of *deceitful* people.

    syn: fraudulent, underhanded; **ant:** honest, straightforward

    family words: deceit, deceitfulness (n); deceitfully (adv)

    Helpful Hint: One who is DECEITFUL is FULL of DECEIT.

4. **illiterate:** (adj) ignorant; uneducated; not knowing how to read or write; (n) an illiterate person, esp. one not knowing how to read or write

    I am *illiterate* when it comes to the intricacies of fixing a car's motor.

    The Literary Club's president urged us to teach *illiterate* people how to read.

    The *illiterate* was embarrassed when he was unable to read the story to his son.

    ant: literate, educated

    family words: illiteracy (n); illiterately (adv)

    Helpful Hint: *Illiterate* = "il-" (not) + "-literate" (able to read)

5. **insubordinate:** (adj) not submitting to authority; disobedient

    The *insubordinate* student who yelled at the teacher was escorted to the principal's office.

    syn: rebellious, defiant, unruly, impudent; **ant:** obedient

    family words: insubordination (n); insubordinately (adv)

    Helpful Hint: *Insubordinate* = "in-" (not) + "-subordinate" (one of a lesser position)

6. **irrational:** (adj) lacking the power to reason; contrary to reason; senseless; unreasonable; absurd

    Your thinking that your dog can sprint faster than a cheetah can is simply *irrational*.

    syn: illogical, unscientific; **ant:** rational, reasonable

    family words: irrationality (n); irrationally (adv)

    Helpful Hint: *Irrational* = "ir-" (not) + "-rational" (same, reasonable)

7. **irritable:** (adj) easily annoyed or provoked; fretful

    Although Linda is usually in a good mood, she is sometimes *irritable* when she wakes up after her nap.

    syn: impatient, touchy, cantankerous; **ant:** calm, composed, agreeable

    family words: irritability, irritableness (n); irritably (adv)

8. morbid: (adj) diseased; gruesome; grisly; horrible

Newspaper reporters are sometimes against relating all the *morbid* facts of an automobile accident, fearing the reading public would be sickened by these gruesome details.

syn: malignant, decaying; **ant:** sound, healthy, robust

family words: morbidness, morbidity (n); morbidly (adv)

9. obstinate: (adj) unreasonably determined to have one's own way; stubborn

He would rather go along with the group's idea than be accused of being *obstinate*.

syn: headstrong, obdurate, unyielding; **ant:** flexible, compliant, amenable

family words: obstinateness (n); obstinately (adv)

10. ornery: (adj) having an ugly or mean disposition; obstinate

Since mules do not always behave as people would like them to behave, the animal is often described as *ornery*.

syn: disagreeable, mulish, unruly; **ant:** pleasant, agreeable, cooperative

family words: orneriness (n)

11. spiteful: (adj) purposefully annoying; malicious; vindictive

Unfortunately, a *spiteful* person will generally look for any way to get even.

syn: having a grudge; **ant:** understanding, benevolent

family words: spitefulness (n); spite (n, v); spitefully (adv)

Helpful Hint: One who is SPITEFUL is FULL of SPITE.

12. stodgy: (adj) heavily built; bulky and slow in movement; stubbornly old-fashioned

The rather *stodgy* animal will never be able to keep the pace of its sleek competitor.

syn: dull, boring, tedious, humdrum; **ant:** lively, entertaining, stimulating

family words: stodginess (n); stodgily (adv)

13. sullen: (adj) showing resentment and ill humor by morose withdrawal; unsociable; gloomy; dismal; sad

Dejected by her loss in this close class election, the runner-up was in a *sullen* mood and chose to go off by herself for a while.

syn: melancholy, depressed, brooding; **ant:** buoyant, enthusiastic

family words: sullenness (n); sullenly (adv)

Helpful Hint: Stuart was *sullen* and disappointed after hearing the depressing news that his family would be moving to another state.

14. tactless: (adj) not having the delicate perception of the right thing to say or do without offending

The store manager's *tactless* manner of responding to his customers' questions was quite unlike the previous store manager's congenial style.

syn: rude, undiplomatic, gauche, impolite; **ant:** tactful, discreet, diplomatic, polite

family words: tactlessness (n); tactlessly (adv)

15. wrathful: (adj) intensely angry; full of rage

Wrathful barbarians hurt and kill angrily and recklessly.

syn: furious, raging, outraged; **ant:** contented, pleased, appeased

family words: wrathfulness (n); wrathfully (adv)

Helpful Hint: One who is WRATHFUL is FULL of WRATH (anger).

26-1 ALL TYPES OF BEHAVIORS AND MOODS

You have seen many of the words below in action. Today you are asked to fill in the blank with the most appropriate word from the columns below. Each word is used only once. If you do not answer them all correctly, please do not be cross, irritable, or ornery. Yet, if you do answer them all correctly, please do not be boastful or tactless when telling others of your deed. So prove that you are not illiterate and begin this activity. Do well!

boastful	illiterate	irritable	ornery	sullen
cross	insubordinate	morbid	spiteful	tactless
deceitful	irrational	obstinate	stodgy	wrathful

1. This _____ guy really had very few polite manners and certainly did not know how to deal with people.

2. Thoughts about ants taking over the world, cars moving sideways at 60 miles per hour, and the sky falling lack common sense and are truly _____.

3. Not having received the award, she entertained some _____ thoughts on how she would show those in charge that she deserved the prize.

4. _____ people are often embarrassed that they cannot read or write.

5. Refusing to obey his teacher's command to return to the classroom, the _____ boy was later punished for his misbehavior.

6. The usually happy player became quite _____ after his team was eliminated from the playoffs.

7. That _____ older man usually took a long time to walk from his car to the supermarket.

8. The man, angered by the inconsiderate motorist who cut him off, was very _____ when anyone asked him about the incident.

9. Rather than listen to the suggestions of the other committee members, the older man remained _____.

10. Lance Armstrong, the Tour de France biking legend, is quite humble and not the least bit _____.

11. Easily annoyed by the slightest thing, the curmudgeon could only be described as one of the more _____ people I know.

12. These newspapers reported on the most shocking and _____ details of the terrible factory fire.

13. We have no proof that this usually honest man could have done anything so _____.

14. My grandfather watched the violent actions of the _____ wrestler as this strong man hit his opponent's head several times.

15. The mule, often associated with being stubborn and doing its own thing, is one of nature's most _____ animals.

26-2   IDENTIFYING THE PERSON

The actions of fifteen different people are described below. On the line next to the number, write the appropriate word next to its action or description. Then write that word's letter number as indicated within the parentheses before the description. Next, write those fifteen letters (in order) at the bottom of the page. If your answers are correct, you will spell out five three-letter words.

boastful	illiterate	irritable	ornery	sullen
cross	insubordinate	morbid	spiteful	tactless
deceitful	irrational	obstinate	stodgy	wrathful

1. _____ ___ (3) one who brags about his or her accomplishments

2. _____ ___ (3) one who never owns up to the truth

3. _____ ___ (5) one who likes to get even

4. _____ ___ (6) one who is unhappy, unsociable, and withdrawn over something

5. _____ ___ (8) one who cannot write a paragraph or read the morning newspaper

6. _____ ___ (5) one who takes a while to move along

7. _____ ___ (6) one whose anger is not easily controlled

8. _____ ___ (9) one who becomes easily annoyed about many things

9. _____ ___ (6) one who wants his or her own way most of the time

10. _____ ___ (2) one who is often hard to approach because he or she is so ill-tempered

11. _____ ___ (4) one whose ideas are often removed from logic and good sense

12. _____ ___ (3) one whose angry disposition is unattractive

13. _____ ___ (5) one who does not know how to act properly and say the right things in social occasions

14. _____ ___ (1) one who does not obey his or her superiors

15. _____ ___ (6) one who concentrates on the horrible and gruesome aspects of people, things, and events

Name: _____ Date: _____ Period: _____

26-3 OBSTINATE IS THE WAY TO GO HERE

Today it is good to be obstinate, or at least to use the word *obstinate*. Why? Ten of these clues are formed from letters found within the word *obstinate*. Fill in those ten answers, as well as the other fifteen clues from Unit 26. So be obedient and see the beauty of being *obstinate* too!

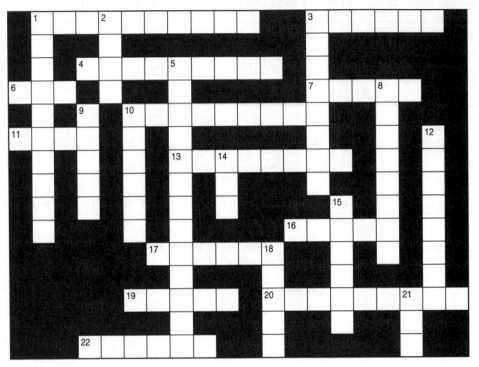

Across

1. lacking the power to reason; contrary to reason; senseless; unreasonable
3. heavily built; bulky and slow in movement
4. dishonest; representing what is known to be false as true
6. a type of metal
7. flavor; to test the flavor of; to eat or drink a small amount
10. unreasonably determined to one's own way; stubborn
11. the second letter of the Greek alphabet
13. inclined to brag; vainly proud
16. ill-tempered; cranky; irritable
17. past participle form of the verb *bite*
19. to change the appearance of wood; blemish on one's clothes or other material; dishonor; guilt
20. easily annoyed or provoked; fretful
22. gloomy; dismal; sad

Down

1. ignorant; uneducated; not able to read or write
2. to help in a crime
3. purposefully annoying; malicious; vindictive
5. not submitting to authority; disobedient
8. not having the delicate perception of the right thing to say or do without offending
9. a musical conductor and a relay team member use this
10. having an ugly or mean disposition
12. intensely angry; full of rage
14. past tense of the verb *eat*
15. gruesome; grisly; horrible
18. loud or disagreeable sound; a sound of any kind; clamor
21. a type of snake

Words, Words, Words!

26-4   CARE TO DO THIS OVER BREAKFAST?

The fifteen words from Unit 26 are waiting to be found. So are ten words (including OJ) that are commonly associated with breakfast. The words are found horizontally, vertically, and diagonally. Do you think you might want to do this Word Find over breakfast? It is up to you. Either way—enjoy!

```
c f g v o l l i r r i t a b l e o b d d
y o h g y r w w d n n a l r z s b o e j
y y f l k x n n r h s c s x h p s a c t
c t m f l r i e w b u t t e r i t s e c
x e t g e y r s r f b l o r l t i t i t
d c r b r e r n a y o e d l m e n f t s
n f y e n d a y t m r s g r m f a u f n
m q c l a y t g h d d s y s c u t l u d
n l b g d l i z f x i j k q s l e d l v
g r j a q q o v u n n h m c u b g b k n
v c h d g y n n l s a m c i l s h h n x
y n r k x e a z t d t f w t l r m a z x
b a c o n i l l i t e r a t e k c r m p
m k l c s v y o y v g r z r n a l w b x
t p c t p s p b j y g m o r b i d x j p
```

bacon	bagel	boastful
butter	cereal	coffee
cross	deceitful	egg
ham	illiterate	insubordinate
irrational	irritable	milk
morbid	obstinate	oj
ornery	spiteful	stodgy
sullen	tactless	tea
wrathful		

Unit 27

HOW MUCH—
OR HOW LITTLE

HOW MUCH—OR HOW LITTLE

1. **abundant:** (adj) very plentiful; more than sufficient; ample; well-supplied

   The church parish members sent an *abundant* number of cards to the ailing minister.

   syn: overflowing, teeming, copious, bountiful; **ant:** sparse, scarce, lacking

   family words: abundance (n); abundantly (adv); abound (v)

   Helpful Hint: If it is ABUNDANT, it is ABOUNDING.

2. **adequate:** (adj) enough or good enough for what is required or needed; sufficient; suitable

   Although this car is certainly nothing special, it is *adequate* for my needs.

   syn: ample, commensurate; **ant:** insufficient, inadequate

   family words: adequateness (n); adequately (adv)

3. **ample:** (adj) large in size, extent, scope; spacious; roomy; more than enough; abundant; plentiful

   During these past seven months, you have had *ample* opportunities to return the library book, but, unfortunately, you failed to do so.

   syn: abundant, capacious, commodious; **ant:** tight, insufficient

   family words: ampleness (n)

   Helpful Hint: Fifteen SAMPLES are AMPLE.

4. **dearth:** (n) scarcity of food supply; famine; any scarcity or lack

   Sadly, due mostly to the current harsh economic times, there has been a *dearth* of contributions and volunteers in our "Help People in Need" program.

   syn: need, paucity, absence; **ant:** abundance, supply

5. **fertile:** (adj) producing abundantly; rich in resources or invention; fruitful; prolific; able to produce young, seeds, fruit, pollen, spores, etc.

   These *fertile* fields have produced a plentiful number of crops these past three years.

   syn: fecund, procreative, yielding; **ant:** sterile, barren

   family words: fertility, fertileness (n); fertilize (v); fertilely (adv)

6. **lavish:** (adj) very generous or liberal in giving or spending, often extravagantly so; prodigal; more than enough; very abundant

   The family's *lavish* mansion included thirty rooms, two pools, and a large sauna.

   syn: profuse, luxuriant; **ant:** meager, skimpy

   family words: lavishness (n); lavishly (adv)

7. **meager:** (adj) thin; lean; emaciated; of poor quality or small amount; not full or rich; inadequate

   The sick man's *meager* frame looked as though he had not eaten in quite a long time.

   Not really wanting to do the math homework, the student gave a *meager* effort at best.

   syn: paltry; **ant:** inexhaustible

   family words: meagerness (n); meagerly (adv)

8. **myriad:** (n) any indefinitely large number; a great number of persons or things; (adj) of an indefinitely large number; countless; innumerable

   Wanting to know every last species of underwater life, the youngster was very interested in the *myriad* fish in the seas.

   syn: multitude, infinity, profusion

   Helpful Hint: *Myriad* means *many. Myriad means many. Myriad means many.*

9. **overflow:** (v) to flow or spread over or across; to flow over the brim or edge; flood; to run over; (n) an overflowing or being overflowed; the amount that overflows; surplus; an outlet for overflowing liquids

Because there was not enough room in the auditorium, the crowd had to *overflow* into the cafeteria.

The crowd *overflow* moved into the cafeteria.

Since the water began to near the sink's top, our science teacher suggested that we make sure that the *overflow* was open.

syn: flood, deluge, inundate (v)

10. **prodigal:** (adj) exceedingly or recklessly wasteful; extremely generous; lavish; extremely abundant; profuse; (n) a person who wastes his or her means; spendthrift

Whereas Johnnie managed his money carefully, his brother was *prodigal*.

The superstar's many fans heaped *prodigal* praise on her.

A *prodigal* is a synonym for a waster or a spendthrift.

syn: extravagant, excessive; **ant:** thrifty, cautious, economical

family words: prodigality (n); prodigally (adv)

11. **saturate:** (v) to cause to be thoroughly soaked or penetrated; to cause (something) to be filled, charged, supplied with the maximum that it can absorb

The cloth was *saturated* with the water that had spilled on it.

syn: imbue, drench; **ant:** dry, dehydrate

family words: saturator, saturation (n); saturated, saturable (adj)

12. **scarcity:** (n) the condition or quality of being scarce; inadequate supply; dearth; rarity; uncommonness

The *scarcity* of the baseball player's rookie trading card forced the buyer to pay dearly for the card.

syn: insufficiency, paucity, shortage; **ant:** wealth, excess, glut

family words: scarceness (n); scarce (adj); scarcely (adv)

13. **scrimp:** (v) to make too small, short; skimp; to treat stingily; to stint; to try to make ends meet; to economize

Those who enjoy living lavishly do not like to *scrimp*.

You are very hungry, so I do not want to *scrimp* on how much food you will be given.

syn: withhold; **ant:** waste, squander

family words: scrimper (n)

Helpful Hint: The hungry diner said to the waitress, "Don't SCRIMP on the SHRIMP! I am very hungry!!"

14. **swarm:** (n) a large number of bees, led by a queen, leaving one hive for another to start a new colony; a moving mass, crowd, or throng; (v) to move, collect, be present in large numbers; to abound; to be filled or crowded; to teem

The number of bees in that *swarm* was easily over one hundred.

Appreciative fans began to *swarm* the performer as she headed for her limo.

syn: mass, horde (n); cluster, bunch (v)

family words: swarmer (n)

Helpful Hint: When it is WARM, people SWARM to the beach.

15. **trivial:** (adj) unimportant; insignificant; trifling

Things that Helene considers very important, her friend considers *trivial*.

syn: petty, paltry, picayune; **ant:** vital, essential, crucial

family words: trivia, triviality (n); trivialize (v); trivially (adv)

27-1   WE WANT NO DEARTH OF CORRECT ANSWERS HERE!

If you know what the word *dearth* means, you will understand that all of the correct answers are in here. Select your answers from the group of words below. Each word is used only once.

abundant	dearth	meager	prodigal	scrimp
adequate	fertile	myriad	saturate	swarm
ample	lavish	overflow	scarcity	trivial

1. The war victims, not having eaten for a long time, appeared _____.

2. His _____ spending habits prevented him from saving money even though he had worked two jobs for the past ten months.

3. Instead of concentrating on the important issues regarding the company's position, the manager spent too much time on _____ matters.

4. Though we could probably use additional help, the number of volunteers we have here today is certainly _____.

5. Even if I sprint to the car, the heavy rains will still probably _____ my clothes.

6. When the rock band entered the arena, a(n) _____ of fans moved toward the band's members.

7. Many people use the word _____ to refer to the number of stars in the heavens.

8. Mr. and Mrs. Jones did not want to _____ on their daughter's wedding so they hired the finest musicians and reserved the most elegant catering hall.

9. Yes, the size of this apartment is _____ enough for two people to live comfortably.

10. There were so many people at the controversial school board meeting that we had to move the _____ into the cafeteria so those people could watch the proceedings on television.

11. The _____ of that baseball player's rookie card has made the card's price extremely expensive.

12. Last month's _____ rainfall made the flowers and grass grow quickly.

13. This nation's _____ farmlands allowed for the production of many different crops.

14. His multimillionaire friend had such _____ surroundings that even the most fashionable magazine photographers never turned down an invitation for a photo shoot.

15. The hungry people in this third world country suffered from a(n) _____ of nutritious food supplies.

27-2 WHAT HAVE YOU WROUGHT?

The verb *wrought* is an interesting word. It is probably best known as part of the first electronic long-distance message sent by Samuel Morse on May 24, 1844, from Washington, D.C., to Baltimore. His words were "What God hath wrought." Today you will show that you know the present tense of the verb *wrought*. Write the correct number in the appropriate boxes of this Magic Square. (One is done for you.) If your answers are correct, the rows, columns, and the two diagonals will add up to the same number. Then you have wrought well!

A=	B=6	C=	D=
E=	F=	G=	H=
I=	J=	K=	L=
M=	N=	O=	P=

Magic Number:

_____

A. swarm	**E.** adequate	**I.** lavish	**M.** myriad
B. scrimp	**F.** trivial	**J.** work	**N.** meager
C. abundant	**G.** fertile	**K.** prodigal	**O.** ample
D. saturate	**H.** dearth	**L.** scarcity	**P.** overflow

1. unimportant; insignificant
2. very generous or liberal in giving or spending, often extravagantly
3. large in size, extent, scope; spacious
4. to cause to be thoroughly soaked or penetrated
5. any indefinitely large number; a great number of persons or things
6. to make too small or short; to treat stingily
7. scarcity of food supply; famine; any scarcity or lack
8. exceedingly or recklessly wasteful; extremely generous
9. very plentiful; more than sufficient; well-supplied
10. surplus
11. present tense of the verb *wrought*
12. enough or good enough for what is required or needed; sufficient; suitable
13. inadequate supply; rarity; uncommonness
14. producing abundantly; rich in resources or invention; fruitful; prolific
15. a large number of bees; a moving mass, crowd, or throng
16. thin; lean; emaciated; of poor quality or small amount

27-3 LARGE OR SMALL OR JUST ENOUGH?

Is each of these words associated with the concept of *large* (L), *small* (S), or *just enough* (JE)? Write the corresponding letters on the line next to the word. If your answers are correct, there should be nine "large" words, five "small" words, and one that is "just enough." When you are finished with each designation, write an illustrative sentence for each of these fifteen words on the lines below. (Continue on the back of this sheet if necessary.)

1. _____ abundant

2. _____ adequate

3. _____ ample

4. _____ dearth

5. _____ fertile

6. _____ lavish

7. _____ meager

8. _____ myriad

9. _____ overflow

10. _____ prodigal

11. _____ saturate

12. _____ scarcity

13. _____ scrimp

14. _____ swarm

15. _____ trivial

27-4   SOUNDS LIKE . . .

Although the activity's title might seem a bit odd at first, it does make sense when you know what you are asked to do here. The Unit 27 word is in Column A. A word (or two) that sounds like Column A's definition is in Column B. On the line in Column C, write the word that is a synonym for Column A's word and that sounds like the words in Column B. (One is done for you.) So perk up your ears, and show how well you know these words and their synonyms!

Column A	Column B	Column C
1. abundant	very bountiful	very plentiful
2. adequate	rebuff	_____
3. ample	gracious	_____
4. dearth	tack	_____
5. fertile	terrific	_____
6. lavish	onerous	_____
7. meager	appreciated	_____
8. myriad	great lumber	_____
9. overflow	head over	_____
10. prodigal	excuse	_____
11. saturate	thoroughly poke	_____
12. scarcity	inadequate reply	_____
13. scrimp	hypothesize	_____
14. swarm	rebound	_____
15. trivial	stifling	_____

Units 25–27   REVIEW TEST

Directions: Please circle the correct **synonym.** Then write the answer's corresponding letter on the line next to the question's number. Each question is worth four points.

1. ____ **boastful**   (a) modest   (b) forgetful   (c) bragging

2. ____ **cross**   (a) tender   (b) irritable   (c) agreeable

3. ____ **myriad**   (a) few   (b) great number of people or things   (c) cause

4. ____ **archaic**   (a) new   (b) antiquated   (c) weird

5. ____ **innovate**   (a) to introduce new methods or devices   (b) to change names   (c) to fluctuate

6. ____ **contemporary**   (a) angry   (b) fluent in several languages   (c) modern

7. ____ **deceitful**   (a) dishonest   (b) local   (c) silly

8. ____ **wrathful**   (a) full of rage   (b) full of cheer   (c) full of knowledge

9. ____ **obsolete**   (a) broken   (b) beginning   (c) no longer in fashion

10. ____ **ornery**   (a) very decorated   (b) having an ugly or mean disposition   (c) sarcastic

Directions: Please circle the correct **antonym.** Then write the answer's corresponding letter on the line next to the question's number. Each question is worth four points.

11. ____ **callow**   (a) materialistic   (b) experienced   (c) watchful

12. ____ **dearth**   (a) life   (b) oversupply   (c) example

13. ____ **irritable**   (a) dirty   (b) composed   (c) sufficient

14. ____ **extinct**   (a) smelly   (b) powerful   (c) living

15. ____ **scarcity**   (a) glut   (b) pause   (c) friendly

16. ____ **prodigal**   (a) economical   (b) rich   (c) holy

17. ____ **ample**   (a) impatient   (b) patient   (c) insufficient

18. ____ **irrational**   (a) reasonable   (b) contained   (c) handsome

19. ____ **sullen**   (a) buoyant   (b) current   (c) unruly

20. ____ **regenerate**   (a) to demolish   (b) to borrow   (c) to return

Units 25–27   REVIEW TEST (continued)

Directions: Please circle the word that correctly **completes** the sentence. Then write the answer's corresponding letter on the line next to the question's number. Each question is worth four points.

21. ____ The wealthy banquet hostess wanted her guests to be impressed by her formal affair so she did not _____ on any aspect of the event.
    (a) regenerate   (b) renovate   (c) scrimp

22. ____ The _____ of termites that filled this section of our basement wall caused structural problems.   **(a) dearth   (b) swarm   (c) scarcity**

23. ____ The _____ lived a wasteful existence, never saving anything.
    (a) veteran   (b) novice   (c) prodigal

24. ____ Embarrassed by his inability to read or write, the _____ dropped out of school.   **(a) contemporary   (b) illiterate   (c) crone**

25. ____ The _____ person's words often hurt and embarrassed others.
    (a) tactless   (b) extinct   (c) stodgy

Unit 28

SOCIAL STUDIES CLASS

SOCIAL STUDIES CLASS

1. **allegiance:** (n) the obligation of support and loyalty to one's ruler, government, or country; loyalty or devotion to a person or cause

    Janine's *allegiance* to her country was exemplified when she joined the army during the war.

    syn: fidelity, adherence; **ant:** disloyalty, betrayal

    family words: allegiant (adj, n); allege (v)

2. **alliance:** (n) union or joining of persons, groups, or countries for mutual benefit; close association for a common objective

    Since the two ancient, smaller cities could not defeat the strongest and largest city in the region, they formed an *alliance*.

    syn: treaty, pact, understanding; **ant:** difference, disparity

    Helpful Hint: When countries are in an ALLiance, they are ALL in it together.

3. **boycott:** (v) to join together in refusing to deal with, so as to punish or coerce; to refuse to buy, sell, or use; (n) an act or instance of boycotting

    Because this company never paid their laborers more than minimum wage, we decided to *boycott* its products and purchase a legitimate company's goods instead.

    The *boycott* of that movie was quite successful since the film production company lost quite a bit of money.

    syn: exclude, ban, blackball (v)

4. **delegate:** (n) a person authorized or sent to speak and act for others; representative, as at a convention; (v) to send or appoint as a representative; to entrust (authority, power) to a person acting as one's agent or representative

    Now that both sides refused to negotiate, we thought it best to send a *delegate* from each side to see if these problem solvers could work out the difficult situation.

    If it is an important matter, my boss will usually do the job herself rather than *delegate* it to one of her workers.

    syn: deputy, envoy, proxy (n); empower, authorize (v)

    family words: delegation, delegacy (n)

5. **enforce:** (v) to give force to; to urge; to bring about or impose (to enforce one's desire)

    Since her only suggesting that the rule be followed was unsuccessful, the teacher now had to *enforce* the rule for it to work out better.

    syn: compel, oblige

    family words: enforcement, enforcer (n); enforceable (adj)

    Helpful Hint: *Enforce* = "en-" (the act of) + "- force" (to pressure)

6. **immigrate:** (v) to come into a new country, region, or environment in order to settle there; to migrate

    Many foreigners *immigrated* to America hoping that they would find good jobs and a better way of life in the new country.

    family words: immigration, immigrant (n)

    Helpful Hint: Those who IMMIGRATE come INTO a country.

7. **liberty:** (n) freedom or release from slavery or imprisonment; rights possessed by the people of a community, state; right or exemption from compulsion

    After spending two months in jail, the released prisoner appreciated his new *liberty*.

    In a democracy, one's *liberty,* the freedom to lawfully do what one desires, is taken for granted.

    syn: independence, emancipation, permission; **ant:** imprisonment, bondage, captivity

8. **militia:** (n) in the United States, all able-bodied male citizens between 18 and 45 years old who are not already members of the regular armed forces; members of the National Guard and of the Reserves (of the Army, Air Force, Coast Guard, Navy, and Marine Corps); originally, any military force; later, any army composed of citizens rather than professional soldiers, called up in time of emergency

   In those years the *militia* was called upon to fight these wars.

   family words: militate (v)

9. **millennium:** (n) a period of 1,000 years; a 1,000th anniversary or commemoration

   Ten centuries constitute a *millennium.*

   How did your family celebrate the *millennium*?

   family words: millennialism, millennialist (n); millennial (adj)

10. **monarchy:** (n) a government or state headed by a monarch (single or sole ruler of a state)

    Whereas our democracy is headed by a president who works along with the Congress and the Senate, a *monarchy* is led by a sole and absolute ruler.

    family words: monarchism (n); monarchal, monarchial, monarchist, monarchical, (adj); monarchially (adv)

    Helpful Hint: *Monarchy* = "mon-" (one) + "-archy" (head or leader)

11. **propaganda:** (n) any systematic, widespread dissemination (publishing or making known officially) or promotion of particular ideas, doctrines, practices, etc., to further one's own cause or to damage an opposing one; ideas, doctrines, or allegations so spread; (now often used disparagingly to connote deception or distortion)

    The dissenting group spread its *propaganda* to try to overthrow the government.

    syn: indoctrination

    family words: propagandism (n); propagandize (v)

12. **ratify:** (v) to approve or confirm; esp. to give sanction to

    We will need at least ten more votes in order to *ratify* this agreement between labor and management.

    syn: endorse, certify; **ant:** veto, oppose

    family words: ratification (n)

13. **reformer:** (n) a person who seeks to bring about reform, esp. political or social reform

    Seeing that the women of her time had few opportunities, the tireless *reformer* worked diligently for equal rights for both genders.

    family words: reform (n, v); reformation, reformism, reformatory (n); reformed (adj)

14. **rural:** (adj) of or characteristic of the country, country life, or country people; rustic; living in the country; having to do with farming

    He preferred living in the *rural* part of the state rather than living in a major city.

    syn: rustic, countrified, pastoral; **ant:** urban, citified, sophisticated

    family words: ruralist, ruralism, ruralization (n); ruralize (v); rurally (adv)

    Helpful Hint: Country AL loved all things RURAL.

15. **urban:** (adj) of, in, constituting, or comprising a city or town; characteristic of the city as distinguished from the country

    She preferred *urban* excitement rather than rural tranquility.

    syn: citified, sophisticated; **ant:** rural, pastoral

    family words: urbanism, urbanite, urbaneness (n); urbanize (v); urbanely

    Helpful Hint: City DAN loved all things URBAN.

28-1   TAKE ONE, THEN TWO, AND THEN #15 DOES IT ALONE

Use the words below to fill in the blanks. Each word is used only one time. On the line next to the question's number, write that word's letter or letters as indicated by the number(s) in parentheses. Each two consecutive answers spell out a three-letter word. Number 15's letters spell out their own word. So if you take one letter, then two letters, and then allow #15 its own three letters, you will spell out eight three-letter words. Good luck!

allegiance	delegate	liberty	monarchy	reformer
alliance	enforce	militia	propaganda	rural
boycott	immigrate	millennium	ratify	urban

1. _____ Since authorities feared possible riots at the controversial concert, part of the state _____ was stationed in the parking lots near the arena. **(2)**

2. _____ Many people were nervous about computer crashes at the start of the new _____ at midnight on January 1. **(3,4)**

3. _____ Civil rights leaders suggested that customers _____ stores that paid their workers less than minimum wage. **(7)**

4. _____ The veterans pledge _____ to our country's flag. **(7,8)**

5. _____ Our boss knows exactly how to _____ work to his staff members in order to get the best production and efficiency. **(6)**

6. _____ In order to protect themselves against larger, more powerful nations, these three countries formed an _____. **(7,8)**

7. _____ Traffic congestion and crowded city sidewalks are two of the many difficulties that _____ officials must face in the coming years. **(5)**

8. _____ The women's rights _____ spoke out against the mistreatment women faced in that part of the world. **(4,5)**

9. _____ In theory, as well as in practice, a democracy, unlike a _____, is ruled by many, not just one person. **(2)**

10. _____ "We will need at least two more votes in order to _____ this amendment," the politician informed the reporter. **(2,3)**

11. _____ Cows, pigs, and cornfields are all part of the _____ setting. **(1)**

12. _____ Please do not believe the _____ that the rebellious, threatening group is distributing. **(5,6)**

13. _____ During the early part of the last century, many Europeans chose to _____ to America in search of an improved way of living. **(7)**

14. _____ I am not at _____ to tell you what was discussed in the closed-door meeting last night. **(5,6)**

15. _____ My principal and her assistant principals will begin to _____ the new dress code that was recently approved by the school board. **(3,4,5)**

28-2   LET'S CALL IT A TIE—AT LEAST IN POINTS

Each boldfaced word has a definition next to it. Some of these definitions are correct; others are not. If the definition is correct, write YES on the line next to the word's question number. If it is not the correct definition, write NO on the line.

　　　Then add up the point values of all the seven YES answers; do the same for the eight NO answers. Use the lines at the bottom of the page to record these point values. Both the YES and NO answers have the same worth, 31 points.

1. _____ (worth 2 points) **ratify:** to give sanction to

2. _____ (worth 3 points) **militia:** an army

3. _____ (worth 6 points) **monarchy:** democratic type of government

4. _____ (worth 1 point) **rural:** pertaining to the city

5. _____ (worth 3 points) **delegate:** to send or appoint as a representative

6. _____ (worth 2 points) **allegiance:** disloyalty towards one's government

7. _____ (worth 3 points) **enforce:** to allow; to discourage

8. _____ (worth 1 point) **reformer:** one who wants the continuation of the existing social and political atmosphere

9. _____ (worth 7 points) **millennium:** period of 1,000 years

10. _____ (worth 6 points) **immigrate:** emigrate

11. _____ (worth 5 points) **urban:** characteristic of the country

12. _____ (worth 3 points) **liberty:** freedom or release from slavery or imprisonment

13. _____ (worth 8 points) **boycott:** to refuse to buy, sell, or use

14. _____ (worth 5 points) **propaganda:** widespread promotion of ideas, doctrines, and practices of one's cause and damage to an opposing cause

15. _____ (worth 7 points) **alliance:** disunion amongst parties

　　YES answers: _____ Total: _____

　　NO answers: _____ Total: _____

28-3   WORDS WITHIN WORDS

All fifteen of Unit 28's words are answers in this crossword puzzle. So are eight other words that are found within some of Unit 28's words. Write the correct answers to these twenty-three clues in their appropriate spaces.

Across

3. part of a race; body part
5. to come into a new country, region, or environment in order to settle there
7. the obligation of support and loyalty to one's ruler, government, or country
10. having to do with the country (as opposed to the city)
12. shape, outline, configuration
14. to join together in refusing to deal with, so as to punish or coerce; to refuse to buy, sell, or use
16. frame of metal bars for holding fuel in a fireplace; to annoy; vex
17. curve or bend; a curved structure
18. period of 1,000 years
19. one who advocates social or political change
20. characteristic of the city (as opposed to the country)

Down

1. government headed by a single or sole ruler of the state
2. right or exemption from compulsion; freedom or release from slavery; rights possessed by citizens
3. envoy or ambassador
4. person authorized or sent to speak and act for others; representative; to entrust another
6. sick
7. union or joining of persons or groups for mutual benefit; close association for a common objective
8. to urge; to bring about or impose
9. narrow, collapsible bed
11. widespread, systematic spreading of ideas advocating one cause and damaging another's cause
13. army
15. to approve or confirm; to give sanction to
16. way to get in and out of a room or a yard

28-4   DO YOU KNOW YOUR U.S. PRESIDENTS?

Match up the fifteen words in Column A with their definitions in Column B. Write the corresponding two-letter answer in the space after the Column A number. If your answers are correct, you will spell out (in consecutive letters) the last names of five U.S. presidents. (Be careful!) Write these names at the bottom of the page. Be patriotic and show your historical knowledge!

Column A	Column B
1. _____ allegiance	**ag.** characteristic of the country, country life, or country people
2. _____ alliance	**an.** comprising a city or town; characteristic of the city
3. _____ boycott	**da.** a period of 1,000 years
4. _____ delegate	**el.** a person authorized or sent to speak and act for others; to entrust to a person acting as one's agent
5. _____ enforce	**ev.** to join together in refusing to deal with, so as to punish or coerce
6. _____ immigrate	**lk.** to approve or confirm
7. _____ liberty	**ma.** freedom or release from slavery or imprisonment; rights possessed by community members
8. _____ militia	**ms.** a government or state headed by a single or sole ruler
9. _____ millennium	**na.** type of army
10. _____ monarchy	**os.** union or joining of persons, groups, or countries for mutual benefit
11. _____ propaganda	**po.** systematic, widespread promotion of ideas, doctrines, or practices to further a cause and damage an opposing cause
12. _____ ratify	**re.** a person who seeks to bring about change, esp. political or social reform
13. _____ reformer	**ro.** loyalty or devotion to a person or cause
14. _____ rural	**ru.** to come into a new country, region, or environment in order to settle there
15. _____ urban	**tt.** to give force to; urge; to bring about or impose

_____

_____

Unit 29

SCIENCE CLASS

SCIENCE CLASS

1. **acquire:** (adj) to get or gain by one's own efforts; to come to have as one's own; to get possession

   The family *acquired* the land through an inheritance.

   My friend *acquired* his father's hair and build.

   syn: obtain, attain, procure; **ant:** lose, forfeit, discard

   family words: acquisition, acquirement (n); acquired, acquirable (adj)

2. **astronomy:** (n) the science of the universe in which the stars, planets, etc., are studied, including their origins, evolution, composition, sizes, and more

   Having acquired a telescope and several books about stars and the planets when he was seven years old, Ed developed an avid interest in *astronomy*.

   family words: astronomical (adj); astronomically (adv)

   Helpful Hint: *Astronomy* = "astr-" (stars) + "-nomy" (law). Thus, *astronomy* is the law of stars.

3. **biology:** (n) the science that deals with the origin, history, physical characteristics, life processes, and more of plants and animals

   Biology majors study the origins, physical characteristics, and life processes of plants and animals.

   family words: biologist (n); biological (adj); biologically (adv)

4. **botany:** (n) the branch of biology that studies plants, their life, structure, growth, and more

   Anyone with a great interest in plant life might consider a career in *botany*.

   family words: botanist (n); botanical (adj); botanically (adv)

5. **condensation:** (n) the act of condensing, as the reduction of a gas to a liquid; the abridgement of a piece of writing; the act of being condensed

   The students were amazed by the *condensation* of that gas into a liquid.

   The book's *condensation* did not do justice to the author's character development skill.

   syn: precipitation, digest

   family words: condensability (n); condense (v); condensed, condensable (adj)

6. **constellation:** (n) the arbitrary configuration of stars, usually named after some object, animal, or mythological being; any brilliant cluster or gathering

   Noting our interest in stars, our science teacher told us to read about the *constellations*, specifically Ursa Minor, Ursa Major, and Andromeda.

   syn: array, collection

   family words: constellate (v); constellatory (adj)

   Helpful Hint: *Constellation* = "con-" (with) + "-stella" (stars)

7. **eclipse:** (n) the part or total obscuring (covering) of one celestial body by another, especially of the sun when the moon comes between it and the earth (solar eclipse); overshadowing or cutting off of the light; (v) to darken or obscure; to outshine or surpass

   The moon passing through the earth's shadow causes a lunar *eclipse*.

   Juan's outstanding musical performance *eclipsed* that of his less talented sister.

   syn: erase, hide, overshadow (v)

8. **ecology:** (n) the branch of biology that deals with the relations between a specific organism and its environment

   His interest in *ecology* motivated Alfredo to organize several "Keep It Clean" and "Don't Be a Litterbug" campaigns in his town.

   family words: ecologist (n); ecological (adj); ecologically (adv)

   Helpful Hint: *Ecology* = "eco-" (habitat, environment) + "-logy" (study of)

9. **evaporate:** (v) to change (a liquid or solid) into vapor; to remove moisture from (milk, vegetables, fruits, etc.) by heating or drying

   This puddle will quickly *evaporate* and disappear once the sun appears.

   syn: vanish, disappear (v)

   family words: evaporation, evaporator, evaporability (n); evaporable, evaporative (adj)

10. **identical:** (adj) the very same; exactly alike or equal; designating twins that are very much alike in appearance

    Since these two drawings are *identical,* they are exactly alike in every way.

    syn: uniform, twin; **ant:** different, separate, distinct, unlike, opposite

    family words: identically (adv)

11. **lunar:** (adj) of or on the moon; like the moon

    The *lunar* observations of the scientist who had already written several books about the moon were recorded and published by his scientific study group.

    family words: lunarian, lunatic (n)

12. **predator:** (n) a person or animal that robs, plunders, or exploits others; one that lives by capturing and feeding off others

    The *predator* quickly captured the prey under the porch.

    family words: predatoriness (n); predatory (adj); predatorially (adv)

13. **prey:** (n) an animal hunted or killed for food by another animal; a person or thing that falls victim to someone or something; (v) to plunder; to rob; to hunt or kill others for food

    After seizing its *prey,* the predator carried it to another section of the forest.

    The larger animal *preyed* upon the frightened smaller one.

    syn: booty, boot, pillage, victim, mark (n); catch, quarry (v)

    family words: preyer (n)

    Helpful Hint: The PREY PRAYED that its predator stayed away.

14. **recycle:** (v) to use again and again, as in a single supply of water in cooling or washing

    Our community members strongly want to *recycle* bottles and cans to use them again at a later date.

    syn: reclaim, restore, regenerate

    family words: recyclable (adj)

15. **soluble:** (adj) that can be dissolved; able to pass into solution; capable of being solved

    Kendra's brother did not believe that sugar is *soluble* in water until he saw the cube dissolve.

    Even though the math problem seems very difficult, it is *soluble* if you take your time and think carefully about it.

    family words: solubility (n); solubly (adv); solubilize (v)

29-1   MAKING SENSE OUT OF SCIENCE

Fill in each blank with a word from the list below. Each word is used only once. If your answers are correct, you have certainly made sense out of science!

acquire	botany	eclipse	identical	prey
astronomy	condensation	ecology	lunar	recycle
biology	constellation	evaporate	predator	soluble

1. My neighbor, who loves to use big words to impress us, refers to rain as _____.

2. As president of the local _____ club, Clarissa urged members to pick up debris and to place cans and bottles in their proper receptacles.

3. Did all of the water in the basement _____, or are there still several small puddles down there?

4. The number of books about the physical characteristics and life processes of plants and animals Wanda owned showed her interest in _____.

5. Yesterday in science class we discussed the moon and many of its _____ characteristics.

6. Although the slighter _____ tried to escape its much larger hunter, this smaller possible victim was no match for the quicker and more agile opponent.

7. We were able to view at least the major _____ with our more powerful telescope.

8. From whom did you _____ the beautiful necklace that you are wearing?

9. Is the material _____ or will it remain in its present solid form?

10. My town's officials stressed how important it is to _____ bottles, cans, and newspapers.

11. The twins are _____, so it is quite difficult to tell them apart from one another.

12. We were forewarned to wear special glasses when we observed the _____.

13. His interest in plants motivated him to seek a career in _____.

14. Since Barry always loved to read about planets and stars, it was no surprise that he studied _____ as his college major.

15. The huge _____ had no trouble capturing and devouring its much smaller victim.

29-2   SCIENCE WORDS

Write the correct letters of the words in the appropriate places. Each word is used only once. Then write the number letter of the answer as indicated by the number in parentheses. (One is done for you.) If your answers are correct, you will spell out two words and a shortened form of a word—all associated with science.

acquire	botany	eclipse	identical	prey
astronomy	condensation	ecology	lunar	recycle
biology	constellation	evaporate	predator	soluble

1. _g_   _e_ _c_ _o_ _l_ _o_ _g_ _y_: the branch of biology that deals with the relations between a specific organism and its environment **(6)**

2. ___   __ __ __ __ __ __ __: the partial or total obscuring of one celestial body by another; to outshine or surpass **(1)**

3. ___   __ __ __ __ __ __ __ __ __ __ __ __ __: the arbitrary configuration of stars **(12)**

4. ___   __ __ __ __ __ __ __ __ __: the very same; exactly alike or equal **(9)**

5. ___   __ __ __ __ __ __ __ __: a person or animal that robs, plunders, or exploits others; one that lives by capturing and feeding off others **(7)**

6. ___   __ __ __ __ __ __ __: the science that deals with the origin, history, physical characteristics, life processes, and more of plants and animals **(6)**

7. ___   __ __ __ __ __ __ __: to use again and again **(4)**

8. ___   __ __ __ __ __ __ __ __ __: the science of the universe in which the stars, planets, and more are studied **(6)**

9. ___   __ __ __ __ __ __: the branch of biology that studies plants, their life, structure, growth, and more **(4)**

10. ___   __ __ __ __ __ __ __ __ __ __ __ __: the act of reducing the volume of or making more compact **(9)**

11. ___   __ __ __ __ __: of or on the moon **(2)**

12. ___   __ __ __ __: an animal hunted or killed for food by another animal; a person or thing that falls victim to someone or something **(2)**

13. ___   __ __ __ __ __ __ __: that can be dissolved; able to pass into solution; capable of being solved **(7)**

14. ___   __ __ __ __ __ __ __: to get or gain by one's own efforts; get possession **(5)**

15. ___   __ __ __ __ __ __ __ __ __: to change (a liquid or solid) into vapor; to remove moisture from something by heating or drying **(2)**

29-3 THE DICTIONARY TO THE RESCUE?

You might need the dictionary for this activity. Then again, perhaps you want to go it alone at first. The fifteen words from Unit 29 are found in Column A. Their origins or derivations are found in Column B. Match the items in Column B with their Column A counterparts by writing the appropriate letter on the line next to the question's number. Write these words at the bottom of this sheet. If your answers are correct, you will spell out four words.

Column A	Column B
1. _____ biology	**a.** moon + shine bright
2. _____ evaporate	**b.** plant + suffix forming nouns
3. _____ predator	**d.** to loosen, release, free
4. _____ identical	**e.** very dense
5. _____ prey	**i.** out, from + to emit vapor
6. _____ lunar	**n.** environment + word, study, thought
7. _____ astronomy	**o.** again + circle
8. _____ constellation	**p.** to prey upon
9. _____ botany	**q.** the same
10. _____ recycle	**r.** star + name
11. _____ ecology	**s.** to seek
12. _____ soluble	**t.** with + to shine (star)
13. _____ acquire	**u.** to seize, to take
14. _____ condensation	**w.** to leave out, fail
15. _____ eclipse	**z.** to live + word, thought, study

_____

_____

Words, Words, Words!

29-4   THE PARADE OF SCIENTISTS

The first names of five very well-known scientists are given as clues in this puzzle. Fill in the last name of each scientist and the fifteen words from Unit 29. If you correctly fill in this crossword puzzle, then you, as the scientists do in this puzzle, can parade around!

Across

2. science dealing with origin, history, and physical characteristics of plants and animals
3. part or total covering of one celestial body by another
8. the very same; alike or equal
9. to get or gain by one's own efforts; get possession
10. to change (a liquid or solid) into vapor; to remove moisture from
15. branch of biology that studies plants, their life, structure, growth, and more
16. Sir Isaac _____
17. that can be dissolved; capable of being solved; able to pass into solution
18. the arbitrary configuration of stars; any brilliant cluster or gathering

Down

1. Marie _____
2. Alexander Graham _____
4. the act of reducing the volume of or making more compact; the act of condensing, as a reduction of a gas to a liquid
5. of or related to the moon
6. a person or animal that robs, plunders, or exploits others; one that lives by capturing and feeding off others
7. the branch of biology that deals with the relations between a specific organism and its environment
9. the science of the universe in which the stars, planets, and more are studied
11. an animal hunted or killed for food by another animal; to plunder; rob
12. to use again and again
13. Benjamin _____
14. Albert _____

Unit 30

ALL ABOUT THE SENSES

ALL ABOUT THE SENSES

1. **aroma:** (n) pleasant odor

    We detected the steak's *aroma* as we neared the restaurant's door.

    syn: fragrance, scent, perfume

    family words: aromatize (v); aromatic (adj); aromatically (adv)

2. **audio:** (adj) related to the ears; acoustic

    Visual pertains to the eyes, and *audio* pertains to the ears.

3. **bellow:** (v) to make a loud deep sound like that of a bull; to roar; (n) a loud, angry roar

    The large animal's *bellow* was so loud that it could be heard almost a half mile away.

    syn: bawl, blare, shout (v); shout, yell, holler, howl (n)

4. **delectable:** (adj) very pleasing; delightful; pleasing to the taste; delicious

    Chefs would be disappointed to hear that their meals were nothing less than *delectable*.

    syn: charming, appealing, savory; **ant:** unappealing, disagreeable, tasteless

    family words: delectability (n); delectably (adv)

5. **din:** (n) loud, continuous noise; confused clamor or uproar; (v) to beset with a din; to repeat insistently or noisily

    That protesting crowd's *din* could be heard from several blocks away.

    The truck's damaged muffler *dinned* the pedestrians.

    syn: riot, racket (n); clatter, clash, bang, blast (v)

6. **durable:** (adj) able to endure; lasting

    Our *durable* tent has lasted for thirteen camping seasons.

    syn: sturdy, solid, strong; **ant:** shoddy, cheap, perishable

    family words: durability (n); durably (adv)

    Helpful Hint: *Durable* = "dur-" (hard) + "-able" (able to do so)

7. **elate:** (v) to raise the spirits of; to make very proud, happy, or joyful

    News that his grandmother's operation was a success *elated* Roberto.

    syn: excite, arouse, stimulate

    family words: elation, elatedness (n); elatedly (adv)

8. **inaudible:** (adj) unable to be heard

    From where we were seated so far back of the auditorium, the orator's words were *inaudible*.

    family words: inaudibility (n); inaudibly (adv)

    Helpful Hint: *Inaudible* = "in-" (not) + "-audible" (able to be heard)

9. **nasal:** (adj) related to the nose

    Geraldo's *nasal* problems started when he broke his nose two years ago.

    family words: nasality (n); nasally (adv)

Words, Words, Words!

10. **oral:** (adj) uttered by the mouth; spoken; using speech; having to do with what is spoken; referring to the mouth

    Oral refers to that which is spoken rather than that which is written.

    Dentists stress the importance of good *oral* hygiene, including semi-annual checkups, daily brushing, and regular flossing.

    syn: verbal, voiced

    family words: oralism, oralist (n); orally (adv)

11. **pungent:** (adj) sharp in smell or taste; acrid; poignant; expressive; biting

    Your nose will easily detect this *pungent* spice.

    The writer's *pungent* satire poked fun at all levels of society.

    syn: (for "sharp in smell") aromatic, tangy, spicy (adj); (for "biting") piercing, penetrating, pointed

    family words: pungency (n); pungently (adv)

12. **putrid:** (adj) stinking due to decay; decomposed; rotten and foul-smelling

    A dump's *putrid* smells can easily sicken people.

    syn: rotting, rancid, decaying, decayed; **ant:** fresh, healthy, pure, wholesome

    family words: putridity, putridness (n); putridly (adv)

13. **tactile:** (adj) related to the sense of touch; that can be perceived by the touch; tangible

    The infant's *tactile* reflexes were most obvious whenever his parents tickled him.

    family words: tactility (n)

14. **tart:** (adj) agreeably sharp to the taste; (n) a small pie or pastry shell containing jelly, custard, or fruit

    Hector made an odd-looking face when he bit into the *tart* apple.

    Instead of ordering a donut in the bakery, my dad opted for a *tart*.

    syn: sour, tangy, acerbic; **ant:** sweet, sugary, honeyed

    family words: tartly (adv)

15. **visual:** (adj) connected with or used in seeing; pertaining to the eyes; visible

    Because of his chronic *visual* problem, Isaac often visits his eye doctor.

    syn: (for "connected with" and "pertaining to the eyes") optic, optical, ocular; (for "visible") observable, discernable, noticeable; **ant:** (for "visible") invisible, imperceptible, unnoticeable, hidden

    family words: visualization (n); visualize (v); visually (adv)

30-1 A CROSSWORD FOR THE SENSES

All twenty of these clues and answers deal with *sense* in one form or another. Some deal with your five senses (and perhaps sixth sense) while others deal with the word *sense* itself. Fill in the crossword puzzle's spaces and make sense out of this crossword for the senses!

Across

1. sense dealing with currency (_____ sense)
2. sense that supposedly everyone has (_____ sense)
5. to a limited degree or extent (_____ _____ sense)
8. pertaining to the eyes; visible
9. pleasing to the taste; delicious
11. an "extra sense" (the _____ sense)
12. pleasant odor
15. able to endure; lasting
16. prefix meaning *not* as in _____ sense
17. agreeably sharp to the taste

Down

1. expression meaning to be logical (to _____ sense)
3. uttered by the mouth; spoken; having to do with what is spoken
4. related to the nose
5. unable to be heard
6. to raise the spirits of; make very proud, happy, or joyful
7. a loud, angry roar
9. loud, continuous noise; to repeat insistently or noisily
10. stinking due to decay; decomposed; rotten and foul-smelling
12. related to the ears
13. sharp in taste or smell; acrid; poignant; biting
14. related to the sense of touch; tangible

30-2   THE FINAL LETTERS

Fill in the blank before each definition with a word from the columns below. Each word is used only once. If your answers are correct, the last letter of each word (in consecutive order) will spell out three consecutive words. Write these words at the bottom of this page.

aroma	delectable	elate	oral	tactile
audio	din	inaudible	pungent	tart
bellow	durable	nasal	putrid	visual

1. _____ stinking due to decay; decomposed; rotten and foul-smelling

2. _____ very pleasing; delightful; pleasing to the taste; delicious

3. _____ related to the nose

4. _____ able to endure; lasting

5. _____ agreeably sharp to the taste; a small pie or pastry shell containing jelly, custard, or fruit

6. _____ to raise the spirits of; make very proud, happy, or joyful

7. _____ to make a loud, deep sound, like that of a bull; to roar; loud, angry roar

8. _____ unable to be heard

9. _____ connected with, or used, in seeing; pertaining to the eyes; visible

10. _____ uttered by the mouth; spoken; using speech

11. _____ related to the ears

12. _____ pleasant odor

13. _____ sharp in smell or taste; acrid; poignant; expressive; biting

14. _____ related to the sense of touch; tangible

15. _____ loud, continuous noise; confused clamor or uproar

_____

30-3 JUST ADD SOME SWEETENERS

Since this vocabulary unit is all about your senses, we have decided to give you a treat. Well, not just one treat—seven sweet treats. Yes, in addition to the fifteen words in this unit, we have added seven sweet words for you to find. The words are arranged horizontally, vertically, and diagonally. Circle the twenty-two words, and then, on a separate sheet of paper, define the fifteen Unit 30 words. Tasty treat? Mmmm.

```
b t h i n a u d i b l e g x t g s d w r
q e z r k h x s l r w h y m z n h z x g
d b l y s y n x v w w m l b p y r q b y
b e k l b x b p c f f r b g w j j n x z
n m l j o v l m v f q q q i y t k h h d
q j y e n w c f p r f n v d s d b j j b
h c g g c n l k o y b a z g y c t m t z
q d m b p t w j m r p s t q j w u g a s
z l o u q e a q d p a a z p g s k i c z
f v c n n l q b l i r l p u n g e n t t
w l a b u a x w l e n q g t q g b m i m
w j k f n t v s j e h z p r h g r k l p
h m e x j e h f s l v t v i w z e y e d
f v i s u a l c o o k i e d u r a b l e
m j s a r o m a t a r t g t a u d i o m
```

aroma	cake	elate	putrid
audio	cookie	inaudible	tactile
bellow	delectable	nasal	tart
biscuit	din	oral	visual
bread	donut	pie	
bun	durable	pungent	

30-4 SENSING YOUR CAPABILITY

The word *capability* has been included with the fifteen words from Unit 30. Why? It will help you get a sense of how capable you are with this activity. Match the words with their definitions by writing the correct number of the definition in the lettered box within the Magic Square. If your answers are correct, the rows, columns, and two diagonals will add up to the same number. Then you will truly, as the activity's title suggests, be sensing your capability.

A=	B=6	C=	D=
E=	F=	G=	H=
I=	J=	K=	L=
M=	N=	O=	P=

Magic Number:

_____

A. delectable
B. nasal
C. din
D. putrid

E. tactile
F. tart
G. capability
H. durable

I. visual
J. audio
K. inaudible
L. aroma

M. oral
N. bellow
O. elate
P. pungent

1. to make a loud, deep sound, like that of a bull; to roar; a loud, angry roar
2. faculty; feeling; sense
3. pleasant odor
4. pleasing to the taste; delicious; delightful
5. unable to be heard
6. pertaining to the nose
7. pertaining to the mouth
8. able to endure; lasting
9. related to the sense of touch; tangible
10. sharp in taste or smell; acrid; poignant
11. to repeat insistently or noisily; loud, continuous noise
12. related to the ears
13. stinking due to decay; decomposed; rotten and foul-smelling
14. visible; pertaining to the eyes
15. agreeably sharp to the taste; small pie or pastry shell
16. to raise the spirits of; make very proud, happy, or joyful

Units 28–30 REVIEW TEST

Directions: Please circle the correct **synonym.** Then write the answer's corresponding letter on the line next to the question's number. Each question is worth four points.

1. ____ **boycott** (a) to end early (b) to refuse to sell, buy, or use (c) to buy, sell, or use

2. ____ **rural** (a) characteristic of lines and circles (b) characteristic of the city (c) characteristic of country life or country people

3. ____ **lunar** (a) pertaining to the water (b) pertaining to the sun (c) pertaining to the moon

4. ____ **pungent** (a) remainder (b) opposite (c) sharp in smell or taste

5. ____ **soluble** (a) that which can be dissolved (b) problematic (c) improbable

6. ____ **enforce** (a) to forget (b) to bring about or impose (c) to arrest

7. ____ **din** (a) confused clamor or uproar (b) pleasant music (c) discolored garment

8. ____ **inaudible** (a) unable to be heard (b) closed (c) crucial

9. ____ **tactile** (a) insensitive (b) fragrant (c) tangible

10. ____ **tart** (a) skinny (b) agreeably sharp to the taste (c) unusual

Directions: Please circle the correct **antonym.** Then write the answer's corresponding letter on the line next to the question's number. Each question is worth four points.

11. ____ **ratify** (a) to veto (b) to fear animals (c) to approve or confirm

12. ____ **liberty** (a) freedom (b) appropriate behavior (c) imprisonment

13. ____ **urban** (a) citified (b) rural (c) punishable

14. ____ **alliance** (a) loyalty or devotion to a cause (b) close association for a common objective (c) disparity

15. ____ **visual** (a) imperceptible (b) pertaining to the eyes (c) attentive

16. ____ **putrid** (a) drooping (b) fresh (c) stinking due to decay

17. ____ **acquire** (a) forfeit (b) get possession of (c) refresh

18. ____ **identical** (a) same (b) different (c) insufficient

19. ____ **durable** (a) perishable (b) capable of being solved (c) beautiful

20. ____ **delectable** (a) unappealing (b) delightful (c) wonderous

Units 28–30   REVIEW TEST (continued)

Directions: Please circle the word that correctly **completes** the sentence. Then write the answer's corresponding letter on the line next to the question's number. Each question is worth four points.

21. ____ The puddle of water had _____ after the sun had beaten down for fifteen minutes.   **(a) evaporated   (b) recycled   (c) bellowed**

22. ____ No human being has ever lived for a full _____.
    (a) millennium   (b) century   (c) decade

23. ____ Each morning my classmates and I pledge _____ to our country's flag.
    (a) alliance   (b) allegiance   (c) bellow

24. ____ Her deep interest in stars and planets contributed to her career in _____.   **(a) biology   (b) botany   (c) astronomy**

25. ____ Her outstanding tournament performances _____ those of her equally talented brother.   **(a) recycled   (b) eclipsed   (c) acquired**

LIST OF WORDS BY UNIT

1 PLACES

asylum	ə sī′ləm	**landmark**	land′märk′
bungalow	buŋ′ gə lō′	**metropolis**	mə träp′əl is
cavern	kav′ərn	**monastery**	män′ə ster ē
depot	dē′pō	**peninsula**	pə nin′sə lə
galley	gal′ē	**plateau**	pla tō′
hearth	härth	**quay**	kē; kwā
labyrinth	lab′ə rinth′	**vestibule**	ves′tə byo͞ol′
lagoon	lə go͞on′		

2 BEG, BORROW, AND STEAL

accumulate	ə kyo͞om′yo͞o lāt′	**larceny**	lär′sə nē
bankrupt	baŋk′rupt′	**mendicant**	men′ di kənt
cache	kash	**mortgage**	mor′gij
counterfeit	kount′ər fit′	**pilfer**	pil′fər
embezzle	em bez′əl	**plagerize**	plā′jə rīz′
entreat	en trēt′; in trēt′	**thief**	thēf
hoard	hôrd	**usurp**	yo͞o zʉrp′
implore	im plôr′		

3 WHAT'S THAT YOU SAY?

anecdote	an′ik dōt′	**interrogate**	in ter′ə gāt′
aver	ə vʉr′	**murmur**	mʉr′mər
braggart	brag′ərt	**mute**	myo͞ot
concur	kən kʉr′	**narrate**	när′āt; na rāt′
counsel	koun′səl	**negotiate**	ni gō′shē at′
fabricate	fab′ri kāt′	**pun**	pun
frank	fraŋk	**reassure**	rē′ə sho͝or′
gist	jist		

4 CLEAN YOUR ROOM!

amend	ə mend′	**imply**	im pli′
cram	kram	**maze**	māz
despair	di sper′	**ordeal**	ôr dēl′; ôr′dēl′
eave	ēv	**prohibit**	prō hib′it
eccentric	ək sen′trik	**scour**	skour
forbidding	fər bid′iŋ	**spacious**	spā′shəs
germinate	jʉr′mə nāt′	**utterly**	ut′ərlē
habitat	hab′i tat′		

5 HOW WE ACT

abnormal	ab nôr′məl	**meddle**	med″l
brood	brōōd	**nurture**	nʉr′cher
casual	kazh′oo ə′l	**oppress**	ə pres′
caustic	kôs′tik	**pamper**	pam′pər
crude	krōōd	**procure**	pro kyoor′
enchant	en chant′	**snare**	snar
hospitable	häs′pit ə bəl	**tamper**	tam′pər
insinuate	in sin′yōō āt′		

6 WORDS FROM MYTHOLOGY

ambrosia	am brō′zhə	**mentor**	men′tər; men′tôr′
atlas	at′ləs	**mercurial**	mər kyoor′ē əl
centaur	sen′tôr′	**nemesis**	nem′ə sis
echo	ek′ō	**odyssey**	äd′i sē
Herculean	Her kyōō′lē ən	**panic**	pan′ik
hygiene	hī′jēn; hi jēn′	**tantalize**	tan′tə līz
iridescent	ir′i des′ənt	**zephyr**	zef′ər
jovial	jō′vē əl		

7 THE BIG AND SMALL OF IT ALL

budget	buj′it	**essential**	e sen′shəl
bulky	bul′kē	**extraneous**	eks trā′nē əs
capacity	kə pas′i tē	**humongous**	hyōō mäŋ′gəs
curtail	kər tāl′	**increase**	in krēs′ (v); in′krēs′ (n)
deprive	dē priv′	**massive**	mas′iv
duplicate	dōō′pli kit; dyōō′ (v);	**morsel**	môr′səl
	dōō′pli kāt′	**penalize**	pē nəl īz; pen′əl īz
dwindle	dwin′dəl	**surplus**	sʉr′plus

8 TELL IT LIKE IT IS

babble	bab′əl	**insist**	in sist′
blurt	blurt	**mumble**	mum′bəl
chatter	chat′ər	**promote**	prō mot′; prə mōt′
consolidate	kən säl′ə dāt	**protest**	prō test′ (v); prə test′ (v);
detest	dē test′		prō′test (v); prō′test (n)
expose	eks pōz′	**rage**	rāj
haggle	hag′əl	**rant**	rant
hilarious	hi ler′ē əs	**understate**	un′dər stāt′

9 THE SCIENCES (NATURALLY!)

chronic	krän′ik	**mutation**	myōō tā′shen
dread	dred	**nutrient**	nōō′trē ent; nyōō′trē ent
genetics	je net′iks	**offspring**	ôf′sprin′
heredity	he red′i tē	**prevent**	prē vent′
immune	im myōōn′; i myōōn′	**species**	spē′shēz
infect	in fekt′	**symbiosis**	sim′bi ō′sis
microbe	mī′krob	**trait**	trāt
molecule	mäl′i kyōōl		

10 MATHEMATICALLY INCLINED

bisect	bī sekt′; bī′sekt	**metric**	me′trik
corresponding	kôr′ə spänd ing	**percent**	pər sent′
decimal	des′ə məl	**perpendicular**	pur pən dik′yōō lər
dividend	div′ə dend	**property**	präp′ər tē
divisor	də vī′zər	**proportion**	prō pôr′shən
estimate	es′tə māt (n); es′tə mit	**quotient**	kwō′shənt
exponent	eks pōn′ənt	**symbol**	sim′bəl
fraction	frak′shən		

11 HOW WE MOVE

ascend	ə send′	**ramble**	ram′bəl
creep	krēp	**scamper**	skam′pər
descend	dē send′	**slink**	slink
dodge	däj	**sprint**	sprint
glide	glīd	**stagger**	stag′ər
hurdle	hurd″l	**strut**	strut
jog	jäg	**vacate**	vā′kāt′; vā kāt′
plod	pläd		

12 WRITE ON!

autobiography	ôt ō bi ä′grə fē	**haiku**	hi′kōō′
biography	bi ä′grə fē	**journal**	jʉr′nəl
comedy	käm′ə dē	**limerick**	lim′ər ik; lim′rik
drama	drä′ma; dram′ə	**myth**	mith
elegy	el′ə jē	**novel**	näv′əl
epic	ep′ik	**short story**	shôrt stôr′ē
epigram	ep′ə gram′	**skit**	skit
essay	e sā′		

13 POPULAR SAT WORDS

abduct	ab dukt′	**frugal**	frōō′gəl
amiable	ā′mē ə bəl; ām′ye bəl	**perceive**	pər sēv′
apprentice	ə pren′tis	**perplex**	pər pleks′
beret	ba rā′	**ruthless**	rōōth′lis
brutal	brōōt′′l	**subtle**	sut′′l
caption	kap′shən	**tenure**	ten′yər; ten′yoor
current	kʉr ənt	**wheedle**	hwēd′′l; wēd′′l
frenetic	frə net′ik		

14 WHAT WE'D LIKE SAID ABOUT US

charitable	char′i tə bəl	**insightful**	in sīt′fəl; in′sit fəl
congenial	kən jēn′yəl	**intelligent**	in tel′ə jent
creative	krē āt′iv	**practical**	prak′ti kəl
diligent	dil′ə jənt	**prompt**	prämpt
enthusiastic	en thōō′zē as′tik	**reputable**	rep′yoo tə bəl
genuine	jen′yōō in; jen′yə win	**respectful**	ri spekt′fəl
humane	hyōō mān′; yōō mān	**unassuming**	un ə sōō′miŋ; un ə syōō′miŋ
humorous	hyōō′mər əs; yōō′mər əs		

15 TO A DEGREE

drought	drout	**multitude**	mul′tə tōōd′
epidemic	ep′ə dem′ik	**numerous**	nōō′mər əs; nyōō′mər əs
feeble	fē′bəl	**puny**	pyōō′nē
gorged	gôrjd	**quench**	kwench
infinite	in′fə nit	**substantial**	səb stan′shəl
intermittent	in′tər mit′′nt	**temperate**	tem′pər it; tem′prit
marginal	mär′jə nəl	**trickle**	trik′əl
monopoly	me näp′ə lē		

16 ALL TYPES OF PEOPLE

amateur	am′ə chər	miser	mī′zər
assassin	ə sas′ən	nomad	nō′mad′
bachelor	bach′ə lər	orator	ôr′ət ər; är′ət ər
bursar	bur′sər	orthodontist	ôr′tho dän′tist
cynic	sin′ik	traitor	trāt′er
dupe	do͞op; dyo͞op	tyrant	tī′rənt
feminist	fem′ə nist′	virtuoso	vur′cho͞o ō′sō
journalist	jur′nəl ist		

17 AN INTERESTING COMBINATION OF WORDS

absurd	ab surd′	meticulous	mə tik′yo͞o ləs
arable	ar′ə bəl	publicize	pub′lə sīz′
bibliography	bib′lē äg′rə fe	rave	rāv
commiserate	kə miz′er āt′	restrict	ri strikt′
deceive	dē sēv′	rustic	rus′tik
fatal	fāt″l	serpentine	sur′pən tēn; sur′pən tīn′
foster	fôs′tər	subdue	sub do͞o′; sub dyo͞o′
glimmer	glim′ər		

18 ALL IN THE FAMILY

adoption	ə däpt′shən	maternal	mə tur′nəl
akin	ə kin′	matriarch	mā′trē ärk′
clan	klan	paternal	pə tur′nəl
fraternal	frə turn′əl	patriarch	pā′trē ärk′
generation	jen′ər ā shən	relative	rel′ə tiv
heritage	her′i tij′	sibling	sib′liŋ
kin	kin	spouse	spous
lineage	lin′ē ij		

19 SKILLED—OR NOT SO SKILLED

adroit	ə droit′	expertise	ek′spər tēz′
anarchist	an′ər kist′	imaginative	i maj′i nə tiv
astute	ə sto͞ot′	inept	in ept′
competent	käm′pə tənt	insufficient	in′sə fish′ənt
crafty	kraf′tē; kräf′tē	masterful	mas′tər fəl
crass	kras	outcast	out′kast′
endowed	en dou′d	skillful	skil′fəl
exemplary	eg zem′plə rē		

20 HERE, THERE, AND EVERYWHERE

abound	ə bound′	plague	plāg
accessible	ak ses′ə bəl	proximity	präks im′ə tē
clutter	klut′ər	random	ran′dəm
copious	kō′pē əs	teem	tēm
cosmopolitan	käz′mə päl′ə tən	tether	teth′er
domestic	dō mes′tik	trek	trek
legendary	lej′ən der′ē	waif	wāf
longevity	län jev′ə tē		

21 SMART—OR NOT SO SMART

acute	ə kyo͞ot′	prodigy	präd′ə jē
brilliant	bril′yənt	quack	kwak
buffoon	bə fo͞on′	rational	rash′ən əl
dense	dens	sage	sāj
imposter	im päs′tər	savvy	sav′ē
incisive	in sī′siv	vigilant	vij′ə lənt
inventive	in ven′tiv	witty	wit′ē
judicious	jo͞o dish′əs		

22 A BIT DIFFERENT

adolescent	ad′′l es′nt	maverick	mav′ ər ik
convict	kən vikt′ (n); kän′ vikt′ (v)	parasite	par′ə sīt′
despot	des′pət	serf	surf
eerie	ir′ē; ē′rē	turncoat	turn′kōt′
fanatic	fə nat′ik	wanton	wän′tən; wänt′′n
fugitive	fyo͞o′ji tiv	xenophobe	zen′ō fōb
lame duck	lām duk	zany	zā′nē
maestro	mīs′trō; mä es′trō′		

23 HOW (OR NOT HOW) TO SAY IT

conversant	kän′vər sənt	forthright	fôrth′rīt
curt	kurt	interrupt	in′tə rupt′
debate	dē bāt′	mediate	mē′dē āt′
dialogue	dī′ə lôg′	paraphrase	par′ə frāz′
digress	di gres′	quibble	kwib′əl
disclaim	dis klām′	retort	ri tôrt′
dissuade	di swād′	verbose	vər bōs′
feud	fyo͞od		

24 GONE!

abdicate	ab′di kāt′	erode	ē rōd′
abstain	ab stān′	kleptomaniac	klep′tō mā′nē ak
annihilate	ə nī′ə lāt′	lack	lak
depression	dē presh′ən	penury	pen′yōō rē
dismantle	dis mant″l	porous	pôr′əs; pōr′əs
dissolve	di zälv′; di zôlv′	purge	purj
eject	ē jekt′	ransack	ran′sak′
elude	ē lōōd′		

25 AGE

anachronism	ə nak′rə niz′əm	geriatric	jer′ē a′trik
antique	an tēk′	innovative	in′ə vāt′
archaic	är kā′ik	novice	näv′is
callow	kal′ō	obsolete	äb′sə lēt′; äb′sə lēt′
contemporary	kən tem′pə rer′ē	regenerate	ri jen′ər it
crone	krōn	renovate	ren′ə vāt′
extinct	ek stinkt′	veteran	vet′ər ən; ve′trən
fledgling	flej′ling		

26 WHO WANTS TO BE CALLED THAT?

boastful	bōst′fəl	obstinate	äb′stə nət
cross	krôs; kräs	ornery	ôr′nər ē
deceitful	dē sēt′fəl	spiteful	spīt′fəl
illiterate	il lit′ər it	stodgy	stä′jē
insubordinate	in′sə bôrd′n it	sullen	sul′ən
irrational	ir rash′ə nəl; i rash′ə nəl	tactless	takt′lis
irritable	ir′i tə bəl	wrathful	rath′ fəl; räth′ fəl
morbid	môr′bid		

27 HOW MUCH—OR HOW LITTLE

abundant	ə bun′dənt	overflow	ō′vər flō′ (v); ō′vər flō′ (v);
adequate	ad′i kwat		ō′vər flō′ (n)
ample	am′pəl	prodigal	präd′i gəl
dearth	durth	saturate	sach′ə rāt′
fertile	furt′l	scarcity	sker′sə tē
lavish	lav′ish	scrimp	skrimp
meager	mē′gər	swarm	swôrm
myriad	mir′ē əd	trivial	triv′ē əl

28 SOCIAL STUDIES CLASS

allegiance	ə lē′jəns	**millennium**	mi len′ē əm
alliance	ə lī′əns	**monarchy**	män′ər kē
boycott	boi′kät′	**propaganda**	präp′ə gan′də
delegate	del′ə gət (n); del′ə gāt′ (v)	**ratify**	rat′ə fī′
enforce	en fôrs′	**reformer**	ri fôr′mər
immigrate	im′ə grāt′	**rural**	rŏŏr′əl
liberty	lib′ər tē	**urban**	ʉr′bən
militia	mə lish′ə		

29 SCIENCE CLASS

acquire	ə kwīr′	**evaporate**	ē vap′ə rāt′
astronomy	ə strän′ə mē	**identical**	ī den′ti kəl
biology	bī äl′ə jē	**lunar**	lōō′nər
botany	bät′n ē	**predator**	pred′ə tər
condensation	kän′dən sā′shən	**prey**	prā
constellation	kän′stə lā′shən	**recycle**	rē sī′kəl
eclipse	i klips′; ē klips′	**soluble**	säl′yōō bəl
ecology	ē käl′ə jē		

30 ALL ABOUT THE SENSES

aroma	ə rō′mə	**nasal**	nā′zəl
audio	ô′dē ō′	**oral**	ōr′əl; ō′rəl
bellow	bel′ō	**pungent**	pun′jənt
delectable	dē lek′tə bəl	**putrid**	pyōō′trid
din	din	**tactile**	tak′təl
durable	dŏŏr′ə bəl; dyŏŏr′ə bəl	**tart**	tärt
elate	ē lāt′	**visual**	vizh′ōō əl
inaudible	in ôd′ə bəl		

WORDS INCLUDED IN THIS BOOK

abdicate	abduct	abnormal
abound	abstain	absurd
abundant	accessible	accumulate
acquire	acute	adequate
adolescent	adoption	adroit
akin	allegiance	alliance
amateur	ambrosia	amend
amiable	ample	anachronism
anarchist	anecdote	annihilate
antique	apprentice	arable
archaic	aroma	ascend
assassin	astronomy	astute
asylum	atlas	audio
autobiography	aver	

babble	bachelor	bankrupt
bellow	beret	bibliography
biography	biology	bisect
blurt	boastful	botany
boycott	braggart	brilliant
brood	brutal	budget
buffoon	bulky	bungalow
bursar		

cache	callow	capacity
caption	casual	caustic
cavern	centaur	charitable
chatter	chronic	clan
clutter	comedy	commiserate
competent	concur	condensation
congenial	consolidate	constellation
contemporary	conversant	convict
copious	corresponding	cosmopolitan
counsel	counterfeit	crafty
cram	crass	creative
creep	crone	cross
crude	current	curt
curtail	cynic	

dearth	debate	deceitful
deceive	decimal	delectable
delegate	dense	depot
depression	deprive	descend
despair	despot	detest
dialogue	digress	diligent

din	disclaim	dismantle
dissolve	dissuade	dividend
divisor	dodge	domestic
drama	dread	drought
dupe	duplicate	durable
dwindle		

eave	eccentric	echo
eclipse	ecology	eerie
eject	elate	elegy
elude	embezzle	enchant
endowed	enforce	enthusiastic
entreat	epic	epidemic
epigram	erode	essay
essential	estimate	evaporate
exemplary	expertise	exponent
expose	extinct	extraneous

fabricate	fanatic	fatal
feeble	feminist	fertile
feud	fledgling	forbidding
forthright	foster	fraction
frank	fraternal	frenetic
frugal	fugitive	

galley	generation	genetics
genuine	geriatric	germinate
gist	glide	glimmer
gorged		

habitat	haggle	haiku
hearth	Herculean	heredity
heritage	hilarious	hoard
hospitable	humane	humongous
humorous	hurdle	hygiene

identical	illiterate	imaginative
immigrate	immune	implore
imply	impostor	inaudible
incisive	increase	inept
infect	infinite	innovate
insightful	insinuate	insist
insubordinate	insufficient	intelligent
intermittent	interrogate	interrupt
inventive	iridescent	irrational
irritable		

jog	journal	journalist
jovial	judicious	

kin   kleptomaniac

labyrinth	lack	lagoon
lame duck	landmark	larceny
lavish	legendary	liberty
limerick	lineage	longevity
lunar		

maestro	marginal	massive
masterful	maternal	matriarch
maverick	maze	meager
meddle	mediate	mendicant
mentor	mercurial	meticulous
metric	metropolis	microbe
militia	millennium	miser
molecule	monarchy	monastery
monopoly	morbid	morsel
mortgage	multitude	mumble
murmur	mutation	mute
myriad	myth	

narrate	nasal	negotiate
nemesis	nomad	novel
novice	numerous	nurture
nutrient		

obsolete	obstinate	odyssey
offspring	oppress	oral
orator	ordeal	ornery
orthodontist	outcast	overflow

pamper	panic	paraphrase
parasite	paternal	patriarch
penalize	peninsula	penury
perceive	percent	perpendicular
perplex	pilfer	plagiarize
plague	plateau	plod
porous	practical	predator
prevent	prey	procure
prodigal	prodigy	prohibit
promote	prompt	propaganda
property	proportion	protest
proximity	publicize	pun
pungent	puny	purge
putrid		

quack	quay	quench
quibble	quotient	

rage	ramble	random
ransack	rant	ratify
rational	rave	reassure
recycle	reformer	regenerate
relative	renovate	reputable
respectful	restrict	retort
rural	rustic	ruthless

sage	saturate	savvy
scamper	scarcity	scour
scrimp	serf	serpentine
short story	sibling	skillful
skit	slink	snare
soluble	spacious	species
spiteful	spouse	sprint
stagger	stodgy	strut
subdue	substantial	subtle
sullen	surplus	swarm
symbiosis	symbol	

tactile	tactless	tamper
tantalize	tart	teem
temperate	tenure	tether
thief	trait	traitor
trek	trickle	trivial
turncoat	tyrant	

| unassuming | understate | urban |
| usurp | utterly | |

vacate	verbose	vestibule
veteran	vigilant	virtuoso
visual		

| waif | wanton | wheedle |
| witty | wrathful | |

| xenophobe | | |

| zany | zephyr | |

ANSWER KEY

1-1   A LARGE CITY, A DOCK, AND MORE

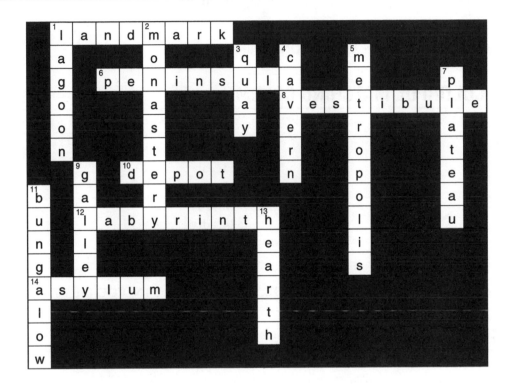

1-2   THE LETTERS C AND R STAND FOR THEMSELVES

1. CAVERN
2. PLATEAU
3. PENINSULA
4. LABYRINTH
5. MONASTERY
6. HEARTH
7. DEPOT
8. METROPOLIS
9. GALLEY
10. ASYLUM
11. LANDMARK
12. VESTIBULE
13. LAGOON
14. BUNGALOW
15. QUAY

Code: A B C D E G H I K L M N O P Q R S T U V W Y

Real: H T C E W K U Q B I G P S D L R M N A Y V O

1-3   FIND THE THREE WORDS

1. cavern	9. galley
2. lagoon	10. landmark
3. asylum	11. vestibule
4. plateau	12. monastery
5. quay	13. hearth
6. labyrinth	14. bungalow
7. metropolis	15. depot
8. peninsula	

The three five-letter words are ALLAY, TONER, and STAGE.

1-4   A COLORFUL MATCHING COLUMN

1. br	9. er
2. ow	10. ed
3. np	11. bl
4. ur	12. ue
5. pl	13. in
6. eo	14. di
7. ra	15. go
8. ng	

The answers are BROWN, PURPLE, ORANGE, RED, BLUE, and INDIGO (all colors).

2-1   START WITH A CAPITAL

A=15	B=6	C=9	D=4
E=12	F=1	G=14	H=7
I=2	J=11	K=8	L=13
M=5	N=16	O=3	P=10

Magic Number
is 34

PATRIOTISM IS IN!

1. je
2. ff
3. er
4. so
5. na
6. da
7. ms
8. fr
9. an
10. kl
11. in

The three famous American patriots are (Thomas) JEFFERSON, (John) ADAMS, and (Ben) FRANKLIN.

2-3 SLIDING ALONG

1. s
2. n
3. o
4. w
5. b
6. o
7. a
8. r
9. d
10. i
11. n
12. g

The popular wintertime activity is SNOWBOARDING.

2-4 NO NEED TO BEG, BORROW, OR STEAL

```
h o a r d   a c c u m u l a t e m m
    e                           o e
    m         p                 r n
    b         i       m         t d
  i e a       l           i     g i
    m z n     f           s     a c
c     p z     k e             e g a
h a g g l e l a r c e n y       r e n
d   c   e o       u               t
w     h   r       p
i     e   e       t
n c o u n t e r f e i t e n t r e a t
d
l
e
```

3-1 RELATING THEM

1. A braggart is not humble. (antonyms)
2. If you counsel another, you advise him or her. (synonyms)
3. You reassure one who lacks confidence. (action)
4. An anecdote is not lengthy. (opposite characteristic)
5. If it is mute, it cannot be heard. (opposites)
6. To fabricate is to make up or invent. (synonyms)
7. One can relate or narrate an anecdote, a short, usually amusing story. (action)
8. Concur (to agree) is the opposite of disagree. (opposites)
9. To aver is to state, and NOT to deny. (opposites)
10. A murmur is soft; a roar is loud. To murmur is to speak softly. (opposites)
11. A pun is a clever, and often amusing, play on words. (characteristic)
12. Frank is the opposite of dishonest. (opposites)
13. The gist of a story is its main point. (synonyms)
14. Interrogate (to question) is the opposite of to answer. (opposites)
15. If you negotiate, you DO NOT stir up trouble. (opposites)

3-2 EGO MAN

1. reassure
2. fabricate
3. gist
4. anecdote
5. frank
6. avers
7. narrate
8. braggart
9. negotiate
10. counsel
11. concur
12. interrogated
13. murmur
14. mute
15. pun

3-3 WHO IS THEODORE GEISEL?

3-4 THREE-LETTER ADJECTIVES

1. tan
2. odd
3. old
4. pot
5. shy

6. big
7. wet
8. dry
9. ice
10. low

3-5 UNITS 1–3 CROSSWORD PUZZLE REVIEW

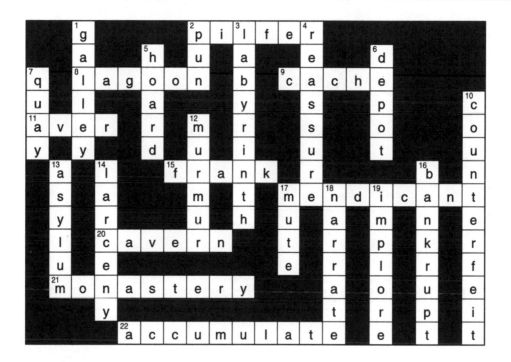

UNITS 1–3 REVIEW TEST

1. b
2. a
3. c
4. a
5. b
6. a
7. c
8. b
9. c
10. a
11. a
12. b
13. b

14. a
15. b
16. a
17. a
18. a
19. b
20. c
21. b
22. a
23. c
24. b
25. a

4-1 FIND THE PROVERB

1. th	8. tc
2. ee	9. he
3. ar	10. st
4. ly	11. he
5. bi	12. wo
6. rd	13. rm
7. ca	

The proverb is "THE EARLY BIRD CATCHES THE WORM."

4-2 THERE ONCE WAS A MAN . . .

1. eccentric	9. germinate
2. eave	10. habitat
3. forbidding	11. Scour
4. despair	12. ordeal
5. utterly	13. maze
6. amend	14. cram
7. spacious	15. prohibit
8. imply	

4-3 LOOK FOR THOSE SECOND LETTERS

1. scour	9. amend
2. ordeal	10. eccentric
3. despair	11. habitat
4. maze	12. prohibit
5. imply	13. spacious
6. cram	14. germinate
7. forbidding	15. utterly
8. eave	

The three words are CREAM, ROAM, and CARPET.

4-4 TWO WORDS AND TWO GIRLS

1. ordeal
2. eave
3. cram
4. prohibit
5. utterly
6. scour
7. forbidding
8. despair
9. germinate
10. imply
11. eccentric
12. maze
13. spacious
14. amend
15. habitat

The two words are AVAIL and UNIT. The names of the two girls are LIZ and UNA.

5-1 CLUMPS OF LETTERS

1. brood
2. pamper
3. enchant
4. oppress
5. tamper
6. nurture
7. abnormal
8. insinuate
9. snare
10. meddle
11. casual
12. hospitable
13. procure
14. crude
15. caustic

Word #1: ROMP
Word #2: CHESS
Word #3: PERT
Word #4: MATE
Word #5: NAME
Word #6: SUIT
Word #7: RUDEST

5-2 WHY START WITH SOMETHING CRUDE?

1. crude
2. oppress
3. meddle
4. brood
5. tamper
6. hospitable
7. insinuate
8. abnormal
9. nurture
10. procure
11. casual
12. caustic
13. pamper
14. snare
15. enchant

5-3 WHAT IS AN AMAZON?

A=13	B=3	C=6	D=12
E=8	F=10	G=15	H=1
I=11	J=5	K=4	L=14
M=2	N=16	O=9	P=7

Magic Number is 34

5-4 MUSIC TO YOUR EARS

1. ro
2. ck
3. bl
4. ue
5. sh
6. ip
7. ho
8. pd
9. is
10. co
11. ja
12. zz
13. re
14. gg
15. ae

The six types of music are ROCK, BLUES, HIP-HOP, DISCO, JAZZ, and REGGAE.

6-1 A MONSTROUS AFFAIR TO SAY THE LEAST

1. odyssey
2. Herculean
3. centaur
4. hygiene
5. mercurial
6. jovial
7. mentor
8. atlas
9. tantalize
10. ambrosia
11. echo
12. iridescent
13. panic
14. zephyr
15. nemesis

6-2 HEADLINES!

1. Ambrosia
2. Mentor
3. Panic
4. Jovial
5. Zephyr
6. Odyssey
7. Tantalize
8. Atlas
9. Herculean
10. Echo
11. Hygiene
12. Centaur
13. Nemesis
14. Iridescent
15. Mercurial

6-3 FIVE WILL GET YOU FORTY

Group A
11. centaur
8. hygiene
1. iridescent
5. jovial
15. panic
Total 40

Group B
9. ambrosia
2. atlas
7. Herculean
12. mentor
10. odyssey
Total 40

Group C
14. echo
3. mercurial
13. nemesis
6. tantalize
4. zephyr
Total 40

6-4 START WITH ZEUS

A=2	B=3	C=15	D=14
E=13	F=16	G=4	H=1
I=8	J=5	K=9	L=12
M=11	N=10	O=6	P=7

Magic Number
is 34

UNITS 4–6 REVIEW TEST

1. a
2. b
3. a
4. c
5. b
6. c
7. b
8. c
9. a
10. a
11. c
12. c
13. b
14. a
15. c
16. a
17. a
18. b
19. b
20. c
21. b
22. a
23. c
24. b
25. a

```
¹d  w   i   n  ²d   l   e                       ³h              ⁴n
            u              ⁵c   u   r   t   a   i   l
       ⁶c   a   p   a  ⁷c   i   t  ⁸y  ⁹m       m              l
   ¹⁰p  o          l   i   c¹¹a   m   a   z   o   n          e
       n          i       c  n   s   n                 ¹²e
       g          c       r  g   s   g                      x
       o          a       e  t   i   o              ¹³p      t
                  t          z   v   u              e        r
   ¹⁴b  u  ¹⁵d   g   e   t     s   e  ¹⁶e ¹⁷s   s   e   n   t   i   a   l
   u       e          e              u          a              n
   l       p                     ¹⁸m  o   r   s   e   l           e
   k       r                         p              i            o
   y       i                         l              z            u
           v                         u              e            s
           e                         s
```

1. ia	9. ha
2. mt	10. mm
3. he	11. ad
4. gr	12. al
5. ea	13. ib
6. te	14. ox
7. st	15. er
8. mu	

Quote: "I AM THE GREATEST."
Name: MUHAMMAD ALI
Occupation: BOXER
He also used to say, "I float like a butterfly and sting like a bee."

7-3 SPINNING AROUND

1. S
2. A
3. T
4. U
5. R
6. N
7. M
8. A

9. R
10. S
11. P
12. L
13. U
14. T
15. O

Three "spinning around" planets are SATURN, MARS, and PLUTO.

7-4 CHANGE A LETTER (OR TWO)

1. (a); plan
2. (b); large
3. (b); space
4. (b); lessen
5. (a); having
6. (c); needed
7. (b); copy
8. (d); needed

9. (a); great
10. (b); set
11. (a); grow
12. (c); size
13. (b); solid
14. (a); piece
15. (d); excess

8-1 IT'S WHAT THEY SAID

1. detest
2. insist
3. promote
4. rant
5. protest
6. blurt
7. mumble
8. babble

9. haggle
10. rage
11. chatter
12. understate
13. consolidate
14. expose
15. hilarious

8-2 YOU ONLY HEAR ITS FIRST LETTER

A=8	B=1	C=13	D=12
E=11	F=14	G=2	H=7
I=10	J=15	K=3	L=6
M=5	N=4	O=16	P=9

Magic Number
is 34

8-3 O! THOSE PREFIXES ENDING WITH O!

1. ge
2. op
3. ho
4. no (1st)
5. bi
6. bl
7. io
8. ps
9. eu
10. do
11. ch
12. ro
13. no (2nd)
14. mo
15. no (3rd)

The six prefixes are GEO- (earth), PHONO- (sound), BIBLIO- (book), PSEUDO- (false), CHRONO- (time), and MONO- (one).

8-4 UNDER THE SEA

1. ca
2. rp
3. fl
4. ou
5. nd
6. er
7. fl
8. uk
9. eb
10. as
11. st
12. un
13. aw
14. ha
15. le

The six sea creatures are the CARP, FLOUNDER, FLUKE, BASS, TUNA, and WHALE.

9-1 SEARCHING FOR THOSE SCIENCE WORDS

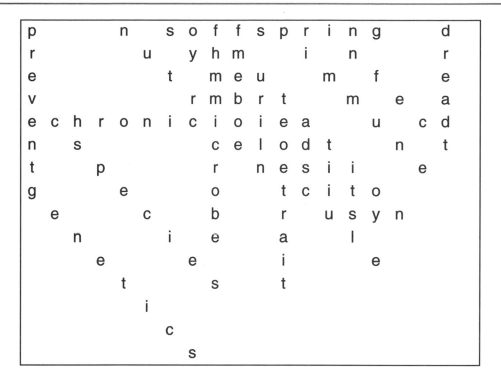

9-2 LET'S START WITH "NO" FOR SOME OF THESE

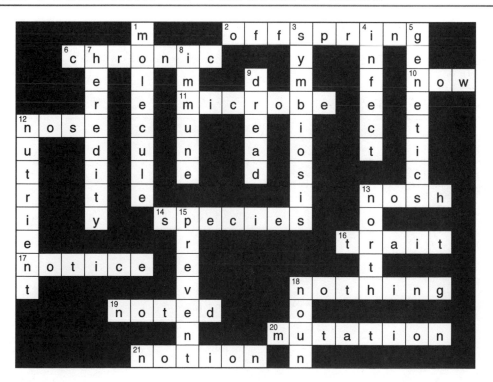

9-3 FINDING THE THREE-LETTER WORDS

1. species
2. heredity
3. symbiosis
4. microbes
5. traits
6. genetics
7. chronic
8. Mutation

9. prevent
10. infect
11. nutrients
12. dread
13. immune
14. offspring
15. molecule

1-3: PRY; 4-6: BAN; 7-9: IMP; 10-12: ERR; 13-15: USE

9-4 FIGURING OUT THE SCIENCE WORDS

1. **heredity**
2. **species**
3. **chronic**
4. **genetics**
5. **microbe**
6. **immune**
7. **infect**
8. **dread**

9. **offspring**
10. **symbiosis**
11. **molecule**
12. **nutrient**
13. **prevent**
14. **mutation**
15. **trait**

Code: A B C D E F G H I L M N O P R S T U V Y

Letter: U M E F T N I C H Y R O P G A L V B S D

UNITS 7–9 REVIEW TEST

1. b
2. c
3. b
4. a
5. a
6. c
7. b
8. a
9. b
10. c
11. c
12. a
13. b

14. b
15. c
16. c
17. a
18. c
19. b
20. b
21. b
22. a
23. b
24. c
25. c

10-1 JUST DO THE MATH

A=1	B=15	C=8	D=10
E=4	F=14	G=5	H=11
I=13	J=3	K=12	L=6
M=16	N=2	O=9	P=7

Magic Number is 34

10-2 OVERHEARD IN MATH CLASS

1. perpendicular
2. divisor
3. bisect
4. symbol
5. estimate
6. property
7. corresponding
8. fraction
9. metric
10. proportion
11. dividend
12. percent
13. quotient
14. exponent
15. decimal

10-3 WHAT IS IT CALLED?

1. metric
2. estimate
3. decimal
4. perpendicular
5. divisor
6. proportion
7. quotient
8. symbol
9. percent
10. bisect
11. property
12. dividend
13. exponent
14. corresponding
15. fraction

10-4 FAMOUS NAMES IN MATHEMATICS

1. ar
2. ch
3. im
4. ed
5. es
6. eu
7. cl
8. id

9. py
10. th
11. ag
12. or
13. as
14. ma
15. th

The famous men were all mathematicians. They are ARCHIMEDES, EUCLID, and PYTHAGORAS. They gained fame in the area of MATH.

11-1 JUST MOVE IT!

1. plod
2. dodge
3. ascend
4. slink
5. vacate
6. glide
7. ramble
8. stagger

9. strut
10. jog
11. descend
12. hurdle
13. scamper
14. creep
15. sprint

11-2 HOW WOULD YOU MOVE IF . . .?

1. sprint
2. stagger
3. plod
4. hurdle
5. descend
6. scamper
7. creep
8. vacate

9. jog
10. strut
11. glide
12. dodge
13. slink
14. ascend
15. ramble

11-3 NEWSPAPER CAPTIONS

1. plod
2. jog
3. slink
4. ramble
5. scamper
6. descend
7. hurdle
8. ascend

9. dodge
10. creep
11. glide
12. strut
13. vacate
14. sprint
15. stagger

11-4 DON'T BE STAGGERING YOUR WAY THROUGH THIS PUZZLE!

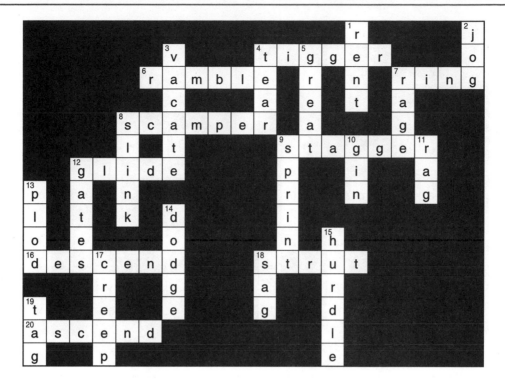

12-1 I'D LIKE TO READ

1. drama
2. essay
3. epigram
4. comedy
5. skit
6. elegy
7. journal
8. epic
9. haiku
10. myth
11. biography
12. autobiography
13. novel
14. limerick
15. short story

Mrs. Flowers READS GREAT BOOKS.

12-2 LEGENDS AMONGST US

1. kit
2. car
3. son
4. joh
5. nhe
6. nry
7. bet
8. tyz
9. ane
10. sac
11. aja
12. wea
13. pec
14. osb
15. ill

The legends are KIT CARSON, JOHN HENRY, BETTY ZANE, SACAJAWEA, and PECOS BILL.

12-3 LITERARY CROSSWORD

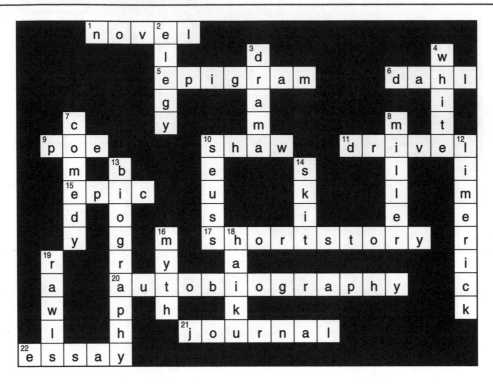

12-4 REALLY RESEARCHING

1. F
2. L
3. A
4. S
5. H
6. B
7. A
8. C
9. K
10. I
11. R
12. O
13. N
14. Y
15. Z

The two literary terms are FLASHBACK (1-9) and IRONY (10-14).

UNITS 10–12 REVIEW TEST

1. c
2. c
3. b
4. a
5. b
6. c
7. a
8. b
9. c
10. a
11. c
12. b
13. a

14. a
15. c
16. b
17. b
18. c
19. c
20. a
21. c
22. b
23. a
24. b
25. c

13-1   LET'S GO FISHING

1. apprentice
2. frenetic
3. perplex
4. amiable
5. ruthless
6. frugal
7. beret
8. perceive

9. abduct
10. caption
11. wheedle
12. current
13. tenure
14. brutal
15. subtle

The four fishing words are REEL (1-4), LURE (5-8), COD (9-11), and NETS (12-15).

13-2   THE FOURTH-OF-JULY SPECIAL

1. jo
2. hn
3. ph
4. il
5. ip
6. so
7. us
8. as

9. ta
10. rs
11. an
12. ds
13. tr
14. ip
15. es

The letters spell out JOHN PHILIP SOUSA, "STARS AND STRIPES Forever."

13-3 TO THE Nth DEGREE

A=1	B=15	C=8	D=10
E=4	F=14	G=5	H=11
I=13	J=3	K=12	L=6
M=16	N=2	O=9	P=7

Magic Number
is 34

13-4 BY A NOSE

1. S
2. O
3. O
4. S
5. O
6. S
7. O
8. O
9. S
10. S
11. O
12. O
13. O
14. S
15. S

14-1 END WITH JAMES BOND

1. insightful
2. reputable
3. practical
4. charitable
5. prompt
6. intelligent
7. creative
8. genuine
9. unassuming
10. enthusiastic
11. humorous
12. respectful
13. humane
14. congenial
15. diligent

The letters spell out the following: #1-2: SIRE; #3-4: TILE; #5-6: ROTE; #7-8: TINE; #9-10: MIST; #11-12: MOPE; #13-15: AGENT.

14-2   DON'T TELL THIS TO BABE RUTH OR MICHAEL JORDAN!

1. ev
2. er
3. yh
4. er
5. ob
6. ec
7. om
8. es

9. ab
10. or
11. ea
12. tl
13. as
14. tr
15. we

"EVERY HERO BECOMES A BORE AT LAST"—Ralph Waldo Emerson (RWE)

14-3   ILLUSTRATIVE EXAMPLES

1. a
2. b
3. b
4. a
5. a
6. b
7. a
8. b

9. b
10. a
11. b
12. a
13. a
14. a
15. b

14-4   AND NOW FOR THE ONE NOUN FORM

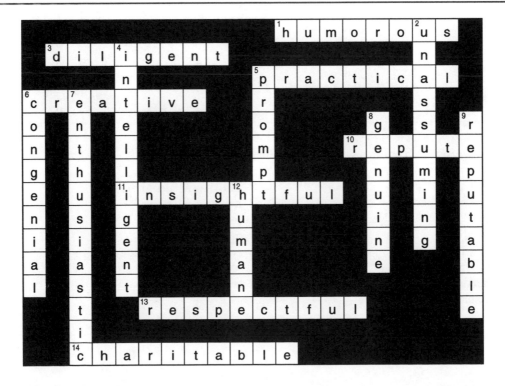

15-1 PLACING THEM IN

1. gorged
2. marginal
3. quench
4. temperate
5. trickle
6. multitude
7. drought
8. infinite
9. monopoly
10. intermittent
11. numerous
12. substantial
13. feeble
14. puny
15. epidemic

15-2 WHERE DID THE WORD *NUMBER* GO?

```
m   m o n o p o l y w e a k     e n g
    a i     t o e x c l u s i v e p u o
s   n n     e e d r o u g h t     i m r
b u   y t   m n s a t i s f y d e g
    o b   i e   p d f l o w       e r e
    r s n   r w e a t h e r     m o d m
    d t     m   r       m       i u m u
    f   e a   t i d a g   o   c s a l
    e   r r n   r t i t r d       r t q
    e   v   l t   i t s e e       g i u
    b   a   i i   c e e r e       i t e
    l   l     n   k n a   d       n u n
    e   s       e l   l t s     i a d c
    c o n s i d e r a b l e   e   l e h
i n i f i n i t e f r a i l p u n y y
```

Here are the words with their associated words:

drought (weather)
epidemic (disease)
feeble (frail)
gorged (greedily)
infinite (no end)
intermittent (intervals)
marginal (border line)
monopoly (exclusive)

multitude (number)
numerous (many)
puny (weak)
quench (satisfy)
substantial (considerable)
temperate (moderate)
trickle (flow)

15-3 TRIPLE THE NUMBER

The synonyms are numbers 1, 5, 6, 7, and 11. They total 30. The antonyms total 90.

15-4 HEY! SOME LETTERS ARE MISSING!

1. drought
2. epidemic
3. feeble
4. gorged
5. infinite
6. intermittent
7. marginal
8. monopoly
9. multitude
10. numerous
11. puny
12. quench
13. substantial
14. temperate
15. trickle

UNITS 13–15 REVIEW TEST

1. a
2. c
3. c
4. a
5. b
6. b
7. c
8. a
9. c
10. b
11. b
12. c
13. a
14. a
15. a
16. b
17. b
18. c
19. b
20. a
21. b
22. a
23. a
24. c
25. a

16-1 WHO SAID IT?

1. orator
2. cynic
3. dupe
4. tyrant
5. bachelor
6. bursar
7. orthodontist
8. feminist
9. miser
10. virtuoso
11. assassin
12. nomad
13. journalist
14. traitor
15. amateur

16-2 ALL SORTS OF PEOPLE

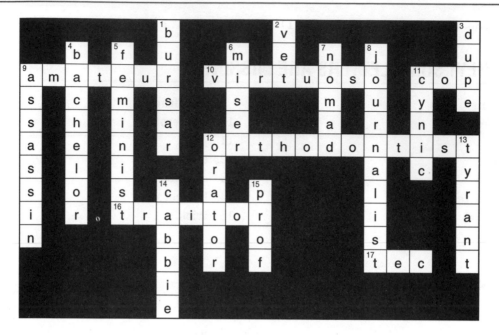

16-3 POLITICALLY SPEAKING

1. assassin
2. amateur
3. cynic
4. orator
5. traitor
6. orthodontist
7. tyrant
8. duping

9. bachelor
10. virtuoso
11. feminist
12. miser
13. nomad
14. journalist
15. bursar

The two words associated with politics are the SENATOR and the GOVERNOR.

16-4 HAVE YOU SEEN THE . . .?

1. bursar
2. feminist
3. tyrant
4. assassin
5. traitor
6. bachelor
7. journalist
8. amateur

9. virtuoso
10. dupe
11. miser
12. nomad
13. orthodontist
14. cynic
15. orator

17-1   COMING OR GOING THERE LATE

1. deceive
2. glimmer
3. publicize
4. absurd
5. subdue
6. bibliography
7. rave
8. rustic
9. fatal
10. meticulous
11. foster
12. serpentine
13. restrict
14. Arable
15. commiserate

The last letters of answers 2-6 spell out RED-EYE.

17-2   PEOPLE WILL NOT BE MAD AT US THIS TIME

```
                                                            b
                                                            i
                                p                       m   b
                    r                   u               e   l
            c           e               b               t   i
            o               s           l               i
        g               t           i                   c
        l   m                   r   c       f           u   g
    f   i   i           m   r   i       o       u           r
    a   m   s       u       a   e   z   c   s   d   e   l   a
    t   i   m   e   a   b   s   u   r   d   e   s   t   e   b   o   n   y   p
    a       e   r       u   m   a   b           h   e   c       u   p   h
    l       r   a       b   o   b   o           a   r   e       s   l   y
            t           d   n   l   o           p   i               e
    r   a   v   e       u   e   e   k       e   v   r   u   s   t   i   c
                        e   y       s   e   r   p   e   n   t   i   n   e
```

17-3   WHO SAID WHAT?

1. N; publicize
2. C; absurd
3. A; subdue
4. E; commiserate
5. H; fatal
6. G; bibliography
7. B; glimmer
8. P; deceive
9. D; arable
10. O; rustic
11. J; restrict
12. F; serpentine
13. R; meticulous
14. Q; rave
15. I; foster

17-4 ALL FIFTEEN

A=15	B=6	C=9	D=4
E=12	F=1	G=14	H=7
I=2	J=11	K=8	L=13
M=5	N=16	O=3	P=10

Magic Number is 34

18-1 IT'S A FAMILY AFFAIR

1. adoption
2. maternal
3. clan
4. spouse
5. kin
6. patriarch
7. generation
8. akin
9. lineage
10. relative
11. fraternal
12. heritage
13. siblings
14. paternal
15. matriarch

18-2 DOUBLE-LETTER WORDS

1. ra
2. bb
3. it
4. fl
5. uf
6. fy
7. va
8. cu
9. um
10. bu
11. ll
12. et
13. ba
14. za
15. ar

The five six-letter words are RABBIT, FLUFFY, VACUUM, BULLET, and BAZAAR.

18-3 NO FEUDING WITHIN THE FAMILY HERE

1. paternal
2. maternal
3. fraternal
4. clan
5. matriarch
6. patriarch
7. sibling
8. kin
9. relative
10. spouse
11. heritage
12. lineage
13. generation
14. adoption
15. akin

18-4 HEADLINES

1. KIN
2. MATERNAL
3. ADOPTIONS
4. SPOUSE'S
5. PATERNAL
6. AKIN
7. MATRIARCH
8. RELATIVES
9. PATRIARCHS
10. SIBLING
11. FRATERNAL
12. CLAN
13. GENERATIONS
14. HERITAGE
15. LINEAGE

UNITS 16–18 REVIEW TEST

1. b
2. c
3. a
4. a
5. a
6. b
7. c
8. b
9. c
10. c
11. b
12. a
13. c
14. a
15. a
16. b
17. b
18. c
19. a
20. a
21. a
22. b
23. c
24. c
25. a

19-1 BE AN EXEMPLARY STUDENT

1. endowed
2. anarchist
3. competent
4. exemplary
5. crafty
6. crass
7. outcast
8. expertise
9. masterful
10. adroit
11. imaginative
12. astute
13. insufficient
14. skillful
15. inept

19-2 POSITIVE AND NEGATIVE WORDS

1. ab (yes)
2. do (no)
3. so (yes)
4. ub (no)
5. tf (no)
6. lu (yes)
7. te (yes)
8. ul (no)
9. ly (no)
10. ly (yes)
11. su (yes)
12. if (no)
13. re (yes)
14. ly (yes)
15. fy (no)

The YES answers spell out ABSOLUTELY and SURELY. The NO answers spell out DOUBTFULLY and IFFY.

19-3 WHICH DOES NOT BELONG—AND WHY?

1. not enough, untalented
2. clumsy, dull
3. incapable, inadequate
4. unskilled, illustrative
5. late, fruitful
6. forgetful, uneventful
7. fit, efficient
8. imaginative, efficient
9. unable, competent
10. inefficient, incompetent
11. one who advocates political continuity
12. lacking talent or quality
13. lacking skill and knowledge
14. lacking creative powers
15. accepted

19-4 INVENTORS AND INVENTIONS

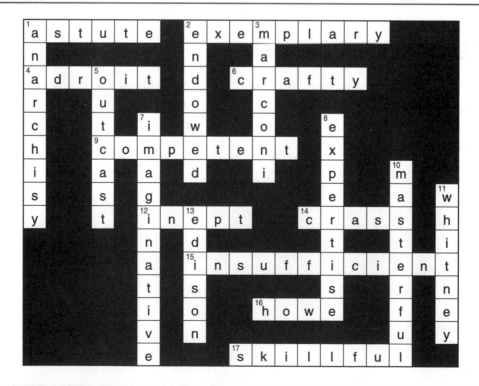

20-1 YOUR MOTHER IS WHAT KIND OF AN ENGINEER?

1. domestic
2. proximity
3. trek
4. random
5. waif
6. clutter
7. abound
8. accessible
9. legendary
10. cosmopolitan
11. plague
12. copious
13. teem
14. longevity
15. tether

20-2 ADVERBS GALORE!

1. ve
2. ry
3. se
4. ld
5. om
6. do
7. wn
8. be
9. lo
10. ws
11. ob
12. el
13. at
14. ed
15. ly

The six adverbs are VERY, SELDOM, DOWN, BELOW, SO, and BELATEDLY.

20-3 MAKING YOUR WAY AROUND ANALOGIES

1. c
2. i
3. r
4. c
5. u
6. m
7. n
8. a
9. v
10. i
11. g
12. a
13. t
14. e
15. d

To circumnavigate is to sail or fly around (the earth, an island, or other area). Thus, if your answers are correct, you have "CIRCUMNAVIGATED around analogies"!

20-4 HOW SIMPLE!

A=2	B=3	C=15	D=14
E=13	F=16	G=4	H=1
I=8	J=5	K=9	L=12
M=11	N=10	O=6	P=7

Magic Number is 34

21-1 DO YOU HAVE THE SMARTS?

1. prodigy
2. sage
3. vigilant
4. rational
5. witty
6. savvy
7. buffoon
8. impostor
9. incisive
10. judicious
11. acute
12. inventive
13. quack
14. brilliant
15. dense

21-2 DO YOU HAVE THE SKILL?

1. ex
2. pe
3. rt
4. is
5. ea
6. bi
7. li
8. ty
9. ma
10. st
11. er
12. yc
13. om
14. ma
15. nd

The four synonyms for skill are EXPERTISE, ABILITY, MASTERY, and COMMAND.

21-3 EXPANDING YOUR VOCABULARY

A. 1
B. 6
C. 8
D. 12
E. 13
F. 2
G. 4
H. 9
I. 10
J. 15
K. 3
L. 5
M. 7
N. 11
O. 14

21-4 WORLD CAPITALS

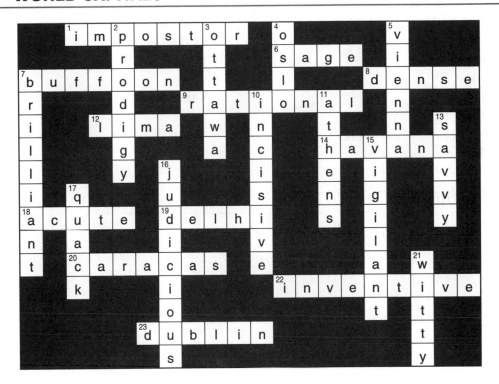

UNITS 19–21 REVIEW TEST

1. c
2. b
3. b
4. a
5. a
6. b
7. c
8. c
9. b
10. a
11. a
12. b
13. c

14. a
15. b
16. c
17. c
18. a
19. b
20. a
21. c
22. b
23. a
24. c
25. a

22-1   A TRAITOR, A CRIMINAL, AND THE REST

1. xenophobe
2. maestro
3. adolescent
4. wanton
5. turncoat
6. lame duck
7. fugitive
8. despot
9. convict
10. parasite
11. maverick
12. zany
13. eerie
14. serf
15. fanatic

22-2   FINDING THE COUNTRIES

1. eg
2. yp
3. tc
4. hi
5. na
6. br
7. az
8. il
9. ye
10. me
11. nc
12. ha
13. dl
14. ib
15. ya

The six countries are EGYPT, CHINA, BRAZIL, YEMEN, CHAD, and LIBYA.

22-3   PEOPLE AND WHAT THEY SAID

1. fanatic
2. maestro
3. convict
4. parasite
5. maverick
6. zany
7. xenophobe
8. fugitive
9. wanton
10. adolescent
11. lame duck
12. serf
13. despot
14. turncoat
15. eerie

22-4 WHERE DID THE WORD *MAESTRO* COME FROM?

A=8	B=1	C=13	D=12
E=11	F=14	G=2	H=7
I=10	J=15	K=3	L=6
M=5	N=4	O=16	P=9

Magic Number
is 34

23-1 IT'S NOT THAT GREEK TO YOU!

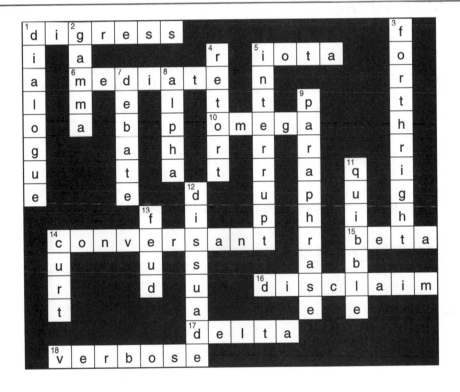

23-2   U-R THAT CLEVER!

1. abr
2. upt
3. fru
4. gal
5. ser
6. umr
7. uta
8. rub

9. agr
10. unt
11. dru
12. idp
13. eru
14. bur
15. lap

The nine "ur" words are ABRUPT, FRUGAL, SERUM, RUT, ARUBA, GRUNT, DRUID, PERU, and BURLAP.

23-3   THIS IS SO EASY!

1. u
2. l
3. t
4. r
5. a
6. c
7. o
8. n

9. v
10. e
11. n
12. i
13. e
14. n
15. t

How easy was doing this puzzle? It was ULTRACONVENIENT.

23-4   A VERY SILLY POEM

1. dialogue
2. dissuade
3. feud
4. quibble
5. curt
6. debate
7. mediate
8. disclaim

9. forthright
10. retort
11. conversant
12. digress
13. interrupt
14. paraphrase
15. verbose

24-1 TWO AT A TIME

1. porous
2. kleptomaniac
3. abdicate
4. penury
5. purge
6. lack
7. dismantle
8. annihilate
9. elude
10. depression
11. dissolve
12. ransack
13. abstain
14. eject
15. erode

#1-2: POLE; #3-4: CAPE; #5-6: PUCK; #7-8; LEAN; #9-10: LURE; #11-12: SOCK; #13-14: TACT; and #15: RODE.

24-2 WATER, WATER EVERYWHERE

1. ca
2. na
3. lb
4. ro
5. ok
6. oc
7. ea
8. nr
9. iv
10. er
11. po
12. nd
13. st
14. re
15. am

The bodies of water are CANAL, BROOK, OCEAN, RIVER, POND, and STREAM.

24-3 "-URY" IS IN

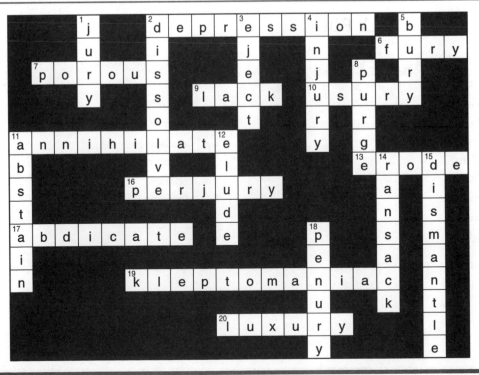

24-4 COUNT ON IT TO BE ONE OF THE FIRST

A=12	B=13	C=1	D=8
E=6	F=3	G=15	H=10
I=7	J=2	K=14	L=11
M=9	N=16	O=4	P=5

Magic Number
is 34

UNITS 22–24 REVIEW TEST

1. b
2. b
3. b
4. a
5. a
6. c
7. a
8. a
9. c
10. b
11. b
12. a
13. b
14. b
15. a
16. c
17. c
18. a
19. b
20. a
21. b
22. a
23. c
24. b
25. a

25-1 THE LAST LETTERS

1. anachronism
2. obsolete
3. callow
4. fledgling
5. innovate
6. regenerate
7. archaic
8. antique
9. crone
10. contemporary
11. renovate
12. veteran
13. extinct
14. novice
15. geriatric

The five words from the last letters of the fifteen words are MEW, GEE, CEE, YEN, and TEC.

25-2 STARTING FRESH

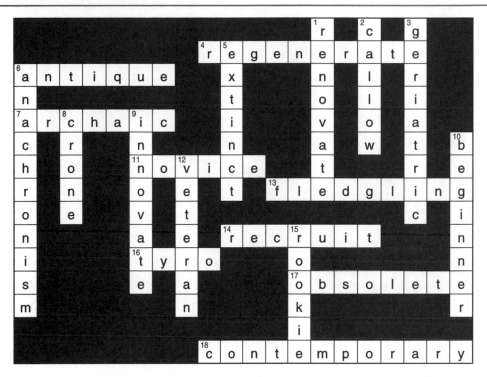

25-3 ONE HUNDRED YEARS AND COUNTING

A=4	B=6	C=11	D=13
E=9	F=15	G=2	H=8
I=14	J=12	K=5	L=3
M=7	N=1	O=16	P=10

Magic Number
is 34

25-4 PONCE DE LEON'S SEARCH

A=7	B=11	C=6	D=10
E=14	F=2	G=15	H=3
I=12	J=8	K=9	L=5
M=1	N=13	O=4	P=16

Magic Number
is 34

26-1 ALL TYPES OF BEHAVIORS AND MOODS

1. tactless
2. irrational
3. spiteful
4. illiterate
5. insubordinate
6. sullen
7. stodgy
8. cross

9. obstinate
10. boastful
11. irritable
12. morbid
13. deceitful
14. wrathful
15. ornery

26-2 IDENTIFYING THE PERSON

1. boastful
2. deceitful
3. spiteful
4. sullen
5. illiterate
6. stodgy
7. wrathful
8. irritable

9. obstinate
10. cross
11. irrational
12. ornery
13. tactless
14. insubordinate
15. morbid

The words spelled out are ACE; NAG; FEN; RAN; and LID.

26-3 OBSTINATE IS THE WAY TO GO HERE

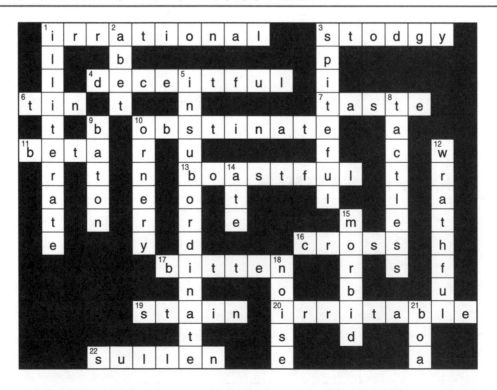

26-4 CARE TO DO THIS OVER BREAKFAST?

```
c       o       i r r i t a b l e o b d
   o       r           n a           s b o e
     f       n         s c s       p s a c
c      f       i e w b u t t e r i t s e
  e         e   r   r b l o       t i t i
    r       e   r   a y o e d     e n f t
      e       a   t   r s g       f a u f
        a     t   h   d s y       u t l u
    b       l i   f   i       s l e   l
        a       o   u   n     m u
      c       g   n   l a     i l   h
      r       e a     t     t l     a
b a c o n i l l i t e r a t e k       m
        s       o       g       n a
        s       j   g m o r b i d
```

27-1 WE WANT NO DEARTH OF CORRECT ANSWERS HERE!

1. meager
2. prodigal
3. trivial
4. adequate
5. saturate
6. swarm
7. myriad
8. scrimp
9. ample
10. overflow
11. scarcity
12. abundant
13. fertile
14. lavish
15. dearth

27-2 WHAT HAVE YOU WROUGHT?

A=15	B=6	C=9	D=4
E=12	F=1	G=14	H=7
I=2	J=11	K=8	L=13
M=5	N=16	O=3	P=10

Magic Number is 34

27-3 LARGE OR SMALL OR JUST ENOUGH?

1. L
2. JE
3. L
4. S
5. L
6. L
7. S
8. L
9. L
10. L
11. L
12. S
13. S
14. L
15. S

Note: In certain instances, some of these designations might be debated.

27-4 SOUNDS LIKE . . .

1. very plentiful
2. enough
3. spacious
4. lack
5. prolific
6. generous
7. emaciated
8. great number
9. spread over
10. profuse
11. thoroughly soak
12. inadequate supply
13. economize
14. abound
15. trifling

UNITS 25–27 REVIEW TEST

1. c
2. b
3. b
4. b
5. a
6. c
7. a
8. a
9. c
10. b
11. b
12. b
13. b
14. c
15. a
16. a
17. c
18. a
19. a
20. a
21. c
22. b
23. c
24. b
25. a

28-1 TAKE ONE, THEN TWO, AND THEN #15 DOES IT ALONE

1. militia
2. millennium
3. boycott
4. allegiance
5. delegate
6. alliance
7. urban
8. reformer
9. monarchy
10. ratify
11. rural
12. propaganda
13. immigrate
14. liberty
15. enforce

The words spelled out are: #1-2: ILL; #3-4: TAN; #5-6: ACE; #7-8: NOR; #9-10: OAT; #11-12: RAG; #13-14: ART; #15: FOR

28-2 LET'S CALL IT A TIE—AT LEAST IN POINTS

1. Yes
2. Yes
3. No
4. No
5. Yes
6. No
7. No
8. No
9. Yes
10. No
11. No
12. Yes
13. Yes
14. Yes
15. No

28-3 WORDS WITHIN WORDS

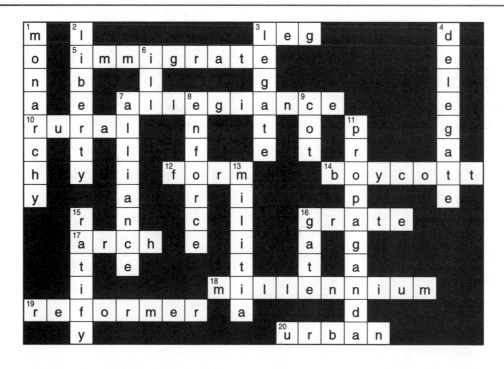

28-4 DO YOU KNOW YOUR U.S. PRESIDENTS?

1. ro
2. os
3. ev
4. el
5. tt
6. ru
7. ma
8. na
9. da
10. ms
11. po
12. lk
13. re
14. ag
15. an

The U.S. presidents are ROOSEVELT, TRUMAN, ADAMS, POLK, and REAGAN.

29-1 MAKING SENSE OUT OF SCIENCE

1. condensation
2. ecology
3. evaporate
4. biology
5. lunar
6. prey
7. constellation
8. acquire
9. soluble
10. recycle
11. identical
12. eclipse
13. botany
14. astronomy
15. predator

29-2 SCIENCE WORDS

1. geology
2. eclipse
3. constellation
4. identical
5. predator
6. biology
7. recycle
8. astronomy
9. botany
10. condensation
11. lunar
12. prey
13. soluble
14. acquire
15. evaporate

The two words and the shortened form of a word that they spell out are GEOLOGY, NATURE, and IV (intravenous).

29-3 THE DICTIONARY TO THE RESCUE?

1. z
2. i
3. p
4. q
5. u
6. a
7. r
8. t

9. b
10. o
11. n
12. d
13. s
14. e
15. w

The four words are ZIP, QUART, BOND, and SEW.

29-4 THE PARADE OF SCIENTISTS

30-1 A CROSSWORD FOR THE SENSES

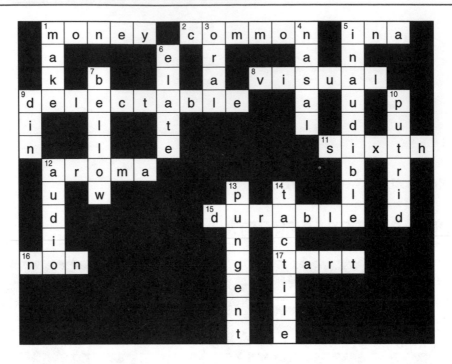

30-2 THE FINAL LETTERS

1. putrid
2. delectable
3. nasal
4. durable
5. tart
6. elate
7. bellow
8. inaudible

9. visual
10. oral
11. audio
12. aroma
13. pungent
14. tactile
15. din

The three words are DELETE, WELL, and OATEN.

30-3 JUST ADD SOME SWEETENERS

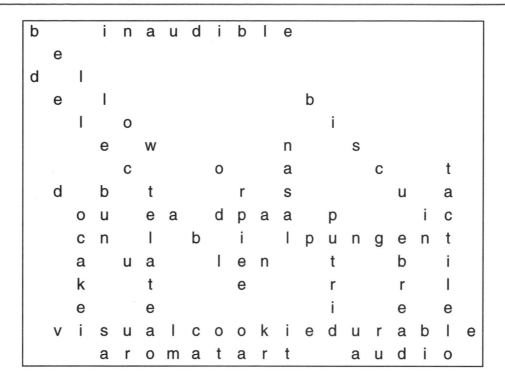

30-4 SENSING YOUR CAPABILITY

A=4	B=6	C=11	D=13
E=9	F=15	G=2	H=8
I=14	J=12	K=5	L=3
M=7	N=1	O=16	P=10

Magic Number is 34

1.	b	14.	c
2.	c	15.	a
3.	c	16.	b
4.	c	17.	a
5.	a	18.	b
6.	b	19.	a
7.	a	20.	a
8.	a	21.	a
9.	c	22.	a
10.	b	23.	b
11.	a	24.	c
12.	c	25.	b
13.	b		

Other Books of Interest

English Brainstormers!
Ready-to-Use Games &
Activities That Make
Language Skills Fun to Learn

Jack Umstatter

Paperback / 320 pages / 2002
ISBN: 0-7879-6583-9

For English and language arts teachers in grades 6-12, here's a unique collection of over 180 fun-filled, ready-to-use activities that help build the skills your students need for test-taking and overall academic success. These activities make learning enjoyable and stimulating while covering the entire English curriculum, including grammar, mechanics, vocabulary, creative writing, literature, research, and critical thinking. You'll find a variety of exciting games such as crosswords, word searches, scrambled words, magic squares, letter substitutions, cryptograms, and word plays—plus activities on story writing, literary analysis, word origins, and more. These exercises can be used to introduce new topics, review skills, complete as homework, or just to take a quick break from the routine!

In short, *English Brainstomers!* give you a ready store of exciting activities that help your students develop their skills and build proficiency across the English curriculum—all while they're having fun!

Jack Umstatter, a master English teacher with over 25 years' experience, is a multiple winner of the Teacher of the Year Award. He currently teaches in Cold Spring Harbor, New York and Oakdale, New York. He is the author of numerous teacher resources such as *Brain Games!* and *Hooked on English!* Both are published by Jossey-Bass. Mr. Umstatter lives in Islip, NY.

Other Books of Interest

201 Ready-to-Use Word Games for the English Classroom

Jack Umstatter

Paperback / 316 pages / 2001
ISBN: 0-13-044536-3

Give your students an exciting new awareness of what they can do with words and what words can do for them! You'll find these activities ideal when you want to spark interest in a new topic, award extra credit, supply substitute teacher plans, or begin or end class with something different. What's more, these 201 reproducible word games make it fun for students to learn and review word origins, vocabulary, spelling, literary devices and other language skills!

These word games are organized for quick access into seven sections: Roots & Limbs of Our Language (Latin & Greek Roots, Prefixes), Tools of Communication (Figures of Speech), World Around You (Celebrities, Math, Science, Music), Land of Literature (Writers, Books), Making Language Work (Grammar & Usage), Taking the Tests by the Horns (Improving Scores), and Just Plain Fun! (Potpourri of 38 Favorites).

Jack Umstatter, a master English teacher with over 25 years' experience, is a multiple winner of the Teacher of the Year Award. He currently teaches in Cold Spring Harbor, New York and Oakdale, New York. He is the author of numerous teacher resources such as *Brain Games!* and *Hooked on English!* Both are published by Jossey-Bass. Mr.Umstatter lives in Islip, NY.

Other Books of Interest

Hooked On English!
Ready-to-Use Activities
for the English Curriculum

Jack Umstatter

Paperback / 304 pages / 1997
ISBN: 0-7879-6584-7

This unique and practical resource gives junior and senior high school English teachers 186 stimulating activities that can be used to review and reinforce concepts across the English curriculum in a challenging and entertaining way. The activities have been tested with students of varying abilities and include a variety of crossword puzzles, word jumbles, word searches, magic squares, crypto-quotes, word scrambles, matching columns, fill-ins, and more.

The book is organized into seven sections including Composition, Usage, Vocabulary, Mechanics & Wordplay, Composition & Speaking, Literature, and Everyday Language. Also included are complete answer keys that can be copied for student self-checking, and "The Internet Connection," a special appendix listing useful sites about authors, lesson plans, literature, writing and research. This is an unparalleled store of stimulating reproducible activities to help your students enjoy English, and it's all ready to use "as is" for homework, tests, extra credit, or any other purpose you wish.

Jack Umstatter, a master English teacher with over 25 years' experience, is a multiple winner of the Teacher of the Year Award. He currently teaches in Cold Spring Harbor, New York and Oakdale, New York. He is the author of numerous teacher resources such as *Brain Games!* and *Hooked on English!* Both are published by Jossey-Bass. Mr. Umstatter lives in Islip, NY.

Other Books of Interest

Brain Games!
Ready-to-Use Activities
That Make Thinking Fun

Jack Umstatter

Paperback / 272 pages / 1996
ISBN: 0-87628-125-0

Here's a unique collection of over 170 reproducible exercises to fill your extra classroom minutes with challenging and practical exercises that stimulate your students to think and reason more intelligently and critically!

Better yet, the exercises are fun, can be used at any time for a variety of instructional purposes, and are perfect for large and small groups as well as independent work.

In short, *Brain Games!* is sure to benefit both you and your students It gives you a ready store of stimulating activities that will build your students' knowledge and critical thinking skills as it sparks their sense of fun!

Jack Umstatter, a master English teacher with over 25 years' experience, is a multiple winner of the Teacher of the Year Award. He currently teaches in Cold Spring Harbor, New York and Oakdale, New York. He is the author of numerous teacher resources such as *Brain Games!* and *Hooked on English!* Both are published by Jossey-Bass. Mr.Umstatter lives in Islip, NY.

Other Books of Interest

Grammar Grabbers! Ready-to-Use Games & Activities for Improving Basic Writing Skills

Jack Umstatter

Paperback/ 352 pages / 2000
ISBN: 0-13-042592-3

This practical resource gives language arts and English teachers a unique collection of over 200 creative, fun-filled, and ready-to-use activities that make teaching and learning grammar more enjoyable for you and your students. All have been tested with students in grades 4 and up and are effective as individual, group, or whole-class activities.

The games and puzzles can be used as introductions, reviews, or homework assignments. They feature a stimulating variety of formats, including crosswords, word finds, concealed quotations, cryptograms, scrambled and hidden words, riddles, magic squares, word generating wheels, jumbles and more, all designed to spark and hold students' interest.

You'll find the 203 ready-to-use activities in *Grammar Grabbers!* give students the tools they need to use grammar more effectively in their writings and make the writing process more enjoyable. As your students become more proficient and comfortable with grammar, they will become more eager to write!

Jack Umstatter, a master English teacher with over 25 years' experience, is a multiple winner of the Teacher of the Year Award. He currently teaches in Cold Spring Harbor, New York and Oakdale, New York. He is the author of numerous teacher resources such as *Brain Games!* and *Hooked on English!* Both are published by Jossey-Bass. Mr. Umstatter lives in Islip, NY.

Other Books of Interest

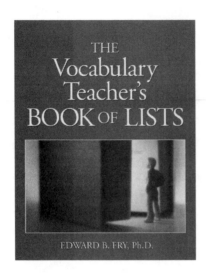

The Vocabulary Teacher's Book of Lists

Edward Bernard Fry, Ph.D.

Paperback/ 400 pages/ 2004
ISBN: 0-7879-7101-4

**A fun way to teach tricky vocabulary rules
to students at all levels**

The Vocabulary Teacher's Book of Lists provides content for literally hundreds of vocabulary improvement lessons for use by elementary, middle, and secondary school teachers, self-improving adults, home schoolers, and students studying for the SATs and ACTs.

Replete with lists of words, books, teaching strategies, and many other useful tidbits of information related to language and literacy, this book picks up where Dr. Fry's bestselling *Reading Teacher's Book of Lists* leaves off. Its primary focus is on vocabulary improvement for reading and writing. It contains a comprehensive section on roots and word origins; extensive lists of words used in science, psychology, and literature; along with an entire chapter on vocabulary teaching methods and options for curriculum content. Other chapters include spelling, homophones, exonyms, affixes, and specialized subject area terms. With a wide variety of levels and lengths, some lists may be appropriate for individual students as extra credit; other lists will help ESL students to master English, and yet other students will use these lists to prepare for college entrance exams.

Based upon extensive scholarship and comprehensive references, Dr. Fry's *Vocabulary Teacher's Book of Lists* bridges popular notions of vocabulary building and word smithing with the more formal academic study of language syntax and lexicon. It is an indispensable resource for both teachers and parents aiming to improve their students' vocabulary and literacy skills.

Edward Bernard Fry, PhD (Laguna Beach, CA), is Professor Emeritus of Education at Rutgers University where, for 24 years, he was director of the Reading Center. He is the author of the bestselling *Reading Teacher's Book of Lists,* now in its fourth edition from Jossey-Bass and the renowned inventor of Fry's Readability Graph.